ALSO BY JOHN CONROY

Belfast Diary: War as a Way of Life

Unspeakable Acts, Ordinary People

Unspeakable Acts, Ordinary People

THE DYNAMICS OF TORTURE

JOHN CONROY

ALFRED A. KNOPF   NEW YORK   2000

THIS IS A BORZOI BOOK
PUBLISHED BY ALFRED A. KNOPF

www.randomhouse.com

Knopf, Borzoi Books, and the colophon are registered
trademarks of Random House, Inc.

Library of Congress Cataloging-in-Publication Data
Conroy, John, [date]
Unspeakable acts, ordinary people : the dynamics of torture /
by John Conroy. — 1st ed.
p.   cm.
Includes bibliographical references and index.
ISBN 0-679-41918-7
1. Torture Case studies.   2. Police brutality Case studies.
3. Political persecution Case studies.   I. Title.
HV8593.c655   2000
323.4'9—dc21   99-28509
CIP

Manufactured in the United States of America
First Edition

For Colette, Matthew, and Sarah

Contents

Introduction ix

1 BELFAST: The Five Techniques 3

2 ISRAEL: Night of the Broken Clubs 11

3 CHICAGO: Getting Confessions 21

4 History and Method 27

5 BELFAST: "No Brutality of Any Kind" 39

6 ISRAEL: A Dangerous Report 48

7 CHICAGO: "The Pain Stays in Your Head" 60

8 Torturers 88

9 BELFAST: Ireland vs. the U.K. 123

10 ISRAEL: The Court-Martial 138

11 CHICAGO: Informants 158

12 Victims 169

13 BELFAST: Life Sentences 184

14 ISRAEL: "The Next Step Is to God" 199

15 CHICAGO: The Public Is Not Aroused 225

16 Bystanders 242

Bibliographical Note 257

Acknowledgments 291

Index 295

Introduction

I feel obliged to say from the start that this book is not fair on three counts. It is not fair to those who have survived torture. It does not do justice to the most brutal regimes in the world today. And, finally, it makes no attempt to portray the work of human rights organizations and the clinics around the world that help torture survivors recover.

On the first count: I think it may be possible to set down on paper a description of all the horrors of torture in such a way that a multitude of survivors might nod and say, "Yes, that adequately portrays the pain that I felt." And yet the end product of such an exercise could be a book too painful for most people to read. Those who managed to reach the final page might find their eyes glazed over and their heart hardened.

Addressing the second count: Those looking for a balanced ranking of human rights violators should look elsewhere. I am aware that there are perpetrators of torture far greater than those I have portrayed here, that in the pages that follow some brutal regimes go unnamed and their methods go unmentioned. I have done this consciously. When I embarked on this project, when I was still unsure as to what form the manuscript would take, dozens of people asked me if I was going to visit various nations well-known for their use of torture. It seemed to me that many of these well-meaning men and women had the idea that torture was something done in some backward civilization by the barely human and certainly ignorant. I was gradually becoming aware, however, that torture is something that most of us are capable of, and so I decided to use case studies that I thought American readers could identify with—"people like us" who deployed the brutal methods I'd heard associated with the Third World.

Once I had decided to go that route, the three case studies included here seemed to choose themselves. I had spent a good deal of time in Northern Ireland working on a previous book, and I was vaguely familiar with a landmark human rights case that began with torture of fourteen Northern Irish men by the British army in 1971. The case offered a certain select population, something akin to a scientific sample. It is common for torturers to vary their techniques, to do one thing to one person and something else to the next. In the case of the "hooded men," the British applied the same techniques to the entire sample, a group of men who came from similar backgrounds, who emerged alive and thus were able to tell their stories, and who I thought might be located twenty years after their ordeal to talk about the long-term effects of the torture. It is common for torturing regimes to deny what they are accused of, and thus accounts of torture often burden the reader with some doubt as to whether the survivor is telling the truth. In the Northern Irish case, however, the government admitted the abuse but denied that it constituted torture, thus offering me an opportunity to focus on both responsibility and definitions.

I was attracted to my Israeli case study in part because the individual torturers stood up in court and admitted that they had done what they were accused of doing (in the Northern Irish case, the torturers' identities were shielded by the government). Thus, no one could argue the incident never happened, nor could I be accused of attaching more weight to the words of Arabs than I did to the words of Jews. Furthermore, while I was still looking for a way to organize this book, I was able to spend a few days observing the court-martial of Colonel Yehuda Meir, the torturers' commanding officer. It was clear to me that he did not fit the Hollywood stereotype of the torturer, and his defense—that he was only following orders—neatly raised the issue of blind obedience to authority. When I approached him, he agreed to be interviewed after the trial ended, and at the time I was not sure I would find many men faced with such accusations who would talk to me.

The third case study unfolded before my eyes in Chicago, my hometown. An upstanding and well-decorated police commander sat as a defendant in a civil suit brought by a most unpopular plaintiff, and it struck me that the case might demonstrate why societies often find it easier to identify with a torturer than with a victim. Here was a court system that American readers would largely regard as just and fair. What better place to show how hard it is to prove that torture has occurred and to explore why torturers are rarely punished?

I recognize that my choice of these three cases will disappoint readers expecting in-depth coverage of more recently publicized incidents and practices. None of these cases will turn up in any current events quiz. Each involved protracted legal proceedings. (The Chicago case, for example, spanned fifteen years from arrest to the culmination of appeals.) I might have chosen cases of more recent vintage, but I would then have produced accusations, denials, and no results, no final sorting-out. I would have been forced to spend a greater portion of my time convincing readers that the incidents occurred, not exploring why they happened.

Lastly, this book may also disappoint those who labor in human rights organizations and treatment centers for torture victims. Their work deserves great attention. It is not provided here. Adding chapters on the efforts of clinicians and human rights activists would have doubled the size of this manuscript, which, with its limited focus, took ten years to produce. Had I tried to be more inclusive I might have never finished. I decided instead to focus on the dynamic of torture, on how an ordinary person becomes a torturer, on what happens to torture victims, on why torturers are rarely punished, and on how torturing societies justify their acts. I trust the human rights activists who helped me along the way and those who read this book will forgive my inattention to their noble work.

Unspeakable Acts, Ordinary People

BELFAST

The Five Techniques

O N NOVEMBER 16, 1971, British Defense Minister Lord Peter
Carrington was moved to denounce Jim Auld, a twenty-year-
old unemployed dental technician, on national television. The British
government had recently tortured Auld and thirteen other Northern
Irish men, and Lord Carrington's denunciation—he claimed the fourteen men were "thugs and murderers"—was meant to justify the torture. In fact, no evidence was ever produced to link Auld or any of the
other men with any crime. None of the men were tried. None were
even charged.

I met Auld twenty years after his ordeal. He had an office above a
bookie's shop in downtown Belfast, and from that office he directed
Challenge for Youth, an organization that provides support for teenagers in trouble. He was then thirty-nine. I would have guessed he was
fifty. He was of medium height, his eyes were light blue, his hair and
beard were graying. His job seemed to be one of those that call only
halfheartedly for a tie, and his was halfheartedly hung around his
neck, his collar open. When I asked him to tell me his side of the story,
it poured out, as if he had been holding it in his throat.

"I was lifted coming home from a party," he told me. "I arrived at
the door to be met by a paratrooper pointing his rifle at me, and he
pulled me into the house. They were holding my parents prisoner
because they were expecting me in. And I was always very apprehen-
sive about that situation—being taken away in the middle of the

night—and at that stage I said to my mother, 'Look, you can see that I am not marked in any way. You can see that I have no black-and-blue marks, no scratches, I am completely clean, and you can see his face. This is the guy who is in charge, so if there are any marks on me later, this is the guy that you need to remember.'

"He was a captain in the paratroopers and he said, 'Look, Mrs. Auld, while your son is with me, I can guarantee you that nothing will happen to him.' And at that they marched me out the door."

Although he didn't know it, Auld was by no means the only man being arrested at that hour. For months, violence in Northern Ireland had been escalating, and in response, British Prime Minister Edward Heath and Defense Minister Carrington decided to resort to "internment," a policy that empowered the government to arrest anyone in the province without charge or evidence and to incarcerate them for an unlimited period. Army intelligence officers compiled a list of potential internees—more than five hundred Catholics whom they believed to be either IRA members, IRA sympathizers, or civil rights activists who would organize demonstrations against the government's new policy. The leadership of the Irish Republican Army, however, had seen it coming, and with few exceptions had moved to safe houses by the time the army began making its sweep early in the morning of August 9, 1971. By midnight, Jim Auld and 341 other Catholics were in custody, the great majority of them having had no involvement in paramilitary activity. It did not take long for the army to discover that its intelligence information was faulty; almost a third of those arrested were released within forty-eight hours.

Auld was taken to Girdwood Barracks, one of the registration points for internees, and from there to the Crumlin Road Jail. Late in the day, the jail authorities handed him back to the military. He recalls, "At that stage some fairly serious physical damage was done to me. Going back to the military camp, I got a tanking from the soldiers, a beating with batons, going back into a small room where I was made to lie on a camp bed.

"In the room there was half a dozen soldiers, military police, and one policeman—4162 was his number, ginger hair, he was about twenty-four, twenty-five; if I saw him today, I'd know him—and they just started beating me while I was lying on the camp bed. They beat me with batons, they kicked me all around the place. They were aiming towards my privates and my head and they were making me keep my hands at my sides. I went unconscious a couple of times and they woke me up. They were screaming at me, 'Keep your hands at your sides! Keep your hands at your sides!' Then every time I tried to keep my hands at my sides they were whacking me, then I was doubling up or trying to get up.

"After a while, the soldiers who were beating everybody started getting a bit sick of it, but the policeman was inflamed at that stage, and he just wouldn't stop, and he ended up saying, 'Fenian bastards, you don't want to be British but you take the Queen's money. You're on the dole and you take her money.' And what annoyed him was that I said, 'Look I'm not working and I don't take the Queen's money. You can stick your Queen's money up your ass.' And he went crazy and he kicked the shit out of me. Turned up the camp bed and he kicked me all round the place. And eventually when I woke up again, I was lying on the camp bed and one of the soldiers who had been beating me gave me a cigarette, he gave me a Number Six, and he lit it and he said, 'Here, you poor bastard, you're going to need that.' And it was the first indication I had that there was something serious gonna happen. And it was him that pushed the cop out of the way and wouldn't let him hit me anymore."

Without warning or explanation, a hood was placed on Auld's head. He was handcuffed and then led to a helicopter. "We seemed to be in the air about a half hour. As soon as it landed I was kicked out and two arms grabbed me and I was trailed along, with the hood on, couldn't see where we were going at all, and they just ran me straight into a post. Straight into my head, flying full force into it, and I just went down. Trailed me inside and stripped me and put on a boilersuit and brought me into this room and put me against the wall, spread-eagled, my hands way above my head so my weight was on my arms and my feet. There was a hissing sound in the background; at that stage I thought it was a pipe hissing."

Auld did not know it, but for reasons still unknown, he and a select group of other Northern Irish Catholics—chosen, it would seem, on a geographic basis—were about to undergo a scientific combination of tortures. The hood over his head was meant to contribute to his sense of isolation and to mask the identity of the torturers. The noise increased in intensity; various survivors described it as the sound of an airplane engine, the sound of compressed air escaping, and the sound of helicopter blades whirring. For a solid week, the noise was absolute and unceasing, an assault of such ferocity that many of the men now recall it as the worst part of the ordeal. The men were also deprived of food and water and were not allowed to sleep (Auld was kept awake for six days). The spread-eagled position was also part of the torture: Auld's feet were placed about a yard from the wall so that his weight rested on his hands, a position that, if held for a long period, produces enormous strain; some of the men were later unable to hold a mug of tea or write a letter. Most of the men were also denied access to a toilet and had to urinate and defecate in their boilersuits.

The combination of tortures—the hooding, the noise bombardment, the food deprivation, the sleep deprivation, and the forced standing at the wall—later came to be known as the "five techniques." In combination, they induced a state of psychosis, a temporary madness with long-lasting aftereffects.

Auld told me that he was petrified with fear. "I didn't know what was going on, where I was, or who was doing what to me. And my hands up against the wall, after ten or fifteen minutes, they started getting numb, so I dropped them down to my side, and as soon as I lifted them off the wall, I got beaten with the batons, just beaten solid. And my hands were forced back up to the wall. And very quickly you got the message that you weren't supposed to move your hands. But you can only keep your hands up for so long. And so what I was doing, I was trying to show them that I was willingly standing against the wall, that I only wanted to start the circulation again in my arms, so I brought one hand down. I was immediately set on again. But you can only stay like that for so long, and again my hands just dropped down. And again, I was set on and knocked unconscious. And I woke up and they threw me back up again. It just went on like that for days. I know that I wet myself.

"The noise started annoying me. At one stage it was a noise at the far corner of the room, and now, at this stage, it was sitting beside me. And I just started getting more and more confused. Every time I dropped they just kicked me all around the place and forced me back up onto the wall. I was eventually brought into a room, and there was a plainclothes guy there and he started asking me questions about the IRA—did I know anybody in the IRA and all that. And I was desperate, and I said, 'Yes, I know everybody. Who did you want? Joe Cahill? Sean MacStiofain?' They were the names that anybody knew. They immediately put the hood down and beat me, dragged me out again and forced me back up onto the wall. And they just beat me.

"After about four days they set me on the ground and lifted the hood up to my nose and they gave me a piece of bread and a cup of water. And I was afraid to take the bread in case they took the water away. Because my mouth was dry, completely dry. And I was afraid— I needed the water, I needed the fluid—and I was afraid to take the bread, so I threw the bread away and I took the water. And he lifted the bread up and he gave it back to me again and he stuck a bit of bread in my mouth. And then he held the cup up and gave me one drink of it and took the whole lot away and put the hood back up. There was obviously two or three of them. As one of them took the bread off, another couple of them threw me back up on the wall. And I remember one of them hit me with a kidney punch or a punch with the baton in my kidneys because I can remember it just knocked all of the wind out of me. And I just went straight down and they all seemed to be in a circle around me beating me.

"And I remember crying at that stage and saying, 'I just can't take this, mister, I am sorry, I just don't know what to do.' And I couldn't do anything, and I just felt so helpless and so isolated that I would have told anybody anything. The interrogations were nothing for me because I wasn't in the position to tell them what they wanted to know. I admitted to being in everything but the crib [with the baby Jesus in Bethlehem], and if they had asked me I would have said, 'Yes, the crib as well, I'm in the background of it there,' because I was just so frightened that I had no fear of anything other than what they were doing to me. I would love to have seen the records of it, to see what I did tell them, because it couldn't be anything but funny, because it is all lies and desperation. When it was happening, it wasn't funny, I can assure you.

"What was in my head at that stage was, how can anybody do this to another human being? And I just couldn't fathom it. I was trying to think the thing through logically and all I could think of was that these people had done so many bad things to me that there was no way that they could ever allow me out alive to tell people. Because it would destroy them. And then I said, 'Then the logical thing is for them to kill me and say that I got killed in a shooting or something, or just make me disappear.' And that was actually in my head, that they were going to kill me."

In the wake of that realization, Auld decided to put himself out of his misery. In falling to the ground he had become aware that a heating pipe ran along the bottom of the wall. "I was saying to myself, 'There is no way that I can take this any longer.' And I was saying, 'If I threw myself down on the ground, I could maybe crack my head or break my neck on this pipe.' And I hit my head off the pipe okay, but all I did was hurt my head. I ended up crying because I didn't die. And they kicked the shit out of me for it because they reckoned that is what I was trying to do."

While all this was going on, Auld thought he was alone in his suffering. In fact, 12 men were being driven into a psychotic state in the same way. Paddy Joe McClean, a schoolteacher from County Tyrone, heard funeral hymns, saw his own casket and a firing squad, and at one point forgot who he was, believing himself to be a farmer from Enniskillen whom he had met only once. His tongue was so swollen from lack of water that he thought he would choke on it, and he later described trying to "vomit his tongue."

Patrick Shivers, a civil rights activist from Toomebridge, felt the same thirst and suddenly saw a table full of containers of fizzing lemonade. He began to pray out loud. He prayed to his son Finbar, who had died at six months of spina bifida. Finbar appeared to him.

Francis McGuigan, an active Republican from Belfast, saw himself in the company of friends and couldn't understand why they wouldn't take off his handcuffs. He prayed for death. At one stage he was asked to spell his name. He failed. His interrogators were much amused and asked him to count to ten. He refused, he told me, because he was afraid he couldn't do it.

Kevin Hannaway, also an active Republican from Belfast, sang the song "Four Green Fields," knew he was going to be shot, and asked for a priest. "I would have liked to have seen my wife and children before I died," he said later.

The men could not tell if it was day or night, or how many days had passed. The one thing Jim Auld knows for certain is that he was missing for nine days. He believes that on the eighth day, he was taken off the wall and brought to a room with a mattress in it. "I was that frightened that it didn't enter my head to take the hood off," he told me. "I was just that petrified. And eventually a Branchman [a member of the Special Branch], a plainclothesman, came in, and he said, 'You should have just taken off the hood.' And he brought me in something to eat, it was like watery stew. And because I couldn't hold it—my hands were useless—he fed me. He gave me a Mars bar, he gave me a Coke, over the period of a day he gave me three or four different meals. And he was continually talking to me about everything in general, just everyday things. And he told me it was over, I wouldn't be going back to the wall, I wouldn't be getting touched again, that he was my friend, that he didn't want anything to happen to me. With hindsight I know what he was trying to do—he was saying, 'You can see me. You know that I've never done anything to you. I've never laid a finger on you.' It was just in case the dirt was gonna hit the wall, he was making sure his back was clean. Because he was the guy I would be able to recognize.

"He was straightening me out, he was bringing me back to sanity. And at that stage, I thought he was God. I thought he was the nicest human being alive. He was my friend and mentor.

"He told me exactly what the process was going to be. He told me we would be going back in the helicopter and landing in the Crumlin Road Jail. And when I got to Crumlin Road Jail I wasn't to look back at the people in the helicopter. I would be set on the edge when it landed, and I was just to slide off and walk to the screws who would be waiting for me. He washed my face and my hands and my feet. My feet were all swollen up, my hands were all swollen up; I was in agony with them, I couldn't do anything. So my face was half clean-looking. And he put the hood back on and he asked me to make sure that it wasn't too tight, that I had plenty of air, and he was very civil about it. And we went back into the helicopter.

"We were gone about twenty minutes. When the helicopter landed, I sat down and there was an arm on my back and it pushed me off, and as that happened, another hand came and pulled the hood off my head, and I was pushed forward towards the two screws.

"And I think it was the first realization for me of how serious the ordeal was that I had been through, because the look that I saw on the screws' faces was one of sheer horror at my appearance. They were absolutely horrified. And the two of them grabbed me and helped me into a minibus and brought me around to the reception in Crumlin

Road Jail. They fed me sweets, and they were running in and out of the cell for three-quarters of an hour, asking me did I want anything, giving me a packet of cigarettes, giving me a box of matches, and continually asking me did I want coffee or tea, until I was moved to D-wing, the basement, the holding cells. I was there overnight, but while I was there, other guys, whose voices I recognized, started talking through the bars, and I got up and I was talking through the bars with them, and I realized then that there were other people who had gone through the same process."

{ 2 }

ISRAEL

Night of the Broken Clubs

IN THE WEST BANK, just south of Nablus, is a small village called Beita, accessible only by traveling a poorly paved road, wide enough for a single vehicle. Drivers going to Beita slow to a crawl to avoid deep ruts, chickens, and donkeys. It is a very poor village, divided into an upper section on a hillside and a lower section in the valley. In upper Beita, Palestinian women walk to and from the communal water supply carrying buckets on their heads.

On January 20, 1988, a group of Israeli soldiers entered Beita to deliver a civics lecture to the inhabitants. The intifada, the Palestinian uprising, was a little more than a month old, and the lecture was in response to an incident a few days earlier in which local youths had set a bus on fire near where the ill-tended road to Beita meets the well-paved road to Nablus. Lieutenant Colonel Yehuda Meir, the commander of the Nablus region, was the featured speaker. Meir, a handsome, dark-haired man, thirty-five years old, was a career soldier who had seen hard duty in Lebanon, Sinai, and the Jordan Valley. He had the carriage of an athlete, he could speak Arabic, he thrived in the field, and he was known as a man who did not command from a chair, as other high-ranking officers did. He lived with his wife and three children in Oranit, a West Bank settlement about forty minutes away from his headquarters in Nablus.

To provide support for that day's mission, Lieutenant Colonel Meir called on a company of about thirty-five soldiers from the Nahal

Brigade. The Nahal is by reputation a good frontline unit, unique in
that those who join it spend two years working on a settlement or on a
kibbutz and two years as infantry soldiers. Nahal troops also undergo
parachute training, though it is more of a morale-boosting course than
something they are likely to be called upon to use. Most members of
the company called upon by Meir had been raised on a kibbutz, and as
kibbutzniks they had been teethed on socialism. A supporter of right-
wing politics would have been lonely in that particular unit.

The company was led by Captain Eldad Ben-Moshe, twenty-three
years old, a thoughtful man who, from his first experience as a soldier
in the West Bank, had believed that Israel should find a way to give it
up. Three years of military service is demanded of young Israelis, and
Ben-Moshe had entered the Israel Defense Forces (IDF) immediately
after high school. He had later gone on to officers' school, and when he
entered Beita that January morning in 1988, he was in his fifth year of
service.

Until that day, Ben-Moshe's group considered themselves lucky,
since they had a fairly good posting considering the times. They functioned as troubleshooters who were called upon to solve problems
other units could not solve by themselves. They lived on a base just
outside Hawara, the village immediately north of Beita, a base surrounded by pine trees, in a beautiful setting, which had been captured
from the Jordanian army during the Six-Day War in 1967. While
waiting to be called out on special assignments, the men had a lot of
time to watch television and to play basketball and soccer.

Lieutenant Colonel Meir, Captain Ben-Moshe, and the Nahal
group entered Beita at dawn. They watched a group of border policemen, armed with a loudspeaker, drive through the village ordering
the men to go to a meeting at the local school. Once the crowd had
assembled, Meir gave his lecture, asking the residents to obey the law,
and his sentiments were repeated by another officer who worked in
the Israeli civil administration, the body that governs daily life in the
occupied territories.

The speeches, however, did not have much of a calming effect. The
troops were stoned on their way out of the village.

Lieutenant Colonel Meir, Captain Ben-Moshe, and the Nahal
group returned to Beita late that afternoon. They found it a different
place. The road was barricaded, tires were burning, and the number

of young men throwing stones had multiplied. Shields, commonly used in other countries to help soldiers and policemen respond to riots, are not normally issued to Israeli troops, and so the Nahal group had nothing to ward off the villagers' projectiles. The soldiers fought back with their standard-issue wooden clubs, but it took them several hours to put down the resistance.

While the battle was in process, Meir sent a messenger to the General Security Service, also known as the Shin Bet, the Israeli secret police, asking for a list of Beita residents who were suspected of hostile activity. The list conveyed to Meir contained the names of eight men of various ages. Some had participated in demonstrations, some were alleged to be "inciters," and one man was believed to have sung nationalist songs. Not one of the eight was suspected of any serious offense or of any involvement in terrorist activity.

Sunset had come and gone by the time the list reached Beita. A few local residents were pressed into service as guides, and Captain Ben-Moshe and his men crisscrossed the village, arresting the eight suspects at their homes. At this point, nothing that had occurred was remarkable or unusual. Ben-Moshe's unit was accustomed to getting lists from the Shin Bet for nighttime arrests, and without knowing any of the charges, they would round up the suspects and transport them to jail.

Once the eight Beita men were in custody, they were handcuffed and made to sit on the floor of the soldiers' bus. Meir then dismissed two intelligence officers who had taken part in the incident. One of them was Mike Herzog, the son of Chaim Herzog, the president of Israel. "You have completed your role," Meir said. "It is not appropriate for the son of the president to be here." A few minutes later, Meir pulled out in his jeep, leading the bus down the rutted pavement.

Meir stopped at the intersection of the Nablus road, and Captain Ben-Moshe and Lieutenants Omri Kochva and Ilan Shani got off the bus to receive further orders. Meir told them that the high command had declared a "strong-arm" policy to deal with the unrest. This may not have been news to the officers. On the previous day Defense Minister Yitzhak Rabin had proclaimed that the intifada would be suppressed with "force, might, and beatings." The *Jerusalem Post*'s account of the proclamation questioned the legality of beating demonstrators but also quoted an unnamed Defense Department spokesman who stressed the utilitarian aspect of the policy. "A detainee sent to Fara'a Prison will be freed in eighteen days unless the authorities have enough evidence to charge him," the paper said. "He may then resume stoning soldiers. But if troops break his hand, he won't be able to throw stones for a month and a half."

Meir explained to the three officers that because of the Palestinian uprising, the jails were packed full. Ben-Moshe, Kochva, and Shani would later testify that Meir told them to take the eight men from Beita into the nearby olive groves and "break their arms and legs."

The three officers had no questions and Meir drove off. The trio then discussed logistics. Captain Ben-Moshe feared that he would lose control of the situation if too many soldiers took part, and so he decided to limit the number of participants. He also ordered Lieutenants Kochva and Shani not to do any beating themselves. Their job, he said, was simply to make certain that their men did not get carried away. One of the officers—it is no longer clear who—came up with the idea of gagging the Arabs with their own scarves, with the flannels used by the soldiers to clean their weapons, or with whatever cloth was handy. Ben-Moshe decided that when the job was finished, his men should release the plastic handcuffs that bound the villagers' hands and return their identification cards, which had been confiscated earlier. The captain also suggested that one man should be beaten only in the arms so that he would be able to walk back to the village to get help for the others.

Once the three officers had worked out the logistics, Ben-Moshe gave the orders to the rest of the men, explaining, as had been explained to him, that the jails were full and that the action they were about to undertake was a reflection of the government's new "strong-arm" policy. He indicated that no one was being forced to take part and said that he was not able to carry out the order himself and would be staying on the bus. He asked for volunteers, and from those who stepped forward he selected those he needed.

While all of this was taking place, the eight men from Beita were sitting on the floor of the bus, still believing that they were going to be taken to jail. They were suddenly ordered to their feet and, once off the bus, were split into two groups. According to Ben-Moshe's orders, one group of Palestinians was to be beaten by Lieutenant Kochva's platoon, the other group by Lieutenant Shani's, and so the two platoons marched their captives off into the woods on opposite sides of the Beita road.

It was the first time the Nahal company had carried out an organized beating and so there was no standard procedure. Some of the Arabs were gagged and some were not. Some had their handcuffs removed before they were beaten and some had their jackets pulled up over their heads so they could not see.

Lieutenant Kochva described the incident to me several years later. He recalled that a light rain was falling, that it was dark amid the trees, and that he had a difficult time keeping track of what was going on. "There were three or four groups that hit," he said, "and it was a really hard situation because of all the screaming. The soldiers were very hard to control. All the frustration of the long day came out. And it was really hard to control the area—it was dark, and when we finished with one, we went and got another, but I couldn't see if any of the soldiers might have gone back and hit one of the ones we had already beaten. And Eldad told us that our job was to see that everything was done only to the arms and legs, and I really tried to do it that way, but I believe that some of the Arabs were hit all over their bodies. Because I couldn't control it, it was really hard to see what was going on.

"And they were hit with clubs, with rifle butts, with kicks, with fists. It was a big mess, everybody hitting and screaming, and somebody escaped, and someone was shouting, 'Escape. Catch him. Catch him.' I remember that the commanders said, 'Leave him, leave him, let him tell the village to come take all the Arabs who had been beaten.' He ran and fell and ran and fell."

A soldier named Shmuel Shefi, who was participating in the beating, saw the escapee collapse on the road, unconscious. Fearing that the man would be run over by a car, Shefi moved him off the pavement.

After a few minutes, the noise and darkness and confusion gave way to a sudden quiet. The men from Beita lay unconscious in the mud. The soldiers walked back to the bus and departed, not certain what would happen to the men in the field, but trusting, somehow, that the eight Palestinians would not die from their wounds, from internal bleeding, or from exposure.

"The situation was a real big mess," Kochva told me. "And we went back to the base, and I remember two soldiers who had stayed on the bus cried afterward."

Captain Ben-Moshe, who had stayed near the bus during the beatings, was troubled by the orders he had given, and when the troops returned to their camp, he told them not to go to sleep. He met first with his officers, and then with all of his men, and he tried to clarify the situation as best he could. He explained that this was not to become the norm, that they did not have license to go out and beat anyone they chose to.

The next day, Ben-Moshe went to see Lieutenant Colonel Meir to express his misgivings about the new policy. When he arrived at Meir's office in the Nablus headquarters, however, he found that the lieutenant colonel was not alone. Meir asked how the action had gone in Beita, and Ben-Moshe outlined his objections, not going into great detail because there were other officers present. Ben-Moshe later recalled that there was a certain lighthearted atmosphere in the room, and Meir responded to Ben-Moshe by saying, "In Nahal, you do things and cry. In Golani, you do things and laugh." Golani is another infantry brigade, one that is perceived as tough—Palestinians would say "cruel"—and unaffected by the angst of the soldier-kibbutzniks.

Later that day, Ben-Moshe did have a private audience with Meir. The lieutenant colonel ordered the young captain to carry out a similar operation that night in Hawara, the village immediately north of Beita on the Nablus road, just a kilometer or two from the Nahal group's base of operations. Ben-Moshe objected. He said that his soldiers were becoming more difficult to control, given the daily provocations of stone throwers inspired by the uprising, and he thought that these new orders would result in a breakdown of discipline, that the men would feel free to break arms and legs whenever they wanted. He also said that he was morally troubled by the order and that as a military tactic he could not believe it would be effective in the long run.

In the end, however, the young captain said that if the planned action that evening constituted an order, he would obey it. He asked, however, if he could speak with Meir's superior, Brigadier General Ze'ev Livne.

That was fine with Meir, who got up and walked into the division commander's office. Meir explained the situation while Ben-

Moshe waited with the secretaries in the outer room, and Captain Ben-Moshe and Brigadier General Livne subsequently had a private conversation about which there is conflicting testimony. What is certain is that Livne offered to visit the Nahal group the following morning, and that Ben-Moshe believed the brigadier general was going to explain the new "strong-arm" policy to his men. It was rare for a man of Livne's rank to address such a small unit, and Ben-Moshe left the office feeling somewhat relieved, certain in the knowledge that Livne had endorsed Meir's order to break arms and legs in Hawara.

At about ten o'clock that night, Ben-Moshe and his group left their base, traveling in a bus, a truck, and a jeep. They were accompanied by Major Dan Gabriel, an officer from the civil administration office in Nablus, who was being taken along because he had a good relationship with the mukhtar of Hawara. A mukhtar is a clan leader, and in the absence of elected officials in Israel's occupied territories, the mukhtar often acts as mediator between the people of his locality and the Israeli civil administration. Some mukhtars are perceived as collaborators, some are seen as functionaries, and some are truly the leaders of their community.

The mukhtar of Hawara is Jihad Hamdan Howary, a large and prosperous man who boasts of two wives, twenty children, a gas station, a good-sized farm, and a factory that makes olive oil. Howary's gas station is situated in the middle of the village on the Nablus road, and he receives visitors in a separate building a few dozen yards from the petrol pumps.

Ben-Moshe and his men pulled into the mukhtar's gas station at about 11 p.m. on January 21, 1988. At that point, only Major Gabriel and one or two of the Nahal's officers knew that the men who were going to be arrested that night were not going to be taken to jail. It was only after Gabriel went off to meet Howary that Ben-Moshe briefed his men. This time he changed the orders slightly. He feared that if he allowed his men to swing at their captives' arms, they would beat the Arabs in the head, and so he ordered them to strike only in the legs. Again, he placed Lieutenants Kochva and Shani in charge of the beaters. Once again, Captain Ben-Moshe did not intend to leave the bus.

It was raining, and the men were not looking forward to tromping through the village to carry out the arrests. They were very pleased when the mukhtar agreed to gather the wanted men himself. "We were very happy to stay in the warm bus, very happy," Kochva told me. "I think it was really nice of the mukhtar to do it."

A mukhtar in Jihad Howary's position is in a difficult spot. Since there are no street names or addresses in Arab villages, it is difficult for the Israelis to find an individual without help from one of the locals. If the mukhtar provides help, he can be seen as a collaborator. If, on the other hand, he refuses, he can be the cause of greater trouble: doors can be kicked in, people can be terrorized, a riot can develop, someone might be shot dead, a curfew might be imposed for days, the houses of the "agitators" might be demolished. Howary's decision may also have been colored by a certain fatalism that is part of the life of Palestinian males: so many have been arrested that it has become an accepted part of the culture, not the traumatic event that it would be in a family in another part of the world. Upon arrest in those days, the men who regarded themselves as innocent would leave their homes hoping that with any luck they would be back in eighteen days, which was the usual holding period at that time. Howary may also have hoped that his cooperation would result in easier treatment for the men who were being arrested, one of whom was his teenage son Muhammad.

And so Howary, showing the customary Arab courtesy, ordered coffee for Major Gabriel, and then, with help from his family, the mukhtar went about gathering the dozen men on the list. Many of them were roused in their bedclothes. They dressed and made their way to the gas station, where they were told to sit on the pavement close to the bus. No one resisted. No one ran away. When everyone had arrived, the men were handcuffed and made to sit on the floor of the bus. Soldiers crowded in around them, and then the troops and their vehicles pulled out.

Going north from Hawara, the Nablus road is particularly beautiful. Green fields stretch into rolling hills, and on those hillsides, the villages of Udala and Awarta stand in silhouette. That night, however, it is unlikely that anyone was paying much attention to the scenery. The bus stopped a half mile up the road, just past the mansion belonging to the mukhtar's brother, and a squad of soldiers and three of the Palestinians got off. The bus drove a short distance up the road while the soldiers escorted their captives into the fields. After walking two hundred to three hundred meters, the soldiers pushed the men into the mud. The villagers had been gagged, but that did not entirely muffle their screams. On the bus, Ben-Moshe ordered the driver to accelerate the engine to drown out the cries of pain. By the time I came to meet some of the participants, it was no longer clear whether the captain had been trying to impair his own hearing or that of the few people who lived nearby.

When the first set of beatings was finished, the soldiers jogged back to the road where their truck was waiting. The truck brought them up to the bus, which had already disgorged another set of prisoners and soldiers. The bus then moved on again, stopped, and three more prisoners were taken off into the fields to be clubbed. When the bus stopped a fourth time, it waited for all of the soldiers to return.

That night, it all went like clockwork. There were no trees blocking the view of the officers and Lieutenant Kochva thought that he had more control over the group of men he was supervising. There was continuing frustration with the quality of the clubs, however, since several broke, as they had at Beita, before the job was finished.

Of the Hawara twelve, one man was chosen to be beaten lightly so that he would be able to get help for the others. Although the officers who took part believe that they saved that place for the son of the mukhtar, they must have made some mistake, since the mukhtar's son ended up in the emergency room of Refideyeh Hospital in Nablus that night, having been beaten not only on the legs but also on the head.

When the job was finished, twelve men lay in the field, some moaning, some unconscious, some floating in and out of reality. The scarves and gags had been removed from their mouths, and the plastic handcuffs had been cut away. When the last group of soldiers had returned to the bus, the driver pulled away. In a couple of minutes, the Nahal group was back at its base.

At least a few among them were having second thoughts. Captain Ben-Moshe called his men together and told them that if they got that order again, it would not be from him. The men stayed up late, talking in small groups. They got little sleep, since they were awakened early the next morning for their promised visit from Brigadier General Livne, who arrived not long after dawn.

Livne was accompanied by a couple of civilians who were anxious to find out what was going on in the territories with this so-called intifada. Livne addressed the troops, but to Ben-Moshe's surprise and dismay, the words Hawara and Beita were never uttered. The brigadier general spoke in generalities, mentioned no orders to break arms and legs, and then left.

Captain Ben-Moshe felt that he had been betrayed.

{3}

CHICAGO

Getting Confessions

A T ABOUT 2 P.M. on February 9, 1982, Chicago police officers
William Fahey, 34, and Richard O'Brien, 33, were in uniform,
cruising an area on the city's south side, when they focused their attention on a brown two-door Chevrolet Impala. Why they decided to stop
the car is unclear. Officer Fahey's widow recalls that her husband had
a sixth sense for spotting a car in which the police might have an interest; even when he was off duty, he had the habit of pointing to other
vehicles and saying, "That car is dirty." On that cold and overcast day
in February, he may have had a feeling that the '78 Impala was dirty.
He would have been right.

The occupants of the car, the brothers Andrew and Jackie Wilson,
had committed a burglary less than an hour before. The proceeds
had not been spectacular: some clothes, a television, a fifth of whis-
key, some bullets, and a jar of pennies. Jackie, 21, also known as
Jacque, Robert, and Bubbles, was driving; he was wanted for parole
violation. Andrew, 29, also known as Joseph, Tony, and Gino, had a
chrome-plated .38 under his hat on the front seat, two outstanding
warrants for his arrest, and a recently acquired predilection for armed
robbery.

The tales told by witnesses and participants diverge at this point,
but it seems likely that Jackie saw the lights flashing on the top of the
police car and pulled the Impala to the curb. Officer O'Brien left the
driver's seat of the police car and approached the Chevy. Jackie got

out, and O'Brien allegedly joked about seeing the two men throw a beer bottle out of the window. He asked Jackie for his license, and when Jackie said he didn't have it, O'Brien frisked him and then decided to search the car.

At about that point, Andrew got out of the passenger seat, and in the next thirty seconds, a tragic sequence was played out: Officer Fahey, having left the passenger seat of the police car, picked up Andrew's jacket from the front seat. He may have found the bullets from the burglary in a pocket. While he was holding the jacket, Andrew stepped behind him and stripped him of his gun. The two men began to struggle for the weapon and slipped in the snow. Andrew Wilson pulled the trigger, perhaps accidentally, perhaps not, and a bullet went through the head of William Fahey.

Meanwhile, on the driver's side, Officer O'Brien had found Andrew's .38 on the front seat. Hearing a shot, he backed out of the car, pointed his weapon at Jackie Wilson, and yelled, "Freeze." Jackie froze. O'Brien, probably unable to see his partner, took a step toward the rear of the car. Andrew Wilson shot him once in the chest with Officer Fahey's gun.

Andrew then yelled at his brother, telling him to disarm O'Brien. Jackie yelled back that the cop was still moving. The older Wilson then climbed onto the back of the Chevy, pumped four more bullets into O'Brien, slid off the car, and picked up O'Brien's gun. The two brothers got back into the Impala and sped off, leaving the two policemen bleeding in the snow.

As the Wilson brothers pulled away, Andre Coulter was driving north on Morgan Street with his friends Dwayne Hardin and Louis Booker as passengers. Coulter pulled to the curb and the three men warily crossed the street. Coulter put his jacket under O'Brien's head while Hardin picked up the radio in the police car and informed the dispatcher that two police officers were down and bleeding. Almost simultaneously, two residents of the 8100 block of Morgan were reporting the same news over the phone. In no time, the scene was crawling with cops.

O'Brien and Fahey were loaded into a police van and driven at speed to Little Company of Mary Hospital. O'Brien was dead on arrival. Fahey died twenty hours later.

THE POLICE BEGAN to track the killers with fragments of information. Andre Coulter said the getaway car was a late-model Chevy Impala, and he thought that the front grillwork might have been damaged. An electrician who had been doing a job at 8209 S. Morgan, a block south of the shooting, reported that the car was brown and a two-door. Other witnesses described the fugitives as two blacks in their twenties, and Tyrone Sims, who had witnessed the shooting from his front window, helped put together a police sketch. A bulletin went out for a 1977–80 Chevrolet Impala, bronze, rust, or burnt orange in color, a two-door model with "possible damage to front grill on driver's side."

The murders had taken place on the turf of Lieutenant Jon Burge, commanding officer of Area 2 Violent Crimes, who was off duty when the incident occurred. Burge was in a car wash about three miles from the scene of the crime when a detective came running through looking for the suspect vehicle. He told the lieutenant of the shootings, and almost simultaneously Burge's beeper went off. He sped to his office to take charge of the investigation. He would not return home for five days.

At that time, Area 2, which sprawls over sixty square miles of Chicago's south side, had its headquarters in a brick building at the corner of 91st and Cottage Grove Avenue. The police who reported there for duty were having a tense winter. On the day Fahey and O'Brien were killed, it may have seemed reasonable to believe that someone had declared open season on policemen. Five law enforcement officers had been shot in the Area, four of them fatally, within little more than a month. (The victims, in addition to Fahey and O'Brien, were two deputy sheriffs, shot during an armed robbery of a McDonald's, and James Doyle, a rookie cop, who was shot dead on a CTA bus while arresting a robbery suspect named Edgar Hope.) As a result, feelings were high when the police set out to find the killers of Fahey and O'Brien. A grid search was set up to find the Impala, and a house-by-house canvass began in the area of the shooting.

Enthusiasm brought excess. Policemen began kicking down doors. Patricia and Alvin Smith claimed that plainclothesmen pointed guns at the head of their twelve-year-old daughter. Adolph Thornton reported that the police had shot his two-year-old German shepherd. William Phillips, 32, a Chicago fireman, complained that he had been arrested for standing on a street corner, that one of his teeth was knocked out in the process, and that he was later charged with disorderly conduct. Doris Miller, a forty-five-year-old postal worker who had never been arrested, was brought in for questioning because she was a neighbor of two suspects; she was handcuffed to a windowsill in an interview room, denied access to a toilet for about fourteen hours, and ultimately had to relieve herself in an ashtray.

The Reverend Willie Barrow of Operation PUSH said that in the neighborhood of the shooting, every young black male in sight was being stopped and questioned, and the *Defender,* Chicago's African American daily newspaper, quoted a woman who said that she had sent her son away because "the police were crazy, picking up kids who clearly did not match the description of the two men who were wanted." The Reverend Jesse Jackson proclaimed that the black community was living under martial law, in "a war zone . . . under economic, political, and military occupation," that the police department was holding "the entire black community hostage for the crimes of two."

Ironically, it was pure luck and citizen cooperation, not the dragnet or the police enthusiasm, that broke the case. Tyrone Sims, the man who had witnessed the shooting from his front window, was shown a large batch of mug shots and tentatively identified Donald White, also known as Kojak, as the shooter. Kojak, it turned out, had nothing to do with the murders, but by the strangest of coincidences, he knew the murderers. He lived next door to the house that the Wilsons had broken into hours before they were pulled over by Officers Fahey and O'Brien. Kojak had taken part in the burglary, and according to police reports, the loot had been divided at his house. He allegedly told the police that Andrew Wilson was plotting the jailbreak of Edgar Hope, the man who had shot the rookie cop on the CTA bus on February 5; that Wilson needed guns for the jailbreak; that the burglary had been carried out with that in mind; and that the burglars had found bullets but no weapons.

A body and fender man named Solomon Morgan, who had known the Wilsons for ten years, also helped police focus on the two brothers.

After the shooting, Jackie Wilson had called Morgan and asked him to paint the Impala and repair the car's grillwork. Morgan realized that the description of the killers' car matched the vehicle he was supposed to paint and repair, and he called the police.

And so the police began to concentrate their efforts on finding the Wilsons, who were separately moving from apartment to apartment on the south and west sides. Pursuing various leads, Lieutenant Burge and his men surrounded a building at 5301 W. Jackson at about 5:15 a.m. on Sunday, February 14, five days after the shooting. Burge was the first man through the door, and he arrested Andrew Wilson without firing a shot.

Not long thereafter, Chester Batey, a policeman with the 8th District tactical unit, received a call from his father, a minister, who said that a member of his congregation knew where Jackie was hiding. Batey flagged down a passing police car, and at 8:05 that Sunday morning, he and assisting policemen from the 2nd District broke into a third-floor apartment at 5157 S. Prairie. The man inside denied he was the subject of the manhunt, but at the police station he admitted he was indeed Jackie Wilson.

BOTH ANDREW and Jackie gave inculpatory statements at Area 2. They were tried together and convicted. Both convictions were reversed on appeal. The two brothers were then tried separately and convicted again. Today, almost twenty years after the murders of Fahey and O'Brien, the Wilson brothers should be a tragic footnote in Chicago's history, a footnote recalled by the children left without a father, by the wife left without a husband, by mothers and fathers left without sons, by the policemen left without comrades.

Instead, Andrew came back to haunt the city, telling a bizarre tale fit for some Third World dictatorship. In a civil suit against the city, the police department, and various detectives from Area 2, Andrew Wilson claimed he was tortured.

Many in the city dismissed the claim as a con's tale, but the judges of the Illinois Supreme Court did not. In granting Wilson a second criminal trial, they wrote, "The evidence here shows clearly that when the defendant was arrested at 5:15 a.m. on February 14, he may have received a cut above his right eye but that he had no other injuries; it is equally clear that when the defendant was taken by police officers to Mercy Hospital sometime after ten o'clock that night he had about fifteen separate injuries on his head, chest, and leg. The inescapable conclusion is that the defendant suffered his injuries while in police custody that day. . . ."

One might be tempted to excuse the police, assuming that in their outrage over the death of a comrade they lost control and beat Wilson up. But Wilson was not complaining of a mere beating. He was complaining of burns and electric shock, the shock delivered by two different devices applied to his genitals, his ears, his nose, and his fingers.

What Wilson didn't know when he filed his complaint was that he was not the first to complain of such treatment at the hands of detectives from Area 2.

{4}

History and Method

TORTURE HAS LONG BEEN employed by well-meaning, even reasonable people armed with the sincere belief that they are preserving civilization as they know it. Aristotle favored the use of torture in
extracting evidence, speaking of its absolute credibility, and St. Augustine also defended the practice. Torture was routine in ancient Greece
and Rome, and although methods have changed in the intervening
centuries, the goals of the torturer—to gain information, to punish, to
force an individual to change his beliefs or loyalties, to intimidate a
community—have not changed at all.

In Rome, strict rules limited who could be tortured in the interest
of gathering evidence. The torturable class, initially limited to slaves,
could be whipped, beaten with rods or chains, stretched on the rack,
exposed to red-hot metal, confined in quarters that required painful
constriction of their bodies or in a device that pulled their legs apart,
all in an attempt to gain information about a crime that they might
or might not have committed. The Romans eventually discovered
what seems to be one of the central aspects of torture, that the class of
people whom society accepts as torturable has a tendency to expand.
In the Roman Empire, the rules changed so that slaves were eligible to
be tortured not just as defendants, but also as witnesses to crimes
committed by others. Then freemen lost their exemption in cases involving treason. By the fourth century, freemen were regularly being
subjected to the same excruciating machines, devices, and weapons

previously reserved for slaves, and the crimes they were tortured for, as either witnesses or as the accused, had become less and less serious. If convicted, the ever-widening torturable class faced torture again— common punishments included crucifixion, mutilation, and the subjection of the allegedly guilty person to the appetites of wild animals in an arena.

The Catholic Church adopted many aspects of Roman law, but was initially opposed to torture. An assembly of cardinals condemned torture in the year 384. By the thirteenth century, however, ecclesiastical sentiment had swung the other way. In 1252, Pope Innocent IV formally announced that heretics deserved torture and that civil authorities had an obligation to do the job. That turnabout is indicative of another pattern of torture: it is easy to condemn the torment when it is done to someone who is not your enemy, but it seems perfectly justifiable when you perceive a threat to your own well-being.

At about the time of Pope Innocent's declaration, legal systems in Western Europe were in a state of flux. For centuries, the prevailing system of determining guilt or innocence in capital crimes had depended upon signs from God. A person suspected of a serious offense would be put through some ordeal—hands would be plunged into flames, hot water, or heated metal, feet would trod upon heated plowshares—and if God regarded the suspect as innocent, he or she would emerge without injury, or at least with injuries so minor that a judge examining the suspect several days after the ordeal would regard them as insignificant.

In the twelfth century, that method of determining guilt came to be recognized as unsatisfactory. A new system of justice evolved, based on old Roman law, in which a conviction could be obtained only with the testimony of two eyewitnesses or a confession from the accused. Circumstantial evidence was significant in cases in which there was only one eyewitness, but taken alone was not enough to convict. Since it was difficult to get two eyewitnesses to many crimes, substantial physical pressure began to be applied to produce confessions, and by the sixteenth century, court-ordered torture was common throughout the Continent.

As in ancient Rome, strict rules governed the application of torture. In judicial proceedings—as opposed to punishment—the methods employed were not supposed to cause death or permanent injury. In his book *Torture,* historian Edward Peters reports that victims were commonly subjected to the rack; the strappado (a procedure, also known as the corda or cola, in which the defendant was hung from the wrists, which were tied behind his or her back, and dropped halfway to the ground, the drop ending with a sudden jerk); various pressure devices that evolved into the leg screw and the thumb screw; extremely tight tying of the hands (chiefly used on women and children); burning the soles of the feet; and sleep deprivation (forty hours was the common period of time). A medical expert was supposed to be present for the torture and a clerk was supposed to make an official record. Legal historian John Langbein, author of *Torture and the Law of Proof* and "Torture and Plea Bargaining" (both of which I am indebted to for the information in this chapter), reports that the German criminal code of 1532 forbade "suggestive questioning, in which the examiner supplied the accused with the detail he wanted to hear from him." The goal was not the confession of guilt—it was recognized that any person might confess just to stop the torture—but the confession of details of the crime. "If the accused confessed to the slaying," Langbein wrote, "he was supposed to be asked where he put the dagger. If he said he buried it under the old oak tree, the examining magistrate was supposed to send someone out to dig it up."

But judges and prosecutors did engage in suggestive questioning, and verification was often shoddy or not done at all. In crimes of witchcraft and heresy, for example, there was no bloody knife to dig up, and so a confession was often taken as the last word. Furthermore, while anyone who was accused of a crime was allowed to recant his or her confession in the courtroom, many declined to do so because they could then be interrogated a second time with the same methods, with their first confession being added to the proofs against them. A third pattern of torture emerges here: in places where torture is common, the judiciary's sympathies are usually with the perpetrators, not with the victims.

And as happened in ancient Rome, the torturable class in Europe expanded. Peters reports that from 1250 until the late eighteenth century, torture was part of the ordinary criminal procedure for most of the states of Europe. Certain people and classes were initially exempt:

children, the elderly, pregnant women, knights, barons, aristocrats, kings, professors, and, usually, the clergy. By the fifteenth century, however, those exemptions had largely disappeared. Everyone could be tortured. What was applied to defendants ultimately was also applied to witnesses.

In Europe during the late Middle Ages and into the Renaissance, torture was both a method of gathering evidence and a favored means of punishment. While petty criminals might be incarcerated for a set term after a trial, prison sentences were more of an exception. By and large, the purpose of prisons was not to punish but to detain people while they awaited trial or execution. For punishment, judges turned to various forms of torture. The German criminal code of 1532, which Langbein says reflected general European practice, provided that traitors should be drawn and quartered, that burglars and murderers be decapitated, that a mother who killed her child be buried alive and impaled, and that other serious criminals could be burned at the stake, drowned, or put upon a device that would smash their limbs. Less serious offenses called for flogging or cutting off the ears, the fingers, or the tongue—usually accompanied by a sentence of banishment. Langbein reports that in England there were eight hundred hangings a year during the reign of Elizabeth I, and as late as the seventeenth century, "traitors were still being castrated, disembowelled, and quartered, felons hanged, heretics burned at the stake; lesser offenders were regularly whipped, their ears shorn, their noses slit."

In Europe, the enshrinement of torture as an acceptable form of legal investigation came to an end in a hundred-year period starting in the mid-eighteenth century. Alternatives to capital punishment and maiming had been developed (imprisonment, the workhouse, transportation to a distant land, and the galleys), and the philosophical underpinnings of those alternatives affected legal reasoning: if there could be punishments less than death, perhaps verdicts did not need to be so certain as to require the accused to confess. Trial by jury, developed in England, began to seem a reasonable alternative to putting a defendant on the rack; if a man's or woman's peers could be convinced by circumstantial evidence, a confession was not needed, and if they were only partially convinced, then perhaps the accused could be partially convicted—in other words convicted of a lesser charge.

Adding impetus to the desire to explore alternatives were the sentiments of influential eighteenth-century philosophers who rejected torture as something that belonged to a dark and superstitious age. Chief among those scholars was the Italian Cesare Beccaria, who argued that torture tested only muscular strength and that truth did not reside in a man's muscles. The abolitionist sentiment among intellectuals had been fueled in part by the expanding definition of the torturable class. Peters points out that there had not been much objection from intellectuals to the torture of people accused of murder, sedition, and betraying their country, but the subjection of magicians, witches, and religious dissenters to hideous pain provoked protest that "was listened to and circulated outside professional or limitedly moralizing circles." A fourth pattern of torture is observable here: it arouses little protest as long as the definition of the torturable class is confined to the lower orders; the closer it gets to one's own door, the more objectionable it becomes.

Prussia abolished all torture in 1754, and other states in Europe followed, with various cantons in Switzerland bringing up the rear in 1848, 1850, and 1851. Judicial torture continued in other parts of the world (Japan, for example, banished it in 1879). Europeans, however, felt that they lived in an enlightened age, that they had eliminated the barbaric practice (in 1874, Victor Hugo proclaimed "torture has ceased to exist"), and that it would soon be as extinct as slavery. It was a strange view, given that prisoners were still being flogged, hung, and subjected to the guillotine, but it was prevalent. In 1929, the *Encyclopaedia Britannica* proclaimed that torture was "only of historical interest as far as Europe is concerned."

It was a wildly inaccurate statement. After the Russian revolution, the Cheka, the Soviet security service, the forerunner of the KGB, employed horrible devices routinely (Peters reports that the Kiev branch would place a cylinder containing a rat on the body of a suspect, then apply heat to the tube, knowing the rat would try to escape the heat by eating its way into the prisoner). Italy was increasingly given to organized brutality after Mussolini ascended to power in 1927. In the two decades that followed, the Third Reich and the Imperial Japanese Army took torture to heights never imagined possible.

After World War II, optimists adopted the belief that torture was done only under despotic or perhaps psychotic regimes, but the revelations in the mid-1950s that France was practicing torture on a widespread scale in Algeria destroyed that notion. In 1958, citing examples from Eastern and Western Europe and calling Hitler merely a forerunner, Jean-Paul Sartre called torture "a plague infecting our whole era."

It was a plague that had been present in the United States for some time. Colonial America was as barbaric as the European continent. In Connecticut, Quakers were branded with the letter H for heresy. In early Virginia, blasphemy was punished by piercing the tongue with a heated bodkin, a tool used for poking holes in fabric and leather. Throughout the colonies there were laws providing for the branding of thieves, forgers, heretics, and burglars, the brand to be applied to the forehead, cheek, or shoulder. The history of slavery in the United States is filled with accounts of torture; former slaves, interviewed in the 1930s by writers working for the Works Progress Administration, reported having been whipped for learning to read, for spilling coffee into a saucer while serving, for praying for freedom. Flogging was practiced in various states well into the twentieth century; in Delaware, the use of the whipping post declined considerably after 1941, when the Delaware legislature passed a law making those who had stolen less than $25 ineligible for the punishment, but it was used on a regular basis until June 1952, and remained a legally sanctioned punishment for another twenty years.

In 1931, the National Commission on Law Observance and Enforcement (commonly known as the Wickersham Commission), a blue-ribbon committee reporting directly to the President of the United States, reported that "the inflicting of pain, physical or mental, to extract confessions or statements is widespread throughout the country." The commission's eleventh report, *Lawlessness in Law Enforcement,* and the book published by the commission's special field investigator (*Our Lawless Police,* by Ernest Hopkins) document police in various cities depriving suspects of food and sleep; confining them in dark, airless cells (in the headquarters of Chicago's Detective Bureau, one hundred people were often kept for hours in a cell meant for six; in Detroit, one cell was regularly so crowded that two jailers were required to shut the door); forcing prisoners to stand for long periods of time; beating people with clubs, blackjacks, rubber hoses, telephone books, and whips; lifting women by their hair; using electric shock devices (in Helena, Arkansas, the sheriff admitted having used an electric chair to get statements, saying he had inherited the device from his predecessor); exposing prisoners to tear gas to get a confession; hanging them head downward out of windows in multistory buildings; handcuffing suspects behind their backs and then lifting them off the ground by their handcuffs; and squeezing the testicles of men in custody (in one case in Cleveland, detectives stripped a man of his clothes and lifted him repeatedly by his genitals).

Since the Wickersham Commission report, the use of torture has surfaced periodically in various parts of the country, even in more modern times. The decades-long plight of prison inmates in Arkansas did not receive national attention until the late 1960s, when various investigations documented the longstanding use of torture at the Tucker State Prison Farm. Techniques included depriving inmates of food, inserting needles under their fingernails, crushing their knuckles and testicles with pliers, and applying electric shock to their genitals with the "Tucker Telephone," a device, invented by the prison physician, that generated an electrical current by drawing on two batteries and a generator taken from an old crank telephone.

The Massachusetts juvenile correctional system was similarly given to torture even in the late 1960s. Officials punished their charges by forcing them to drink from toilets, to kneel on a stone floor with pencils under their knees, to remain naked for days in dark concrete cells, and to submit to falanga—a form of torture in which the soles of the feet are beaten.

In the 1980s, police in New Orleans and New York were convicted of torturing suspects. In New Orleans, suspects were suffocated with plastic bags and hit on the head with telephone books. In New York, police used a stun gun to shock men charged with minor crimes; in one case a high school senior who had never been arrested before emerged from the police station with twenty-five pairs of burn marks on his back, abdomen, and buttocks. Police suspected that he had sold $10 worth of marijuana to an undercover officer. The victim denied he had done so and charges against him were eventually dismissed. In Los Angeles, substantial amounts have been paid to victims of the K-9 unit in out-of-court settlements. Evidence indicates that policemen allowed their German shepherds and rottweilers to bite suspects— guilty and innocent—as a reward for finding them. More than nine hundred people were bitten by Los Angeles police dogs during a three-year period ending in early 1991; by contrast, in a three-year period ending in 1993, Chicago police dogs bit only thirty-two people.

Other accounts of torture have risen in police stations and prisons in small towns and in big cities throughout the United States. No one argues that it is an epidemic, no one argues that it is as bad as it was in the days of the Wickersham investigation, and no one equates the United States with the world's most notorious human rights offenders. At the same time, however, no one can dispute that it happens here.

WHEN PRESENTED with a list of cruel tortures, it is hard not to fixate on the more exotic methods, yet a man or woman who is beaten can be in as much pain as someone subjected to more elaborate techniques. Some of the most brutal tortures are the simplest, requiring no imagination, no technology, and little effort on the part of the torturer.

Depriving someone of food, for example, is remarkably economical and as effective as the most elaborate methods. Depriving a man or woman of sleep is only slightly more difficult and is equally effective. Menachem Begin, prime minister of Israel from 1977 to 1983, was tortured as a young man in the Soviet Union, and in his book *White Nights: The Story of a Prisoner in Russia,* he tells of fellow prisoners who had endured extreme tortures under other regimes and had not cracked, but who lost their will to resist when subjected to sleep deprivation: "In the head of the interrogated prisoner, a haze begins to form. His spirit is wearied to death, his legs are unsteady, and he has one sole desire: to sleep, to sleep just a little, not to get up, to lie, to rest, to forget. . . . Anyone who has experienced this desire knows that not even hunger or thirst are comparable with it. I came across prisoners who signed what they were ordered to sign, only to get what the interrogator promised them. He did not promise them their liberty; he did not promise them food to sate themselves. He promised them—if they signed—uninterrupted sleep! And they signed. . . . And, having signed, there was nothing in the world that could move them to risk again such nights and such days. The main thing was—to sleep."

Sleep deprivation falls into a category of tortures, seemingly more commonly used now than in the past, that are favored because they leave no marks on the victim. Depriving prisoners of sleep or food, forcing them to stand for long periods of time, confining them in positions that cause acute muscle strain, depriving them of the use of a toilet, all allow interrogators to proclaim that they never laid a finger on the men or women in their charge.

Humiliation of the prisoner often adds an additional layer to the torture, producing self-loathing in the prisoner, again with little effort by the torturer. In the mid-1970s, for example, police in Northern Ireland humiliated suspects by forcing them to eat mucus from an interrogator's nose, by riding them as if they were horses, by covering their heads with soiled underwear, and by making a prisoner stand with his undershorts at his knees while the interrogators made insulting remarks about his genitals. The Nazis resorted to humiliation on a grand scale, forcing concentration camp inmates to live in their own excrement. At Bergen-Belsen there was one latrine for thirty thousand women. At Auschwitz there was no toilet paper. Holocaust survivors tell of being beaten or set upon with dogs for leaving their work posts to relieve themselves; many inmates were forced to go about their duties with urine and feces running down their legs. Cleanliness was impossible, but those who gave in completely to that humiliation often died. In his memoir *The Holocaust Kingdom,* Alexander Donat tells of how he and his fellow inmates used a portion of the ersatz coffee they were given in the morning to wash. He noted that some prisoners, driven by hunger, abandoned the wash and drank all the liquid. "This was the first step to the grave," Donat wrote. "It was almost an iron law: those who failed to wash every day soon died."

Torture aimed at a victim's mind is often as effective as the use of the most brutal force. Mock executions, for example, while causing no physical harm, can cause extreme mental anguish. In an article published in the *Chicago Tribune* on May 23, 1994, Yossi Melman, an Israeli journalist, described one such incident in which he was a participant. In 1970, Melman was in the Israeli army, assigned to a platoon patrolling Gaza, when he and his comrades came across a middle-aged Palestinian working in an orchard. After establishing that the man was not involved in anything suspicious, one of the soldiers told him that he had been found guilty of terrorist activities and that he was about to be executed. "The soldier tied him to the tree and blindfolded him with a handkerchief," Melman wrote. "The man's sobs racked his body. I saw death in his eyes. He begged for his soul and his family and screamed that he was innocent. Now my colleague was joined by two of our mates. . . . [They] counted in Arabic, 'One, two, three,' and noisily pulled the triggers. Of course there was no actual shooting as the rifles were not loaded. We all burst out laughing. The first soldier walked up to the Palestinian, took off his blindfold, and untied him. The Palestinian's trousers were wet. He fell to his knees and kissed the feet of the 'liberating' soldier, who gave him, in return, a contemptuous kick and ordered him to get up."

Other psychological methods of torture were recounted by a Honduran torturer named Florencio Caballero in a conversation with *New York Times* reporter James LeMoyne in 1988. Caballero, a former officer in the Honduran army, said that he had been trained on an army base in Texas by instructors from the CIA and the U.S. Army. "They taught us psychological methods—to study the fears and weaknesses of a prisoner," Caballero said. "Make him stand up, don't let him sleep, keep him naked and isolated, put rats and cockroaches in his cell, give him bad food, serve him dead animals, throw cold water on him, change the temperature. . . . The Americans didn't accept physical torture." Caballero provided LeMoyne with the name of one of his victims, who verified that at mealtimes she had been presented with rats and birds, that freezing water had been thrown on her naked body at half-hour intervals for extended periods of time, that she had been forced to stand for hours without sleep, and that she had been prevented from using a toilet.

From 1973 to 1985, Uruguayan authorities attempted psychological torture on a large scale. After having been tortured in more common ways (near drownings, electric shock, burnings, hanging from the wrists, knees, and ankles), inmates incarcerated in Libertad and Punta de Rieles prisons were subjected to conditions calculated to cause psychological pain. In his book *A Miracle, a Universe,* Lawrence Weschler quoted the director of Libertad saying of the prisoners under his charge, "We didn't get rid of them when we had the chance, and one day we'll have to let them go, so we'll have to take advantage of the time we have left to drive them mad." To that end, rules at the two prisons were changed daily. A door that was always to be kept open was suddenly supposed to be kept shut. Prisoners were ordered to bathe when there was no water. They would be directed to wash eating utensils that were already clean. Prisoners on labor detail would clear the ground of stones, stacking them in piles, only to have a subsequent work crew tear down the piles and redistribute the stones. A day might be spent in total silence or with loudspeakers blaring music so loudly that speech was impossible. Singing, smiling, and laughing were forbidden. Visits from a child would be terminated as soon as the parent made an affectionate gesture. The sane would be given insane cellmates. At the end of years and years of such treatment, a released prisoner and his family could expect to be billed thousands of dollars for the room and board that the state had provided.

Psychological methods like those used by the Hondurans and the Uruguayans present the difficulty of defining torture. Is ordering someone to carry out a pointless task torture? No. Is it torture to forbid someone to sing? Clearly not. Is a whole regime designed to drive someone crazy torture? Yes, but at what point does that regime become torture and when is it simply cruel treatment?

Defining precisely what constitutes torture has long been the source of controversy. One rule of thumb is that it is easiest to define when some country other than your own is employing it. Thus a given method deployed by our army is not torture, though it might be if it were done to us.

In 1975, the United Nations defined torture as "any act by which severe pain or suffering, whether physical or mental, is intentionally inflicted by or at the instigation of a public official on a person for such purposes as obtaining from him or a third person information or confession, punishing him for an act he has committed, or intimidating him or other persons. . . . Torture constitutes an aggravated and deliberate form of cruel, inhuman or degrading treatment or punishment." The definition also stated that torture did not include pain or suffering that might arise from legitimate imprisonment if the conditions of detention were consistent with the Standard Minimum Rules for the Treatment of Prisoners adopted by the UN in 1955. In 1984, the definition was refined a bit further. "Discrimination of any kind" was added to the list of motivations for torture and the authorization of such treatment was clarified with the clause "when such pain or suffering is inflicted by or at the instigation of or with the consent or acquiescence of a public official or other person acting in an official capacity."

The 1975 definition, unanimously approved by the member nations, was a significant accomplishment. It provided an undisputed standard that could be applied in legal proceedings, and it placed the infliction of mental suffering on the same footing as the infliction of physical pain, a significant development at a time when some torturers were realizing that a victim's scars, burns, and broken limbs could make for damning evidence while a victim's psychological scars and torment were less easily displayed. The UN definition, however, has proved to be not so easily interpreted in court. When does pain or suffering become "severe"? What exactly constitutes "cruel, inhuman or degrading" treatment?

And despite the member nations' unanimous approval of the definition, the practice of torture has continued largely undiminished, even in countries that voted for the measure. In 1999, almost twenty-five years after the passage of the United Nations definition, Amnesty International recorded incidents of torture or ill-treatment in more than one hundred nations.

{5}

Belfast

"No Brutality of Any Kind"

WHEN JIM AULD arrived at the Crumlin Road Jail in August 1971, he was one of a dozen survivors of the "five techniques." Two other men would go through the same ordeal in October. The initial twelve were housed on the same wing of the prison and were so relieved that the torture was over and that they were still alive that even now they recall those first days in the jail with some fondness. Gerard McKerr remembers it as "an absolute high." Pat Shivers compared it to a childhood outing: "It was like going to Butlin's Holiday Camp." Patrick McNally recalls howls of laughter; one of the men, he told me, complained about something in the jail, and Joe Clarke, another survivor of the treatment, stood up, put a pillowcase over his head, assumed the spread-eagled position, and didn't have to say that life had certainly taken a sudden turn for the better.

But the twelve men were far from well. Schoolteacher Paddy Joe McClean had lost more than forty pounds. Michael Donnelly, a bricklayer from Derry, was unable to use his hands except as clublike instruments. Seeing his livelihood on the line, he complained to the jail doctor, who stuck pins in Donnelly's hands to test his reactions. "I had no feeling at all," Donnelly told me in 1991, "and he said, 'I think you'll be all right in three or four months.' "

Kevin Hannaway's nose was swollen, his teeth had gone through his lip, and as a result his face was distorted beyond recognition.

39

Hannaway's two brothers had also been interned but had not been tortured, and having heard through the grapevine that Kevin had arrived, they went looking for him in the jail yard. Hannaway watched them walk right past him.

Pat Shivers, whose dead son had appeared to him during the torture, went into the exercise yard for the first time and was greeted by a prisoner who said, "Where have you been? Your wife has been looking for you all week. The papers say that you disappeared off the face of the earth." Shivers later said that until that point he had forgotten that he was married.

At that point, none of the men could figure out how the group of twelve had been chosen, though it was clear that geography had something to do with it. The British army had divided Northern Ireland into three brigade areas, and among the dozen men in the Crumlin Road Jail there were four men from each area. Since none of the men had been interrogated before the hooding treatment began, some thought that the treatment was an experiment, not a means of getting information. If you wanted information, they reasoned, the most efficient method is first to ask for it—the torture might prove to be unnecessary. In the years since the torture, other theories have surfaced, none ever confirmed: The men were chosen randomly. They were chosen because the army wanted a cross section of people with Republican views. They were chosen because they were to be guinea pigs, that the interrogation techniques, once refined, were to be used on another dozen men who were being held in isolation in the Crumlin Road Jail and who were the real targets of the experiment. They were chosen because the army's intelligence was wildly inaccurate (only a few of the fourteen men were involved in paramilitary organizations). They were chosen because the army didn't know who the leaders were but thought that by mistreating everyone at the three holding areas, their natural leaders would emerge. They were chosen not for what they could tell the British army but for the intimidating effect that torturing them would have on the communities the men had come from.

In those first days in the jail, the twelve survivors decided to expose what had been done to them, and they asked three professional men who had been interned to witness their statements. Jim Auld recalls that his statement was taken by a Belfast pharmacist. "I can remember him saying, 'Look, there's no way that I can write this, because if I write this, people aren't gonna believe it. Water it down a bit.' " And so Auld watered down his story.

The accounts were given to newspapers, which were also reporting the less scientific abuse of other men arrested in the same sweep. Some told tales of severe beatings, of being harassed by dogs, of being thrown out of a helicopter not knowing it was only a few feet above the ground. Some men were forced to do push-ups, sit-ups, and other exercises for hours at a time. A group of men at the Ballykinler army camp claimed they had been awakened in the middle of the night, forced to run in a circle and simultaneously urinate, then say "Good night, sergeant" and "Good night, corporal" to their keepers, and later bid "Good morning" to a dog. Still others said they had been forced to run over rough ground in their bare feet.

The newspaper stories were dismissed by Brian Faulkner, prime minister of Northern Ireland, who guaranteed that "no brutality of any kind" had occurred.

British Prime Minister Heath, however, appointed a commission, headed by Sir Edmund Compton, to investigate the charges. Compton and his two fellow commissioners arrived in the province on September 1, three weeks after internment had been introduced. They were not welcomed by the internees, who felt that the committee was going to produce a whitewash: Compton had let it be known that he would be holding private hearings and that he would not allow the cross-examination of witnesses. Of the 342 men who had been arrested, only one appeared before the committee.

Compton, however, was satisfied that he had the internees' side of the story because he possessed newspaper accounts of their treatment. He and his two colleagues then proceeded to interview members of the army and the police, who found in Compton a willing listener who seemed to know nothing about the dynamics of torture. Compton came to believe, for example, that the men who had been forced to perform strenuous and degrading exercises all day had been ordered to do so to keep warm. He later referred to the exercises as "position changes" and, in an interview in 1991, indicated to me that the men had merely been told to roll from side to side.

Compton's report was issued on November 16, 1971. The hooding, he wrote, had indeed occurred. "The hood . . . reduces to the mini-mum the possibility that while [the prisoner] is in transit or with other detainees, he will be identified or will be able to identify other persons or the locations to which he is moved. It thus provides security both for the detainee and for his guards. . . . We were told that in fact some complainants kept their hoods on when they could have removed them if they wished."

The continuous noise, Compton wrote, "prevents their overhearing or being overheard by each other and is thus a further security measure. . . . A diet of bread and water . . . may form part of the atmosphere of discipline imposed upon detainees while under control for the purpose of interrogation. . . .

"Mr. Auld's complaint that he was refused permission to relieve himself was denied. It was not clear to us how a man in the required posture, hooded and surrounded by a loud noise, was expected to indicate his need. We were told he would have to use gestures. Such gestures might initially be construed merely as an attempt to move from the required posture. If this were so, he would be put back in the posture in the manner described, at any rate to start with. We were however told that lavatory facilities were available and were regularly used under escort by all the interrogatees, with the exception of Mr. McClean. . . . It was Mr. McClean's own fault that he did not use them."

The report also indicated that the posture the men were forced to assume was not stressful; that Joe Clarke's hands were not beaten but rather massaged in order to restore circulation in them; and that Paddy Joe McClean's black eye and the contusions on his arms and chest must have occurred accidentally while in transit.

In Compton's version of events, the men were provided with water and bread at six-hour intervals, and those who claimed they had been starved had actually failed to take the food that was offered. Jim Auld did not stand at the wall for six days, Compton said, but for forty-three and a half hours, which, according to the army's alleged record, was longer than anyone else. According to Compton, Pat Shivers had been on the wall for twenty-three hours, Gerard McKerr for fifteen, and Paddy Joe McClean for twenty-nine. Michael Donnelly, the bricklayer whose hands were useless when he arrived at Crumlin Road Jail, had been at the wall for only nine hours, according to Compton.

"These methods," Compton wrote, "have been used in support of the interrogation of a small number of persons arrested in Northern Ireland who were believed to possess information of a kind which it was operationally necessary to obtain as rapidly as possible in the interest of saving lives, while at the same time providing the detainees with the necessary security for their own persons and identities."

Compton did conclude that the men had been deprived of sleep, that the bread and water diet was insufficient, and that the hooding, the noise, and the physical methods used to keep the men at the wall did amount to ill treatment. He then went on to draw a most remarkable conclusion:

"Where we have concluded that physical ill-treatment took place, we are not making a finding of brutality on the part of those who handled these complainants. We consider that brutality is an inhuman or savage form of cruelty, and that cruelty implics a disposition to inflict suffering, coupled with indifference to, or pleasure in, the victim's pain. We do not think that happened here."

Upon its release, Compton's report was debated in the House of Commons. Home Secretary Reginald Maulding assured those who criticized the interrogation methods that "there was no permanent lasting injury whatever, physical or mental, to any of the men concerned," and he went on to say that vigorous methods were needed to fight a ruthless enemy like the IRA. Lord Balniel, junior minister of defense, said that there was no evidence of torture, ill treatment, or brainwashing, and that the methods employed had produced "invaluable" information. Defense Minister Lord Carrington went a bit further, telling television reporters that the men who had been subjected to the techniques were "thugs and murderers."

The Compton Report prompted two British intelligence experts to write letters to the *Times,* then the United Kingdom's most prestigious daily newspaper, commenting on the five techniques. In a letter published on November 25, 1971, Cyril Cunningham, who had served in the Ministry of Defense from 1951 to 1961, called such interrogations "blunt, medieval and extremely inefficient." Those who would employ such methods, Cunningham wrote, were "singularly stupid and unimaginative." As senior psychologist in charge of Prisoner of War Intelligence, Cunningham had made a comprehensive study of international interrogation techniques for the ministry and had concluded that sheer ignorance on the part of politicians and commanders resulted in favoring interrogators "whose only qualification is a loud voice and an overbearing manner." "The best interrogator I ever met," Cunningham said in his letter, ". . . had the demeanor of an unctuous parson."

Two days after Cunningham's letter, the *Times* published a similar protest from L. St. Clare Grondona, who had served as commander of the Combined Services Detailed Interrogation Centre during World War II. Writing of the treatment provided German prisoners, Grondona said that interrogations were always carried out with regard to the Geneva Convention, that the interrogators therefore had to be "as wily as they were resourceful," and that the methods used were "processes of 'painless extraction' seasoned with legitimate guile. More often than not a 'guest' would be unaware that he had given us useful data. Courtesy was extended to every prisoner so long as his behavior warranted this—and it usually did. Comfortable quarters were provided, and prisoners' fare was precisely the same as for British personnel. It is the simple truth to say that if one of our interrogators had suggested submitting any prisoner to any form of physical duress (which would certainly not have been permitted) he would have been a laughingstock among his colleagues. Nevertheless, the intelligence we obtained (all the items of which were carefully correlated) was of inestimable value."

At the time that the Compton Report was issued, Home Secretary Maulding announced that there would be a second inquiry, one that would consider "authorised procedures for the interrogation of persons suspected of terrorism." Three men were given responsibility for the inquiry: Lord Parker of Waddington, who was to be the chairman, John Boyd-Carpenter, and Lord Gardiner.

The trio, known as the Parker Commission, met in secret and heard evidence from no detainees. In the end, they were unable to reach a consensus. On January 31, 1972, Lord Parker and Mr. Boyd-Carpenter filed a majority report, and Lord Gardiner filed a sharply dissenting minority report.

In the minority report, Gardiner revealed that planning for the interrogation had begun in March, five months before the men were arrested; that officers of the English Intelligence Centre had taught the techniques to members of the Royal Ulster Constabulary at a seminar in Northern Ireland in April; and that officers from the center were present when the hooded men went through their ordeal.

Gardiner said that the medical experts who had appeared before the committee had testified that the foundation of the five techniques had been laid by the KGB in Russia, who had first tried sensory isolation as a method of inducing mental disorientation. "Sensory isolation is one method of inducing an artificial psychosis or episode of insanity," he said, and he pointed out that such states had a way of becoming permanent.

To provide some contrast to the suffering the hooded men had endured, Gardiner quoted from a 1959 article in *The Lancet*. The article told of a sensory isolation experiment in which a hospital recruited twenty volunteers from its staff and placed them in a room with a constant noise. The volunteers were required to wear goggles that impaired vision and gloves made of padded fur. They were allowed to walk about, they could sleep on mattresses, and they were fed normal meals four times a day. During mealtimes they were allowed to remove the gloves and goggles and chat with colleagues on the hospital staff. They were paid for their experience and asked to stay in the room for as long as they could.

Two of the twenty volunteers gave up after five hours. By the end of forty-eight hours, two-thirds of the volunteers had quit, citing unbearable anxiety, tension, and panic attacks. Gardiner emphasized that these were volunteers in their own hospital, who knew they would not be mistreated, who had not been beaten, who had not been deprived of food or sleep, and who had not been forced to stand in a painful position.

Gardiner concluded that there was nothing in domestic law that allowed a soldier or policeman to do what had been done, that no army officer and no cabinet minister could lawfully have authorized the use of the procedures, and that the procedures were morally unjustifiable, an assault, and a crime.

The majority report filed by Lord Parker and Mr. Boyd-Carpenter reached a distinctly different conclusion. The two men reported that British forces had previously used some or all of the techniques in Palestine, Malaya, Kenya, Cyprus, the British Cameroons, Brunei,

British Guiana, Aden, Malaysia, and the Persian Gulf. Parker and Boyd-Carpenter went on to quote without question the army's justification for their use. The army claimed that seven hundred IRA members had been identified, that arms caches, safe houses, communications and supply routes, future plans, and responsibility for about eighty-five unexplained incidents had all been revealed. In addition, the army claimed that massive numbers of weapons had been discovered after internment began, and that the great part of that haul resulted from information obtained from the "interrogation in depth," the euphemism employed by the government for the torture.

The army's claims, however, were easily disputed. Membership in the IRA is a crime in Northern Ireland. If seven hundred IRA members had been identified, why weren't even a small fraction of that number immediately arrested and charged? If the interrogation was so successful, why were the men who allegedly gave so much information, those men whom Lord Carrington identified as "thugs and murderers," never charged with any crime themselves—not even with membership in an illegal organization?

The great increase in weapons confiscated had other, far more likely explanations. First, the British security forces arrested and interrogated hundreds more people after the implementation of the internment policy; one would expect that increased intelligence would result from a dramatic increase in interrogations. Second, and more important, the government's internment policy had proven to be a tremendous recruiting device for the IRA. Bombings, assassination attempts, and armed robberies escalated enormously as new members swelled the ranks of the guerrillas. Statistics from the four-month periods before and after the introduction of internment show that in the latter period there was a tenfold increase in the number of soldiers and policemen killed. In 1972, the year after internment was introduced, the number of shootings rose by 605 percent. A more likely reason for any alleged increase in the number of weapons confiscations was that in the wake of the internment arrests, hundreds more weapons were acquired, moved, used, and openly displayed.

Parker and Boyd-Carpenter's majority report also downplayed the medical effects of the five techniques. They claimed that any mental disorientation could be "expected to disappear within a matter of hours at the end of the interrogation," though "in a small minority of cases, some mental effects may persist for up to two months. There is no evidence of a mental effect lasting longer, though fairly all the medical witnesses were unable to rule out that possibility." They went on to say that the hooded men had an advantage over the volunteers in various experiments of sensory bombardment in that the hooded men "enjoyed a break during which medical examination and later interrogation took place" and were also "members of an organization bound together by bonds of loyalty which would help them hold out." In fact most of the men were not members of any paramilitary group, there were long-lasting effects, and being interrogated by one's torturer is hardly "a break." Many torture survivors report that some of the worst anguish they experienced occurred in the intervals between torture sessions.

Parker and Boyd-Carpenter went on to suggest that any mental effects that did not disappear at once might be self-induced, the result of anxiety caused by "guilty knowledge" and "fear of reprisals" if the detainee had let down "his fellows" and given information during the interrogation.

Parker and Boyd-Carpenter also reported that one of the benefits of the techniques was that they had the potential to establish the internee's innocence and thereby facilitate his release. They concluded that in the future there was no reason "to rule out these techniques on moral grounds."

Despite that conclusion, Prime Minister Edward Heath announced that the government would stop using the techniques. Mr. Heath declined to be interviewed for this book, so his motives for that decision cannot be produced here. He may have been moved by Lord Gardiner's moral arguments, but it seems more likely that he was feeling international pressure: in the European Commission of Human Rights, the Republic of Ireland had done something truly remarkable. Outraged by the treatment accorded the Irishmen interned on the other side of the border, the Republic dispensed with cautious diplomacy and filed suit against the United Kingdom. The suit alleged that the fourteen hooded men had been tortured.

{6}

ISRAEL

A Dangerous Report

AT THE END OF January 1988, news coverage of the Israeli government's response to the intifada tended to focus on the new "strongarm" policy and not on individual incidents. The events at Beita and Hawara passed without mention in the Israeli press.

In March, two months after ordering the breaking of limbs in the two villages, Lieutenant Colonel Yehuda Meir was promoted to the rank of colonel and transferred out of the West Bank to the command of a civil defense unit. That same month, Captain Ben-Moshe's group was rotated out of Nablus to a refugee camp in the Gaza Strip. Ben-Moshe left the army shortly thereafter to attend university, where he planned to study accounting.

Some time that spring, Lieutenant Omri Kochva, who had overseen some of the beatings at Beita and Hawara, went home on leave to Na'an, the kibbutz where he had been born and raised. It happened that his best friend, Yoram Rabin, was also home on leave. The two had been born weeks apart in the summer of 1967, had grown up sleeping in the same room, had attended school together, and had joined the army at the same time. Kochva had a compact, athletic build and seemed a natural warrior; when he joined the army he chose a combat unit—the Nahal Brigade. Rabin, tall and thin, with wire-rimmed glasses, was the intellectual of the pair and a fanatic collector of the music of the Beatles and John Lennon. He had problems with his back, so rather than join a front-line unit, he had signed on with the military police, where he became an investigator.

Before the intifada, military police assigned to the occupied territories had investigated every shooting and every complaint that was formally filed. If someone living in Gaza or the West Bank complained about a soldier stealing something or molesting someone, or if a human rights group complained about mistreatment somewhere, the complaint would be investigated (though perhaps not to the complainant's satisfaction). The protest had to be formally filed, however. A story of soldiers breaking the law that appeared in the newspaper would not be investigated unless a complaint was filed.

The intifada, however, taxed the military police investigative staff to their limits. Where they might have had two or three people shot by soldiers in a busy week, they now might have twenty or more shot in a single day. Complaints from various human rights groups were arriving in record numbers. In order to cope with the increased workload, the military police became more selective about which complaints they investigated, working only on those they regarded as both important and likely to lead to some solid and useful evidence. "And so every day twenty reports—or a lot of reports—arrived," Rabin told me in an interview in January 1993, "and were just stapled together and put in the closet without being investigated."

At that point, military police investigators did not consider the occupied territories to be a prestigious assignment. Ambitious investigators like Lieutenant Rabin wanted to be working in the forensic laboratory, the polygraph office, or in some unit investigating "real crime." The intifada was considered something else: children and teenagers throwing stones at soldiers, and soldiers sometimes shooting them dead. "We were going to the elite units," Rabin said, "and after everyone had thrown stones at them, we questioned them. 'Okay, you shot him because he threw stones at you [today] or because he threw stones at you yesterday?' Nobody wanted to do it. Nobody wants to serve in MPI Nablus. They want to serve in Lebanon and to ride in helicopters looking for drug smuggling. And the paratrooper says, 'Oh, you don't want to investigate? I don't want to be here either. I don't want to run after children.'

"It was a bad time—bad work for the paratroopers, bad work for the investigators. Everything was gray, nothing was black and white.

It was a shitty situation politically, socially. It was not a war. It was not the '67 war, it was not the '73 war, it was not even the '82 war that was in dispute. So everybody wanted to close one eye."

Not long after the start of the intifada, the caseload of the investigators in the West Bank was so heavy that reinforcements were called for. Rabin was transferred from a base in the south of Israel to Jerusalem in order to help out. For investigator Rabin, there was a bright side to the transfer to Jerusalem: in covering the West Bank, he could drop in and visit his friend Omri Kochva at the base near Nablus. The friendship had been an unlikely one on the kibbutz: the athlete-farmer-warrior and the intellectual with the John Lennon glasses. The friendship was even less likely in the military, since Israeli combat soldiers generally despise military police investigators. Rabin recalls that Kochva would introduce him to fellow soldiers by saying, "There is MPI, but this is my friend. He is MPI, but he is good."

When the two men were home on leave at the same time in the spring of 1988, both were twenty-year-old lieutenants. At some level, Kochva was troubled by what had occurred at Beita and Hawara, and in a conversation one afternoon, months after the beatings, he told Rabin about the incidents.

Rabin was amazed. It was like nothing he had ever heard before, and he did not think that it reflected the government's new policy. "When he first told me that story, I didn't tell him, 'Wow, that amazes me, it is against Jewish morals, or against all humanity,' " Rabin told me. "He was my friend. I didn't think that he made crimes against the universe."

Rabin did think, however, that his friend had been given an order that violated the rules taught in textbooks in military police school. The two friends then had a fierce debate about the legality of the action, a debate that continued over the course of several days. Kochva argued that there was one law for the military police and another for combat soldiers, and that the textbooks of the investigator did not reflect the real pressures of the battlefield. Rabin vacillated, wondering if in fact that might be true, but for the most part the MP maintained his position. After several days, Kochva changed his mind and told Rabin that he believed the orders had indeed been illegal.

As an investigator with responsibility for events in the Nablus area, Rabin wanted to investigate the beatings in the two villages. He told me that he was motivated not by outrage, but by the hope that if he did a good job on the case, he would get a promotion and a transfer to a more prestigious assignment. The Beita and Hawara cases were a rare opportunity, first, because they involved charges against a high-ranking officer (by that time, Meir had been promoted to colonel), and second, because the investigation would be initiated by someone within the ranks of MPI. Most of the cases Rabin worked on were initiated by commanders in the field who called to report a shooting, all of which were supposed to be investigated.

Rabin could not, however, simply go back to his base and open a file. "I had to have a formal reason to open a case because my commander decides what to open and what to close. So if I told him I need a car to go to Nablus to talk with a lieutenant of my kibbutz who wants to open a big file, he would say, 'Why? Do you want to revenge something? Why would an officer in the paratroopers go to the military police?' "

Rabin believes that suspicion would have been reasonable. "Everybody hates the MPI," he says. "Nobody wants to testify, to go to trial. [As a soldier], if something happens to me, I expect that you will not tell about me, and if something happens to you, you expect that I will not tell about you. So the MPI comes and investigates or doesn't come and investigate, but no soldier ever calls them. That is the idea.

"Even in this case, with the soldiers who cried [after the beatings], who found it hard, and who were from the Left [of the political spectrum], there was something stronger than all that emotion—a principle inside the individual soldier, the knowledge that no one will go to the military police and file a report.

"You have to understand the atmosphere. A soldier who is in Nablus does not know where the base of the military police is. He does not know if he has to go to Jerusalem or Tel Aviv, to the prosecutor or to the military police. He does not know if he can call in a complaint on the phone or if he is supposed to write it out. He knows nothing about it. You have to be so determined and so idealistic to fight for an incident to come out that no reasonable person would do it."

AFTER HIS LEAVE ENDED, Rabin returned to his office with the hope that there might be a piece of paper somewhere in the files that would support his friend's story. He knew from experience that no soldier would have complained, and he doubted that any of the Arabs had filed a report. "They are afraid," Rabin told me. "They see a military policeman and a paratrooper and they don't know the difference, so they won't come." Rabin thought there was a chance, however, that Red Cross field-workers laboring in the West Bank might have run into one of the wounded Palestinians, and so he pulled out the binders that contained old Red Cross reports, reports that had been discounted and dismissed upon arrival.

The task was not easy, since the Red Cross files its complaints in English, and at that point Rabin didn't know much of the language. He read through the pages looking only for the words "Hawara" and "Beita." He found them on a report dated May 2, 1988, a report that also bore the handwritten remarks of the MPI sergeant who had filed it away. In Hebrew, the sergeant had written "too exaggerated."

"I went to my commander and asked him to translate," Rabin told me. "He read the report to me. I said, 'What you just read is true and I will prove it.' He said, 'Okay, okay, you have work to do,' something like that. He said, 'Okay, who told you it is true?' I said, 'A friend of mine.' He said, 'Okay.' And he kept on doing the usual thing. And I kept on saying, 'No, it is true. I know it is true.' I was a lieutenant, but I was a little soldier, you understand."

Rabin's commander gave him permission to open the file, but he did not share the young lieutenant's enthusiasm. "He didn't pay it great attention," Rabin recalled, "because a lot of investigations are nothing because the Arabs lie, or the Arabs tell the truth and the soldier lies and you will never know who lies and who told the truth."

Rabin continued, "So on the weekend, I went to Na'an and I said, 'Omri, I found it, and my major told me to open the file.'" Omri was uneasy. He liked Yehuda Meir, knew that Meir liked him, and was uncomfortable testifying against the colonel. Kochva also feared that he might be prosecuted himself, and in light of that, Rabin arranged a meeting with Colonel Menachem Finklestein, the chief military prosecutor. According to Kochva and Rabin, Finklestein promised that if prosecution did result from the investigation, it would be directed solely against Meir.

And so, on June 28, 1988, five months after the beatings, Kochva told his story for the record. Rabin recalls that there was still considerable doubt within MPI despite Kochva's story: "Everyone said, 'It was exaggerated. The one who gave you the testimony is dreaming.' " No one in the office paid it much attention. Rabin, saddled with his usual heavy caseload, plodded on, fitting in interviews with Captain Ben-Moshe and the rest of the unit when time permitted. In order to protect his friend Omri as the source of the investigation, Rabin always brought another investigator along when he did an interview, and so that officer's name, and not Rabin's, appeared at the bottom of each set of testimony.

"I remember that two of the soldiers cried when they testified," Rabin said. "One of them told me, 'I didn't tell this to my father, I didn't tell it to my girlfriend, because I think it was bad, and sometimes I think about it at night.' And he cried. I don't remember if he had been one of those who was hitting or if he was one of those on the bus.

"It is sad to tell, but a lot of the people who did the beating felt nothing about it—'If it was against the order, okay. If it was not against the order, okay.' But it didn't affect them personally. He is eighteen years old and the legal concepts have not been explained to him. I say, 'Okay, on that day, what happened?' He says, 'I took, I run, I hit, I do that, bye.' He signs [his statement] and goes. So when someone tells you what happened and he starts to cry, it is a much stronger feeling, so much so that I had a tightness in my throat. Because I didn't explain that it is against the morals, it is against this, against that, against what you learned in school. I just said, 'You can tell me what happened.' And he knows it is bad, and he starts to cry."

Rabin was well acquainted with Colonel Meir because the two had conferred on numerous other cases that had risen when Meir was commander of the Nablus region. "So when I came to him, he said, 'Okay, what is it this time?' I told him it is not ordinary testimony. I told him, 'There were these events in Hawara and Beita and what do you have to say? You don't have to say anything if you don't want to, but if you say something, it can be used against you in your file, etc., etc.' And so he said, 'Okay, I don't want to say anything. Get out of my office.' He had known about the investigation for quite a long time, but he was very angry when I came to him."

As is typical in Israeli military police investigations, Rabin made little attempt to gather information from the Arabs. He talked to none of the victims, nor did he visit the hospitals they might have been rushed to. When he prepared his final report, he wrote that the investigation had begun as a result of a complaint from the Red Cross, and he listed the date of that complaint as the starting point for the investigation. In a further effort to protect his friend, he placed Omri Kochva's testimony last among the witnesses, although anyone sorting the documents by date would have noticed that Kochva had been the first to be interviewed.

Rabin submitted his file about five months after the start of his investigation, ten months after the beatings had taken place. His report, charging Meir with "breach of authority," was a particularly damaging file, both because of the nature of the offense and because no one of Meir's rank had been charged with misconduct at that point in the intifada. After reading the file, Rabin's superiors told him that he could not be listed as the author because a lieutenant was not of sufficient rank to charge a colonel with an offense. That infuriated the young investigator. "I had told everyone it was true, and everyone, including my commander, had said, 'Oh, it is nothing, nothing, nothing.' And then in the end they said, 'Oh, we can't put your name on this.' So it was quite an insult."

Rabin insisted that his name should appear, and in the end a compromise was reached. The final draft, dated November 15, 1988, carried two signatures: Rabin's and his commanding officer's.

"So we sent the file to the [military] district attorney," Rabin told me, "and he said, 'Oh, this is very dangerous.' And he sent it higher and higher and higher."

The file ended up on the desk of Brigadier General Amnon Strashnow, the judge advocate general, the equivalent of the attorney general for the Israel Defense Forces. Strashnow had two choices. He could order Meir to be court-martialed for a variety of charges reflecting the grievous bodily harm inflicted and the issuing of manifestly illegal orders, or he could call Meir in for a disciplinary hearing on a charge of exceeding authority. If he chose a court-martial, Meir could face a twenty-year sentence if convicted. If Strashnow chose a disciplinary hearing, the most severe sentence that could be handed down would be a "severe reprimand"—in essence, a black mark in Meir's military file.

Strashnow made his decision in March 1989, five months after

Lieutenant Rabin's report was completed and more than a year after the beatings. Chief of staff Dan Shomron called Meir into his office to deliver the decision. "Good morning," Shomron said. "Severe reprimand."

Colonel Meir was then thirty-seven, two years and some months away from qualifying for his pension. Judge Advocate General Strashnow, Chief of Staff Shomron, and chief of army personnel Brigadier General Yirmi Olmert decided that Meir should terminate his active army duty, but do so in such a way that his pension would not be jeopardized. They arranged for Meir to be loaned to the General Security Service—the Israeli secret police—for two years. The GSS agreed to pay Meir's army salary, and he would thus be able to retire at the age of forty at a colonel's rank, pension intact.

At that point, the Israeli public still knew nothing about Beita, Hawara, and Colonel Meir's orders. When military police investigator Rabin heard what had come of his report, he was disappointed. "Omri and a lot of people in the MPI said, 'Oh, that is proof that in the MPI it is one way, in the field it is another way. It is not the same law. When there is a political question involved and when the minister of defense [Yitzhak Rabin] wants it one way, it will be that way. The law is not equally applied [to officers and common soldiers]. Meir was a high officer, and it wasn't good for the army, and so nothing happened and they buried it.'

"It was against all of the things that I learned in my course in the military police," Rabin told me. "I was quite amazed."

The army's arrangements with Meir, however, eventually leaked to the press. On April 28, 1989, Alex Fishman, a reporter with the Israeli daily *Hadashot,* wrote an article entitled "Who Is Afraid of Colonel Yehuda Meir?" Fishman indicated that chief of staff Shomron had suffered a slip of the tongue, the press had begun making inquiries about Meir, and the GSS then began to have second thoughts about employing someone who was about to become famous. Fishman knew that a cover-up had taken place, but he did not know exactly what was being covered.

At about the same time, Yossi Sarid, a leftist member of the Israeli Knesset, heard that a senior army officer was about to be appointed to a job in the GSS because the army was not interested in his continued service. Sarid called the army and the GSS and said the arrangement was not acceptable, that if a man was not fit to serve in the army, he was not fit to serve in any Israeli security force.

After hearing that Sarid was interfering with the appointment, Colonel Meir arranged a meeting with the Knesset member. Meir was open with Sarid and asked for his help. He said that what had occurred at Beita and Hawara was not unusual, that what had happened there had happened elsewhere, and that he had simply been following orders given to him at the time. Sarid was sympathetic. He had been opposed to Defense Minister Rabin's beatings policy from the start and believed that Rabin should be held accountable for what had resulted. Sarid asked Meir to lend him the army's investigative file so that he could make an informed decision. Meir left the office believing that Sarid was going to keep the information confidential and that the parliamentarian was in his corner.

Sarid took the file home, began to read it, and grew more horrified as he turned each page. He later wrote that he suffered considerable anguish in deciding whether to help "an unfortunate person" who had trusted him, or whether to expose the incident. He chose the latter, and on May 4, 1989, he published an article in the daily *Ha'aretz* entitled "The Night of the Broken Clubs." "In the new Israel," he wrote, "any atrocity is possible." He then went on to describe in detail what had taken place in Hawara, leaving out the names of the soldiers and officers who had been the perpetrators.

The Association for Civil Rights in Israel, a small organization funded mostly by American foundations, was inspired by the controversy. Dan Simon, an ACRI staff lawyer who spoke Arabic, went to Hawara and found four of the victims. It was the first time that any Israeli had asked them to talk about the incident, which had occurred almost a year and a half earlier. The four men signed affidavits and gave power of attorney to ACRI. As was to be expected, none of the men knew the names of the soldiers who had beaten them, and at that point, ACRI knew the name of only one person involved in the incident: Colonel Meir. As a result, the rest of the perpetrators— Captain Eldad Ben-Moshe, his deputy Captain Ziv Gefen, Lieutenants Omri Kochva and Ilan Shani, Major Danny Gabriel, and the soldiers who did the beatings—were not named when ACRI filed suit in the Israeli High Court of Justice. The suit asked the court to order Judge Advocate General Strashnow, chief of staff Dan Shomron, and chief of personnel Yirmi Olmert to order the trial of Meir in military court.

Joshua Schoffman, ACRI's legal director, argued that Judge Advocate General Strashnow had acted with extreme unreasonableness and a lack of good faith, that Meir was clearly guilty of unlawfully and intentionally causing grievous bodily harm, and that he should have been charged accordingly. Other soldiers and officers of lesser rank had been court-martialed for far less serious offenses, Schoffman said, and the Meir case clearly indicated that the law was not applied equally when the higher ranks were involved.

The IDF's defense, initially laid out in a letter to ACRI and later presented to the High Court, leaned heavily on the argument that the incidents had taken place at the beginning of the intifada, a short time after the "strong-arm" or "firm hand" policy had been introduced. Strashnow said that there had been a lack of clarity regarding orders on using force, that a hazy situation had resulted from conflicting statements in the press and the absence of an unambiguous order from the chain of command. Furthermore, Strashnow said, considerable time—fifteen months—had passed between the events and the bringing of charges, and the punishment that had been imposed, the forced resignation, was very significant to a man whose whole professional life had been in the employ of the army. That punishment, Strashnow said, was designed to send a clear message to other soldiers that such behavior would not be tolerated.

In various motions before the court, ACRI pressed for details of the army's investigation and its arrangement with Meir, and over the course of six months, the High Court justices ordered Strashnow and the IDF to produce various documents. In the fall, months after it had filed its suit, ACRI learned that Meir had actually not yet left the army; because the transfer to the GSS had not gone through, the colonel was on leave with pay until a place could be found for him in some public institution. Strashnow still wanted Meir to get his pension. "Along with respecting the rights of Palestinians," Strashnow said, "one must also consider the rights of an officer who has served in the Israeli army for twenty years."

The IDF continued to resist ACRI's request for a copy of the actual agreement with Meir, but was eventually forced to turn it over. One clause in the agreement stated that the IDF would "not initiate official exposure of the case," flatly contradicting Strashnow's claim that Meir's reprimand was intended to send a message to other soldiers.

The High Court's decision to accept the case was unprecedented, as courts in Israel, like courts in the United States, are not accustomed to compelling prosecutors to charge someone with a crime. Under the doctrine of separation of powers, prosecution is supposed to be initiated by prosecutors, not by judges.

Few people were more concerned about the High Court's decision to intervene than military police investigator Yoram Rabin. Rabin told me that after the High Court accepted the case, Colonel Finklestein, the army's chief prosecutor, told him that the case had moved beyond the control of the prosecutor's office, that anything could happen. Finklestein allegedly made it clear that his promise to charge only Colonel Meir could be rendered null and void by an order from the High Court to prosecute everyone. As a result, Rabin feared that he had put his friend Omri Kochva in jeopardy of a court-martial and a jail sentence.

High Court justices Moshe Beiski, Yaakov Kedmi, and Dov Levin issued their decision on December 24, 1989. (Beiski, the presiding judge who wrote the first opinion, had been saved from German death camps during World War II by German industrialist Oscar Schindler; Beiski had been one of the lucky Jews whose names were on Schindler's list.) Addressing Strashnow's argument that a considerable amount of time had passed between the beating incidents and the drawing up of charges, Beiski noted that criminal proceedings sometimes took place years after the commission of the offense. If the passage of fifteen months was a legitimate excuse, Beiski asked, why had the judge advocate general gone ahead and charged Meir anyway, albeit with a lesser offense?

Beiski also dismissed the defense that Colonel Meir's forced retirement from active duty was sufficient punishment (Meir had been formally dismissed from the IDF payroll on November 1), comparing the case to that of a doctor or lawyer who has committed a crime. The doctor would be both disbarred and prosecuted, Beiski said, and the same should hold true for Meir. Beiski also said that Strashnow and the IDF command had provided no clear reason why the Meir case did not represent a case of discrimination in favor of a high-ranking officer, as many lower ranking soldiers had been both forced to retire and subjected to a court-martial.

Beiski reserved his strongest sentiments for Strashnow's argument that there was a "lack of clarity as to the use of force" at the time. "Is it at all possible," Beiski wrote, "to speak of a 'lack of clarity' and 'haziness' when the matter is one of an order to remove people from their homes, bind their hands and gag their mouths, beat them with clubs in order to break their hands and feet? . . . Acts of this sort arouse every cultured person and no haziness or lack of clarity can excuse them."

Justice Kedmi wrote that he would have been more impressed with the dismissal of Meir if it had been immediate and decisive, done in a manner that expressed abhorrence of and revulsion toward Meir's conduct, rather than in a way that looked more like resignation under agreed conditions with care that none of the conditions would be painful. Kedmi concluded that Strashnow's ruling was "intolerable," that Meir's acts were "in complete contradiction to the fundamental values of the people of Israel and to the basic norms of conduct as expressed in Israeli law," and that the order to break arms and legs was clearly illegal without explanation to anyone who heard it, down to the last soldier.

Justice Levin, writing last, asked, "What here is hazy? What here is not clear?" The acts performed in Hawara and Beita were so serious, Levin said, that "everyone involved in initiating or carrying out those acts should pay the penalty for such."

It was the first time in Israel's history that the High Court had overruled the judge advocate general. Strashnow was ordered to court-martial Meir, and in January 1990, Meir was charged with aggravated assault, intentionally causing bodily harm, and conduct unbecoming an officer.

Despite Judge Levin's admonition that "everyone involved" should be penalized, no one else was indicted.

{7}

CHICAGO

"The Pain Stays in Your Head"

ANDREW WILSON's complaints were given little credence and not much of a hearing until seven years after he had murdered Officers Fahey and O'Brien, when his civil suit came to trial before U.S. District Court Judge Brian Barnett Duff. Wilson was charging that after his arrest, various policemen beat him upon his arrival at Area 2; that they put a plastic bag over his head so that he could not breathe; that they burned him, first with a cigarette and later with a radiator; that Detective John Yucaitis administered electric shock and Lieutenant Jon Burge carried it to great lengths; that Detectives Patrick O'Hara and William McKenna participated in the conspiracy by making no mention of the torture in their reports on the case; and that it was a de facto policy or custom of the city of Chicago and the police department to mistreat persons suspected of killing police officers—in other words, that the ill treatment was widespread and well known, even at the highest levels of the department, and nobody did anything about it. Wilson was asking for $10 million in damages. The outcome would have no effect on his criminal conviction.

Although Wilson was suing six defendants (the four detectives, former police superintendent Richard Brzeczek, and the city), it soon became apparent to everyone in the courtroom that the real contest was between Andrew Wilson and Jon Burge. Burge was the commander of the unit that interrogated Wilson and was allegedly the perpetrator-in-chief. On the surface, the battle seemed to be a mismatch of tremendous proportions.

Jon Burge was born a few days before Christmas 1947, the second son of Floyd and Ethel Burge. Floyd, of Norwegian descent, worked for the phone company in a blue-collar job, and Ethel, who was of German, English, and Irish descent, went to work when her son Jon was about ten years old. She wrote a fashion column for the *Chicago Daily News,* did some modeling, organized fashion shows, and once wrote a book in the "Dress for Success" vein.

Jon Burge was a good student in high school and went off to the University of Missouri with great expectations, but he managed to flunk out not long after his arrival; in an interview in 1989 he told me that he had been enjoying himself too much to study, and so was asked to leave. After he returned to Chicago he worked as a stock clerk in a grocery store for eight months and then joined the army, where he eventually attained the rank of staff sergeant. Along the way he served time as a drill instructor and attended military police school at Fort Benning, where he acknowledged he received some training in interrogation. He volunteered twice to go to Vietnam. The first time he was sent to Korea. The second time he got what he asked for.

In Vietnam he served as a military policeman assigned to the 9th Infantry. He was twice awarded the army commendation for valor, both times for leaving a bunker to drag wounded men to safety amid incoming fire. He also was given the Bronze Star for meritorious service, the Vietnamese Cross of Gallantry, and a Purple Heart (which he says was given to him for a shrapnel wound that laid him up for "about fifteen minutes"). He took an honorable discharge in August 1969, went to work in a gas station, and applied to join the police. In March 1970, at the age of twenty-two, he was officially accepted.

On January 26, 1972, Patrolman Burge, age twenty-four, responded to a call of "woman with a gun" at a drugstore in a poor black neighborhood on Chicago's south side. When he arrived, he saw Erma Moody, twenty-two, talking on the telephone and pointing a .22-caliber derringer at her throat. First she told Burge not to come any closer. After a few minutes she said she wanted to go home to check on her baby, and Burge and another officer escorted her there. Once in her home, Mrs. Moody, still with the gun at her throat, said she would like to see a member of the clergy. Burge made the call, and he and the three priests who responded did their best to soothe the distraught woman. After about an hour and a half, Burge began to feel that Mrs. Moody was likely to pull the trigger, and he signaled to the other officer that he was going to make a move for the gun. Burge pounced. Erma Moody pulled the trigger. Nothing happened since Burge had managed to jam his thumb into the firing mechanism. In recognition of that effort, the police department gave Burge his first department commendation.

Burge was commended again in 1980 for an incident that occurred while he was off duty. He was in a middle-class neighborhood on the far south side when he spotted a car containing three men and felt that, as Officer Fahey might have said, the car was dirty. He stopped and waited. One of the men got out and walked into a nearby Fotomat. A few minutes later, the man left the store in a hurry and jumped into the car. Burge ran into the Fotomat, learned it had been robbed, and chased the fugitives in his own car. He had no radio to call in a request for aid. He was carrying a five-shot snub-nose revolver, had no extra ammunition, and had no idea how much firepower the three thieves were carrying. When they stopped at a red light, Burge pulled his gun, snuck up behind them on foot, ordered the trio out of the car, and placed them all under arrest. He had the three lying in the middle of the street, their hands on their heads, when help finally came.

And so had gone Burge's career. In 1989, when the Wilson case came to trial, Burge's personnel file contained thirteen commendations and a letter of praise from the Department of Justice. He had been promoted repeatedly, and when he took his seat in Judge Duff's courtroom he was commander of the Area 3 detective division and outranked 99 percent of the policemen in the city.

ANDREW WILSON declined to be interviewed without being paid, and what I know of his background comes largely from police records and a presentencing report written by social worker Jill Miller in 1988. Miller's report indicates that Andrew Wilson was the third of nine children, that he was born on October 8, 1952, that his father worked as a machine operator in a soap plant fifty miles from Chicago, and that his mother worked as a waitress in various restaurants. While the parents were working, the Wilson children were taken care of by relatives and by the oldest child, a daughter named Bobbie, who was two years older than Andrew. The children perhaps hungered for attention, but their material needs were taken care of. When Andrew was eleven, the family moved into a split-level, three-bedroom house in Morgan Park, a house described in Miller's report as neat, clean, and nicely furnished, with an electric organ and a small library. Miller also indicated that the family regularly attended church services and that all of the Wilson children could play the organ by ear.

Andrew, however, probably had some sort of cognitive difficulties from birth. When he was in first grade, he was diagnosed as "educable mentally handicapped" (EMH) and was thereafter tracked as a slow learner. Between the ages of seven and fifteen, he was given three IQ tests, scoring 73, 78, and 70, scores that would indicate he was close to being labeled retarded. Yet various professionals who have come in contact with him as an adult have said that he is of average intelligence. Miller's report concludes that Wilson was not diagnosed properly as a child, that his low IQ scores were probably the result of a learning disability that was never identified or treated.

Andrew Wilson never learned to read. At eleven, he began to skip school and to periodically run away from home, sleeping in old cars in the neighborhood. His parents told correctional officials that they would "whup him. . . . It didn't help. . . . We just couldn't control him." Andrew told Miller that the standard punishment was being "whupped" with an extension cord. At thirteen, he was sent to a school for children with behavioral problems. At fourteen, he started stealing. He was committed to another special school, ran away after six weeks, and was then committed to the Audy Home, Cook County's juvenile detention facility. At fifteen, he recorded his first conviction for burglary, after which he spent time in a reformatory and in a juvenile detention center in southern Illinois.

At the age of fifteen, he was given a neurological exam, the results of which suggested an organic brain dysfunction. A reformatory doctor put Wilson on tranquilizers for emotional disturbance and hyperactivity and on an anticonvulsive medication used for treating seizure disorders. Miller's report indicates that Wilson functioned well on the medication, well enough that after about two years, doctors decided that he might be able to function normally without it. His prescriptions were stopped about three months before he was paroled. Miller notes that he experienced some difficulty afterward, including anxiety, irritability, and depression. She goes on to say, "It appears from all available records and Andrew's statements that he was never again given a neurological exam nor assessed for his need for anticonvulsive medication."

Andrew was sixteen at the time of his release. He returned to the family home in Morgan Park and his parents found him jobs. He worked on a cleaning crew, and in 1970 labored briefly as a busboy at a German restaurant on Chicago's north side. But he again took to theft. He was arrested in 1969, 1970, and 1971 for burglary and served brief sentences.

At some point after his release from the juvenile facility in 1969, Wilson began a relationship with a woman who lived in his family's neighborhood. The couple never married and never lived together, but their relationship survived several of Andrew's jail terms. The couple had two daughters, born in 1971 and 1973. Miller reports that Wilson's girlfriend believed that he was a good father and said that he was very generous with his daughters. During Wilson's subsequent stays in prison, he took up knitting and crocheting, and his daughters, who were then teenagers, told Miller that their father had knitted them numerous scarves, hats, and headbands. "The girls reported that when they talk to him on the phone he 'tries to teach us manners . . . wants us to be polite. . . . Dad always talks to us about school . . . how important school is, especially reading. . . . He tells us . . . "Do good, and when you read in class, read for me." ' " Both daughters are bright and academically successful.

Wilson, however, largely knows them by phone, since in the last twenty-five years he has been on the street for a total of about four months. In 1975, he took up armed robbery. He was thereafter sentenced to eight to sixteen years for the robbery of a suburban police officer and a coffee shop.

When he entered the penitentiary in the wake of those convictions, Wilson was described by prison officials as aggressive, hostile, negativistic, uncooperative, and in need of basic education. He was sent to Menard prison, where he worked in the kitchen until he received a conduct report for "unauthorized possession of state property"—five pieces of fried chicken and three oranges. He attended Protestant services, participated in religious counseling, and was eventually reassigned to the kitchen. His correctional counselor noted that Wilson responded well to personal counseling. He was paroled in October 1981.

During the next three and a half months he saw his daughters almost every day and did odd jobs at a beauty parlor in exchange for being allowed to sleep there. He also returned to his old profession. His police file indicates that he participated in four armed robberies in the four months before his encounter with Officers Fahey and O'Brien. In one incident, he and his brother Jackie are alleged to have robbed a camera store by pulling guns on the two clerks, tying them up with tape, and leaving them in the basement, after which the brothers relieved three customers of their cash and walked out with enough equipment to open a small store. In another incident, Andrew was alleged to have robbed a clothing store, leaving Jackie behind posing as a victim so that he could give a phony description to the police.

On February 4, 1982, Andrew, disguised as a postman, carried a package to the home of fifty-six-year-old Levada Downs. When she opened the door to take the package, Andrew pulled a gun, Jackie stepped out of hiding, and the brothers forced their way inside. They tied up Mrs. Downs, ransacked her house, and fled with $700 in currency and her .38 Colt. Officer O'Brien would find that Colt on the front seat of the Impala a few days later.

Miller, summarizing Wilson's personal characteristics, called him "an institutionalized person. Having spent much of his life since 1967 in institutions, he functions well in that setting. His ability to function in the community is severely limited. . . . Emotionally, he functions at an adolescent level. He has been impulsive and has been unable to accept delayed gratification. . . . He has learned not to work for what he has wanted; he chose, instead, to take it."

Miller's analysis, however, was not public knowledge. In the public mind, Andrew Wilson was known only by the label "cop killer." So when opening arguments on his civil suit began in Judge Duff's courtroom, the odds against him were more than considerable. He was a murderer. Burge was a war hero. Anarchy was suing order. The underclass was having a go at the establishment. In more than one sense it seemed to be a confrontation of black versus white.

JUDGE BRIAN BARNETT DUFF is an avuncular Republican with gray hair, a winning smile, an aversion to the death penalty, and a fondness for quoting Shakespeare from the bench. He is not, however, a popular man in the federal courts. In 1989, the *Chicago Lawyer* surveyed 348 attorneys, both prosecutors and defense lawyers, who practiced in federal court, asking them to rate the twenty active judges on the federal bench in the Northern District of Illinois. The survey asked eight questions dealing with knowledge of the law, ability, fairness, efficiency, and courtesy. "Of the eight questions, Duff was rated worst on five and second worst on one," the *Lawyer* reported in its March 1989 issue.

For the Wilson case, the courtroom was laid out with three tables, one behind the other, on the judge's right; the jury box was on his left. Wilson's attorneys occupied the first table, a most unfortunate placement, as they were to find themselves directly in the judge's line of fire. Wilson was represented by the People's Law Office, a group of lawyers that many people in the legal community refer to, sometimes with a trace of irony, as the PLO. Three other firms had been assigned to defend Wilson but had found ways to bow out or evade the responsibility, and Wilson had rejected a fourth firm before settling on the People's Law Office. The PLO's attorneys were a geographically unlikely trio: Flint Taylor, a lanky man with graying hair who hails from the Boston area; Jeffrey Haas, a bearded, dark-haired attorney who has traces of his Atlanta upbringing in his speech; and John Stainthorp, who wears sideburns reminiscent of Civil War generals and who hails from Preston, a city in northern England. Taylor and Haas first worked together as lawyers for the survivors of the police raid on the Chicago headquarters of the Black Panthers on December 4, 1969, during which the Chicago police killed Panther leaders Fred Hampton and Mark Clark; Taylor and Haas, after a thirteen-year legal battle, won $1.85 million in damages from the city, the county, and the federal government for the survivors of the raid and the families of Hampton and Clark. The People's Law Office has since taken on many unpopular defendants in criminal cases and has a steady track record of civil rights suits, many against the police. In style they are zealous (their opponents in the Wilson case were to accuse them of conducting a holy war), fearless, and rarely concise.

The city's lawyers—James McCarthy and Maureen Murphy, both from the office of the corporation counsel—sat behind Wilson's attorneys. They played second fiddle to the third table, where sat William Kunkle, defender of the four accused policemen, and his associate Jeffrey Rubin. Kunkle, a partner in the prestigious firm of Phelan Pope and John, brought to court a righteous air and a keen legal mind. Before entering private practice he had labored as a county prosecutor for twelve years, rising to the rank of first assistant after Democrat Richard Daley became state's attorney in 1983. In those twelve years he prosecuted some of Cook County's most notorious criminals, including serial killer John Gacy, Andrew Wilson, and five other men accused of killing law enforcement officers. After entering private practice, Kunkle served the U.S. Congress in the ethics investigations of House Speaker Jim Wright and Representative Newt Gingrich, and he has twice been on the short list of candidates to become U.S. Attorney of the Northern District of Illinois.

Kunkle is also a man who takes up a lot of room. At a defense table that seated four policemen of considerable heft (their average weight was well over two hundred pounds), Kunkle could have been mistaken for one of the defendants but for the quality of his courtroom attire. A brutal cross-examiner, Kunkle fills a court with his sarcasm, his incredulity, his anger at a witness he doesn't like—criminal or upstanding citizen, it makes no difference. It is far easier to imagine a judge being intimidated by Kunkle than Kunkle being intimidated by a judge, and there were many times in Judge Duff's courtroom when it seemed the real power was not on the bench.

Kunkle and Wilson had faced off in courtrooms twice before. Kunkle had prosecuted Wilson in 1983 and won a conviction using Wilson's alleged confession, and he had prosecuted him again in 1988—after the Illinois Supreme Court ruled the confession could not be used—and had prevailed a second time. Kunkle was by no means circumspect about how he felt about the plaintiff. During the course of a deposition taken at Pontiac penitentiary in December 1988, Wilson broke down while he was talking about being electroshocked. Kunkle's response was to smile broadly and say, "I love to see him cry."

ANDREW WILSON did not attend court on a daily basis, and so his
appearance on the witness stand, seven days after the start of the
trial, drew a good number of spectators, among them policemen, lawyers, and relatives of Officer Fahey. Wilson was clean-shaven, a short,
trim, balding man, neatly dressed in a blue sweater, blue shirt, and
tinted glasses. After swearing to tell the truth, he sat down and, in
response to John Stainthorp's questions, stated his place of residence
as Pontiac prison and his term as natural life without possibility of
parole.

> Q. How old were you when you left the Chicago public
>   school system?
> A. I don't know.
> Q. . . . Did you graduate from elementary school?
> A. No.
> Q. At the time that you last attended a Chicago public
>   school, were you able to read?
> A. No.
> Q. And are you able to read today?
> A. No.
> Q. Are you able to write?
> A. What I know how.
> Q. By that you mean you can copy letters?
> A. Yes.
> Q. Do you know how to spell words?
> A. The ones I know.
> Q. Do you know how many words you know?
> A. It's not that many.

He went on to relate the events of February 14, 1982, from his point
of view. He claimed that upon leaving the apartment where the arrest
had taken place, Burge told his men not to assault the prisoner,
adding, "We'll get him at the station." Wilson said that upon arrival at
Area 2 headquarters, he was taken into a small room, thrown to the
floor, and beaten; that he was kicked in the eye, a kick that tore his
retina; and that someone had taken a plastic bag out of the garbage can

and put it over his head, causing him to suffocate until he bit a hole in the bag. That session ended, Wilson said, when Burge walked in and told the assembled cops that "he wouldn't have messed my face up, he wouldn't have messed me up"—in other words, that Wilson's assailants had screwed up, that they should not have left any marks.

Wilson testified that he was then taken to Interview Room Number 2, and that Burge said something on the order of "My reputation is at stake and you are going to make a statement." According to Wilson, Detective Yucaitis entered the room a short time later carrying a brown paper bag, from which he extracted a black box. Yucaitis allegedly pulled two wires out of the box, attached them with clamps to Wilson's right ear and nostril, and then turned a crank on the side of the box. "I really can't explain it," he said. "The first time he did it, it just hurt. I can't explain it. When Burge was doing it, I can explain more because he did it more. . . . It hurts, but it stays in your head, okay? It stays in your head and it grinds your teeth. . . . It grinds, constantly grinds, constantly. . . . The pain just stays in your head. . . . It's just like this light here like when it flickers, it flickers . . . and your teeth constantly grinds and grinds and grinds and grinds and grinds and grinds. All my bottom teeth was loose behind that, these four or five of them, and I tried to get the doctor to pull them. He said he wouldn't pull them because they would tighten back up."

Wilson said, "I kept hollering when he [Yucaitis] kept cranking, but he stopped because somebody come to the door, so he went out the door and see what they wanted." When Yucaitis came back, Wilson said, he put the device back in the bag and left. Wilson testified that Burge returned with the black box about an hour later.

> Q. What, if anything, did Commander Burge say when he
> came into the room?
> A. He said "fun time."

According to Wilson, Burge put one clip on each of his suspect's ears and started cranking. Wilson says that although he was handcuffed to a ring in the wall, he could move his shoulders, and so was able to rub the clamps off his ears. "So they got tired of me rubbing the wire off my ear. So he unhandcuffed one of my hands, unhandcuffed the left hand, and he tried to stretch me across the room and the radiator was right there, so he was trying to stretch me across, across the room, and I wasn't going. So the officer, the other officer was there, he helped him, and they both stretched me across . . . they hooked me onto the other ring over there."

Wilson said that he was now unable to rub the clamps off his ears; each of his outstretched arms was handcuffed to a ring in the wall, and between the rings was a radiator that his chest sometimes touched.

> A. . . . So I don't know if he put it back on my ears or what, but it didn't last long because he put it on my fingers, my baby fingers, one on one finger and one on the other finger and then he kept cranking it and kept cranking it, and I was hollering and screaming. I was calling for help and stuff. My teeth was grinding, flickering in my head, pain and all that stuff. . . .
>
> Q. While you were stretched across in this fashion, were you aware of whether or not the radiator was hot?
>
> A. I wasn't paying no attention, but it burned me still. But I didn't even feel it. . . . That radiator . . . it wouldn't have mattered. That box . . . took over. That's what was happening. The heat radiator didn't even exist then. The box existed.
>
> Q. . . . After Commander Burge stopped with the crank machine, what happened next?
>
> A. He got the other one out. It's black and it's round and it had a wire sticking out of it and it had a cord on it. He plugged it into the wall. . . . He took it and he ran it up between my legs, my groin area, just ran it up there very gently . . . up and down, up and down, you know, right between my legs, up and down like this, real gentle with it, but you can feel it, still feel it. Then he jabbed me with the thing and it slammed me . . . into the grill on the window. Then I fell back down, and I think that's when I started spitting up the blood and stuff. Then he stopped.

Twice in the course of his testimony about Commander Burge and the electrical devices, Wilson came close to breaking down. The first time came after Stainthorp asked, "And when he brought the brown paper bag back, what did he do with it?" Wilson's reply was "I want to leave," and the judge declared a short recess. The second time came a few minutes later, when Wilson said that somehow, during the course of the electroshock, the alligator clip had come loose and he had gotten it in his hand, but the maneuver had done him no good, because he was simply shocked there as well. He lost his ability to continue the story and was urged by Stainthorp to take a minute and compose himself.

Wilson said that later, after the electroshock was finished, he was taken to another police station for a lineup, and that there he got a mouthful of the lieutenant's gun. Burge, he said, "was playing with his gun . . . he was sticking it in my mouth and . . . he kept doing it, he kept clicking it and he had it in my mouth and stuff. So he finally pulled it out."

At 6:05 p.m., after thirteen hours in the custody of Area 2 police, Wilson gave a statement in which he confessed to the murders of Officers Fahey and O'Brien. The statement was taken by assistant state's attorney Larry Hyman in the presence of a court reporter and Detective O'Hara. After their departure, Wilson was left alone with another detective and Mario Ferro and William Mulvaney, the two officers assigned to the police wagon that was to transport the prisoner to the lockup at Chicago police headquarters downtown. Wilson claims that he was beaten again, and that his penis was grabbed and squeezed by one of the wagon men, the same officer who would later club him on the head with a gun. Wilson says that the detective told Ferro and Mulvaney to have the lockup keeper put Wilson in an occupied cell so it could be said later that other prisoners had caused his injuries.

If that plan existed, it ran into a hitch when the lockup keeper refused to take custody of Wilson, not wanting to be held responsible for his injuries. At that point police procedure dictated that Ferro and Mulvaney should take Wilson to a hospital for treatment. Patricia Crossen, a nurse who was working in the emergency room at Mercy Hospital, testified that Ferro and Mulvaney entered at about 11:40 p.m., saying they had come just for the paperwork, that if Wilson knew what was good for him he would refuse treatment. Crossen said that Wilson initially refused treatment, but changed his mind when a black orderly assured him he had the right to be treated. Wilson ended up being examined by Dr. Geoffrey Korn, who testified that, just as he was about to suture a wound in Wilson's head, Officer Mulvaney pulled out a gun. Korn refused to treat the prisoner while the gun was out of its holster and walked out of the room. After being left alone with Ferro and Mulvaney in the examination room, Andrew Wilson decided to refuse treatment, signed a statement to that effect, and was returned by squadrol (formerly known as a paddy wagon) to the lockup at 11th and State.

The following morning, Wilson was taken to Cook County Jail. Ordinarily, jail authorities take only a mug shot of an arriving prisoner. In Andrew Wilson's case they took pictures of his whole body so as not to be blamed for his injuries. The following day, Dale Coventry, the public defender appointed to defend Wilson, arranged to have more pictures taken of the prisoner, paying particular attention to Wilson's ears, chest, and thigh.

Blowups of the Coventry photos were the most troubling evidence against Commander Burge. The chest shots showed marks where Andrew Wilson said he had been burned against the radiator. A blowup of the shot of his thigh also showed a very large burn mark. The shots of the ears, however, were the most curious: they showed a pattern of U-shaped scabs that seemed inexplicable unless one believed that alligator clips had indeed been attached to Wilson's ears.

THE CROSS-EXAMINATION of Andrew Wilson by William Kunkle, the policemen's attorney, revealed that the police would not contest that those U-shaped scabs came from alligator clips. In Kunkle's version, however, there was no electrical current: he wanted the jury to believe that Andrew Wilson had found a roach clip between the time he left Area 2 and the time he entered Cook County Jail and that he had placed the clip on his ears and nose in order to support his cock-and-bull story that he'd been subjected to electrical shock. Kunkle claimed that Wilson had gone to this extreme because he realized he had confessed to a death penalty offense and he needed to do something to have that confession suppressed.

Kunkle appeared absolutely convinced of the righteousness of his cause as he began his cross-examination of Wilson. The former prosecutor began by asking Detectives O'Hara and McKenna to stand up (McKenna and O'Hara had been the first interrogators of Wilson, at least in the police department's version of the chain of events, and they were the primary authors of the "cleared and closed" report on the case). Kunkle asked Wilson if either of the two detectives had ever laid a hand on him. Wilson said no. (Wilson's attorneys were arguing that O'Hara and McKenna were the nice guys in a good guy/bad guy team, that the two men had taken Wilson's statement but had chosen to overlook and cover up his torture.) Then Kunkle went to work on the character of Andrew Wilson, trying to change the jury's impression of him from victim to predator, from a bloody and burned human being to a man who made his living with a gun.

Q. Mr. Wilson, between August of 1981 and your arrest on February fourteenth of 1982 did you have a job?
A. No.
Q. Were you doing any kind of work to support yourself?
A. On advice of my counsel I am not going to answer that . . . on the grounds that it might incriminate me.
Q. How were you getting money during that period of time?
A. . . . On the advice of my counsel I'm not going to answer that on the grounds it might incriminate me.
Q. . . . Mr. Wilson, you testified on direct that you went to Mosely [school] for being truant, but you didn't recall playing hooky, is that right?
A. Yes.
Q. Did they teach you any reading at Mosely?
A. No.
Q. What did they teach you at Mosely?
A. How to fix shoes.
Q. Did you ever get a job fixing shoes?
A. No.
Q. Did you ever have a job of any kind?
A. Yes.
Q. When?
A. I don't know what year. I was washing dishes.
Q. When was that?
A. In the '70s.
Q. How long?
A. I don't know.

Q. A month, a year, ten years?

A. Oh, I don't know about—probably a month.

Q. Any other jobs?

A. I paint.

Q. Painted?

A. Yes.

Q. When did you paint?

A. In the '70s.

Q. . . . How many painting jobs did you have?

A. Only one.

Q. Any other jobs?

A. No—yes, working at the Warner's Drugstore.

Q. When was that?

A. I think it was in the '70s.

Q. How long?

A. It didn't last long, maybe a week or so.

Kunkle's cross-examination was quite theatrical. When he tore open an envelope, you could hear the rip from one end of court to the other. He tossed guns onto the defense table almost carelessly. He came across as superior, even arrogant, and Wilson seemed cowed at some times, hostile at others.

Kunkle got Wilson to admit he had seen roach clips in various jails and prisons. And Wilson changed a small detail of his story: it suddenly came to him that he had been wearing boxer shorts when he was arrested, not long underwear; that admission might affect the jury's belief in his claim to have been burned on the thigh by the radiator. (The police and the city contested not the existence of the thigh burn, but the time at which it was received. Wilson might have received it, for example, the day before he was arrested.) Wilson also claimed that when an assistant state's attorney and a court reporter arrived to take his confession on February 14, 1982, he told both men that he had been tortured; both men would later take the stand and say they had been told nothing of the sort. Wilson claimed he had never been read his rights; the statement recorded by the court reporter that day, however, opens with the state's attorney reading the Miranda litany. Mercy Hospital documents indicate that Wilson said that he had received his injuries after falling outside the police station (the documents also indicate that the policemen present were encouraging Wilson to refuse treatment); on the witness stand, however, Wilson denied making any statement about falling.

Kunkle also raised questions about the allegation that Burge had put a gun in his prisoner's mouth. If it had happened in the lineup room at Area 1, as Wilson said it did, Burge would have had to have been a little reckless, as anyone on the other side of the one-way mirror would have been able to witness the act.

Under Kunkle's questioning, Wilson also admitted that in earlier testimony he had claimed that one of the cops at Area 2 had burned him with a cigarette, and that he had omitted mention of that burn this time around. Wilson claimed he had not mentioned it because the burn was on his shoulder, and his shoulder bore a tattoo, and he knew that juries generally do not like tattoos. Kunkle asked Wilson exactly what his tattoo depicted. Wilson said it consisted of a rose, a noose, and two shovels, that it had been done by a jailhouse artist, and that it had absolutely no significance.

Omitting mention of the cigarette burn in order to hide his tattoo seemed to be about the only attempt Wilson had made to refine his performance for the jury. He was sometimes short-tempered, sometimes sullen, and his posture throughout his testimony conveyed the impression that he was ready to duck an incoming punch. He referred to a court reporter as "the ponographer" and to various policemen as the "heavyset stud," the "young stud," and the "blond-haired young dude." A witness trying to impress the jury would have cried at the points where Wilson choked up; Wilson asked for a recess, as if he were too proud to cry in public.

Commander Burge, on the other hand, sat tall and erect and seemed completely at ease on the stand. At one point, when the judge and the lawyers retired for a sidebar, the blond commander conversed with the U.S. marshal, an attractive young woman, and he laughed, seeming unthreatened, almost unbothered by the proceedings. During another sidebar, he joked with the courtroom artist, who sat a few feet away, motioning as if he could hold back a double chin. Burge is the first to admit that he is not in peak physical condition; in one deposition he described himself as fat, and when I asked him to describe himself during the course of an interview he said, "Overweight. I'm six-foot-one, hog-headed, red-faced, about forty pounds overweight and not in as good a shape as I would like to be in." He defined "hog-headed" as having a round face and a large head.

Kunkle took Burge through each of Wilson's charges, which made for a series of forthright denials. The attorney then asked the commander his net worth, which would become a factor in assessing damages if the jury sided with Wilson. Burge, who has never married and who has no dependents, said that his assets were minimal: he owned neither house nor car, had some equity in his boat, a few thousand in a money market account, a few thousand in the police credit union, a few thousand in debts. He concluded that his net worth was a negative $17,000. Kunkle walked him through his military career, asking him about his decorations; Burge listed them matter-of-factly, making no great attempt to milk them for the sympathy they could engender. Kunkle asked about his police career, and he sketched it in with no elaboration, making no mention of his department commendations.

The bulk of Burge's testimony dealt with the manhunt for the killers of Fahey and O'Brien, the arrest of Andrew Wilson, and Wilson's passage through Area 2. In Burge's version, Wilson's only injury was the scratch on his eye; he was not certain whether Wilson had the injury before the police found him or if he sustained it when the police, applying reasonable force to a dangerous man, shoved Wilson to the floor to handcuff him at the moment of his arrest. Burge maintained that he had instructed his men to treat Wilson "with kid gloves"; that Wilson was taken directly to an interview room at Area 2; that he gave an oral statement admitting his role in the shootings to Detectives O'Hara and McKenna between 7:00 and 7:40 a.m.; and that he gave a written statement eleven hours later.

Wilson attorney Flint Taylor, trying to disturb the image the commander projected as a cool-headed professional, addressed the witness as "Defendant Burge." Under Taylor's cross-examination, Burge admitted that he was familiar with electrical devices operated by a crank, saying he had used field telephones during his service in Vietnam. Burge said that there had been a POW compound on the base he served on in Vietnam, but he denied having heard of any torture that might have gone on there. Taylor was incredulous.

"Never had any discussions about that the whole time you were there, is that right?"

"No. I was in the U.S. Army, counselor."

Taylor was not able to pierce that denial, the jury heard nothing else linking Burge to torture in Vietnam, and the PLO attorney went on to ask Commander Burge about the investigation of the murders of Fahey and O'Brien. Burge said that he had gone without sleep for five and a half to six days, that he drank a lot of coffee, that he smoked two packs of cigarettes a day, and that it was the biggest investigation he had ever handled. He said that the arrest had not been handled as he would have liked to have done it: just before it happened, deputy superintendent Joseph McCarthy had shown up with about five men from Gang Crimes South, the same unit that Fahey and O'Brien had been assigned to, and announced that they were going to be in on the action. Burge thought that it was a bad idea for friends and comrades of the dead officers to participate in the raid, but since McCarthy was deputy superintendent, Burge knew he was outranked and felt he had little choice in the matter.

Burge's most peculiar admission, however, was that he had personally interviewed Sebastian Ragland, a man who confessed to the killings of Fahey and O'Brien not long after the shootings. Ragland had had nothing to do with the crime, and Detective O'Hara, who first interviewed him, told Burge that Ragland would have confessed to killing Cock Robin. Burge interviewed him anyway. Yet once Wilson was arrested, Burge said that he let the men under him question the prisoner and that he never even entered the interview room. Burge maintained that he had seen Wilson only once all morning—when the prisoner was taken to the bathroom and was escorted past the commander's open door. The commander said he had heard no screams, no cries for help, and that at any given moment, between ten and a hundred other policemen would have been on the second floor of Area 2, ostensibly within hearing distance of such screams and cries.

Detective Yucaitis followed Burge to the stand and was equally personable and at ease. He denied striking, shocking, beating, or kicking Wilson, and said that his only role was to drive Wilson back to Area 2 after the arrest and to stand guard outside the interview room where he was held.

There was some dispute about exactly which interview room Wilson had been taken to. Burge initially indicated that Wilson had been taken to Interview Room Number 1, but later said he could not remember which room the prisoner had been taken to. Other detectives maintained that Wilson was in Interview Room Number 2, and that the radiator in that room had never worked.

In support of the theory that Wilson was not burned by any radiator, Kunkle produced Dr. Raymond Warpeha, a balding man with a thick mustache and glasses, director of the burn center at Loyola Medical Center and chairman of the center's Division of Plastic and Reconstructive Surgery. On the witness stand he claimed to have diagnosed and treated six thousand to seven thousand burns, three thousand of them major. In preparation for the trial, he said that he had seen photos of the radiators at Area 2, reviewed Wilson's medical records, and examined the prisoner. The records seemed to reflect some disagreement on the part of the various medical personnel who had examined Wilson at Mercy Hospital and at Cook County Jail. Some had labeled the marks on Wilson's chest as burns, while others had referred to them as abrasions. Warpeha concluded that the doctors and the nurse who had diagnosed Wilson's injuries as burns were mistaken; the wounds on Wilson's face, chest, and thigh, Warpeha said, were friction abrasions—wounds caused by friction, not by heat (such as a "rope burn" or a "floor burn"). Such wounds are dry, do not blister, and do not produce fluid. Analyzing the photographs of Wilson's injuries from the jail, Warpeha said that the blistering that should have occurred had the prisoner been burned was simply not present.

Warpeha's diagnosis was important because it allowed the jury to consider the possibility that Wilson's chest had been scratched and not burned, and that the scratches had occurred when Wilson struggled with Officer Fahey, or when he crawled up on the car to shoot Officer O'Brien, or when he rode in the squadrol from Area 2 to the lockup at 11th and State.

Wilson's attorneys also presented an expert witness, Dr. Robert Kirschner, deputy chief medical examiner of Cook County. Kirschner has an unusual countenance—a beard, no mustache, and dark, deep-set eyes—and he was an unusual witness. As a forensic pathologist employed by the county, he spent a good portion of his time working with policemen and testifying for the state. His job, day in and day out, was to determine what weapons, devices, or accidents could have caused various injuries or death, and as a result he was recognized as an expert in the identification of burns. Furthermore, in his spare time Kirschner did human rights work, and he had taken part in investigations in Argentina, Kenya, Czechoslovakia, and the West Bank under the auspices of Amnesty International, Physicians for Human Rights, and the American Association for the Advancement of Science. He served on the clinical committee of the Chicago-based Marjorie Kovler Center for the Treatment of Survivors of Torture and had taught other physicians how to diagnose and evaluate victims of torture.

In a deposition taken five days before the trial started, Kirschner explained that he had become involved in the Wilson case when John Stainthorp, having heard that the doctor was an expert on torture, called the medical examiner's office and asked Kirschner to look over Wilson's file. "I said I would review it," Kirschner said, "and I told Mr. Stainthorp again that I was very skeptical because I have been around the medical examiner's office for ten years, [had a] lot of close contact with the police, and I think I have a fair idea of what goes on in the police stations when people are in custody . . . and I said I just never heard of anything like this in Chicago, and I said that it does seem very unlikely to me that this would be the case. But Mr. Stainthorp sent me the medical records and portions of Andrew Wilson's deposition . . . and I must say I read it . . . and I called Mr. Stainthorp and said, 'This guy has been tortured. I think there is a very high degree of medical certainty to say this man has not only been beaten and/or kicked, which, let's face it, occurs in custody, but that this man has received electric shock.' "

In that deposition, Kirschner went on to say that Wilson's description of what had happened to his body and his difficulty in telling the story without breaking down were consistent with the experiences of others who had been tortured with electric shock. "These are not the kinds of things that are faked. . . ." Kirschner said. "This is not general knowledge . . . or things you pick up through your general reading. . . . This is not information that I would expect to be floating around the prisons, passed from one prisoner to another."

Kirschner was clearly a very dangerous witness, far more dangerous than even Andrew Wilson, and Kunkle did not want the doctor's

opinions to be heard in open court. With the jury out of the courtroom, Kunkle argued that the federal court had never recognized a
torture expert and had never recognized torture as a field of scientific
expertise; that even those working in the field had written that there
had not been enough studies done to draw a scientifically sound profile
of torture victims. Furthermore, Kunkle argued, Kirschner had no
personal experience with the machinery of electroshock and that the
doctor had never seen anyone who had had an electrical device
attached to his or her ears.

Judge Duff said it was "a tough call." He professed admiration for
Kirschner's work and at one point suggested that more attention be
paid by Kirschner's human rights colleagues to abuses committed by
the British in Northern Ireland. In the end, however, the judge sided
with Kunkle. Kirschner was allowed to testify as an expert in identifying burns but was not allowed to say anything about torture or about
the credibility of Andrew Wilson's account. Duff also ordered that
Kirschner's curriculum vitae should be purged of any mention of torture and human rights activity before it was submitted to the jury.

Kirschner's testimony stood in stark contrast to Dr. Warpeha's. The
deputy chief medical examiner said that when forensic pathologists
set about determining whether a wound is a burn or an abrasion, one
key factor is the border of the wound. An abrasion, Kirschner said, is
always accompanied by a scraping of the skin, while a burn is marked
by very sharp margins. Kirschner, pointing to photos of Wilson's
wounds, stated that the chest, thigh, and cheek injuries had very sharp
margins, that there was no evidence of scraping, and that there was
also evidence of blisters. The wounds, he said, were therefore second-
degree burns.

In making his diagnosis in his own study, Kirschner had been
viewing eight-by-ten-inch blowups of Wilson's injuries, and it was
only just before he entered the courtroom that he saw the same
exhibits blown up to two feet by three feet. He carried a magnifying glass with him, and in the course of explaining that the wounds
on Wilson's ears were punctate abrasions, he noticed in one of the
enlargements a mark that was both darker than the others and slightly
out of line. While on the stand he came to the conclusion that that particular mark was probably not a punctate abrasion, but a spark burn.

The remark, delivered casually, was particularly threatening for the defendants. Their roach-clip defense could support abrasions. It could not withstand a spark burn.

When Kunkle got the chance to cross-examine Kirschner, he worked up a great deal of indignation, mocking the doctor's eleventh-hour magnifying glass discovery. He asked Kirschner how many live burn patients the doctor had examined. Kirschner, who works on the dead, said he had seen fewer than a dozen, and that only two or three of those had radiator burns. Kunkle tried to raise suspicion about Kirschner's objectivity by working on the fact that the doctor had waived his usual fee for serving as an expert witness; the implication Kunkle wanted to impart was that the doctor had some vested interest in the case, that Warpeha was more trustworthy because he had to be paid.

In the end, however, after hearing testimony and/or a deposition from two expert witnesses, one emergency room nurse, and four doctors who had seen Wilson between February 14 and February 17, it was difficult to imagine what medical conclusions the jury would come to. The nurse clearly said she saw burns, the doctors recorded burns, lacerations, and/or abrasions, and the two experts were poles apart.

IN AND AROUND the medical testimony, the policemen's stories, and Wilson's account, there was also a case building against the city of Chicago. Wilson's suit alleged that there was a custom, policy, or practice of allowing police officers to "mistreat those persons suspected, charged with, or otherwise allegedly connected with the shooting or killing of Chicago police officers" and allowing the police to "exact unconstitutional revenge, punishment, and retribution." To that end, Wilson's attorneys produced four victims of the police department's enthusiasm in searching for the killers of Fahey and O'Brien.

The first victim presented was Mrs. Julia Davis, a middle-aged black woman who seemed depressed, intimidated, and out of her element when she took the stand. She testified that during the canvass of the neighborhood around the site of the shootings, police had broken down her door, ransacked her bedroom, and seized her son, Larry

Milan, hitting him with a billy club and a flashlight in the process. She said that her son, who had died in 1984, was held for three days and came home with bruises on his back and legs.

James McCarthy, the city corporation counsel, went after Mrs. Davis by asking if it was the first time the police had been to the house. It wasn't. Larry Milan was a prominent member of the Black Gangster Disciples, a powerful Chicago street gang, and was known to the police. "Isn't it true," McCarthy asked, "that your son spent time in prison for arson?" Mrs. Davis said it was true, although it seemed to have nothing to do with the matter at hand. McCarthy went on to ask why Mrs. Davis had never filed a complaint against the officers who had allegedly beaten her son and broken down her door. With no sense of outrage in her voice, Mrs. Davis replied, "I thought the police could do anything they wanted."

Roy Wade Brown, a stocky, well-dressed twenty-six-year-old with a shaved head and a gravelly voice, also testified against the city. Brown said that he too had been a member of the Black Gangster Disciples, that he had put that life behind him, and that he was studying to become a minister and running a store that sold candy, potato chips, and chili. Brown testified that on the day that Fahey and O'Brien were shot, he was in Mrs. Davis's house, watching TV with Larry Milan, when the police broke through the door. He said he was taken into custody; that one of his interrogators put fingers in his ears and applied pressure; that another policeman put a plastic bag over his head, cutting off his air supply; that his interrogators put his finger in a bolt cutter and threatened to cut it off; that they hit him repeatedly on the thighs with a paddle; and that he was taken to the roof of the police station and was told he would be thrown off if he didn't tell what he knew about the shootings of Fahey and O'Brien. He didn't know anything. He said he was so frightened, however, that he would have done anything to appease the police, and so he gave his interrogators the name of a member of a rival gang.

Maureen Murphy, who was defending the city along with McCarthy, cross-examined Roy Brown. She asked if Brown had not pled guilty once to intimidating a witness; if he had not had to leave Chicago for two years because he had hit a member of another gang with a bat; if his friend Larry Milan had not been arrested for raping a sixteen-year-old girl the day before he and Brown filed a complaint against the police for being abused. She asked Brown if he was willing to lie to get even with an enemy, as he had apparently done, she said, when he gave an innocent man's name to the police who were investigating the Fahey and O'Brien murders. Her implication was, of course, that he would lie again, this time to get even with the police.

IT OFTEN SEEMED there were two cultures in conflict in the courtroom. One was black, poor, given to violence, and often in trouble with the law. The other was white, respectable, given to violence, and in charge of enforcing the law. The city's attorneys wanted the jury to doubt the victims because they had criminal records or associations. Wilson's attorneys wanted the jury to conclude that in February 1982, the police could and did run amok. Ideally, an impartial arbiter might have sorted out the claims before they were aired in federal court. In Chicago, however, the agency established to fill that role is the police department's Office of Professional Standards, an office that at the time seemed designed to fuel the notion, voiced by Mrs. Davis, that the police can do anything they want. In 1982, the year Wilson committed the murders, the OPS rejected 96 percent of the complaints filed against policemen, and that was a fairly typical year. One can either conclude that the vast, overwhelming number of citizens who complain are liars or that the system does not work.

Andrew Wilson's OPS case is a prime example. OPS investigations usually begin when a citizen files a complaint against a policeman. Wilson's case, however, was opened not by citizen Wilson, but by order of police superintendent Richard Brzeczek, a fact that should have raised the case to a position of great prominence. Brzeczek ordered the head of OPS to open a file after receiving a letter from Dr. John Raba, medical director of the hospital that serves the inmates of Cook County Jail. Raba listed Wilson's injuries, mentioned the allegation that Wilson had been electroshocked, and urged that Brzeczek conduct a "thorough investigation."

The OPS investigation was handled by Keith Griffiths, a pale, blond-haired man with a plump face, a mustache, and a demeanor that might lead a stranger to think he was a librarian or an accountant, not an investigator. After being sworn in, he explained that his supervisor had handed him the Wilson file on August 22, 1983, a year and a half after Brzeczek ordered the OPS to investigate. Griffiths testified that, at that point, someone had collected a few letters and some transcripts of a hearing at which Andrew Wilson had told the story of his arrest and interrogation. The file did not contain the name of the person who had assembled the material, or even an indication that someone from the OPS had actually done any investigating. Griffiths testified that his supervisor told him to "write a summary," which, according to OPS procedure, meant that he should do no more investigation, that he should simply read the file's contents and come to a judgment about the case. No one ever told Griffiths to give the case high priority, and so it became a back-burner assignment. He handed in his three-page summary 706 days after receiving the file, and in all that time no one from the department asked him a single question about it. On the basis of the file's contents, Griffiths recommended a finding of "not sustained," and so, three years after Andrew Wilson was arrested, Burge and his colleagues were cleared.

When Police Superintendent Brzeczek sent a copy of Dr. Raba's letter to the OPS, he also sent a copy to State's Attorney Richard Daley. Brzeczek wrote that he had publicly stated that he would scrupulously investigate every allegation of police misconduct, but he was wary of jeopardizing the prosecution's case against Andrew Wilson and so was asking for guidance on how to proceed. When he took the witness stand in Judge Duff's courtroom, Brzeczek testified that Daley had never replied to the letter.

Daley was elected mayor of Chicago in April 1989. Later that year, I asked him to comment on Brzeczek's allegation. Through his press secretary, he said that he acknowledged that he had not written the police superintendent but that he had tried to investigate Wilson's complaints through the state's attorney's special prosecutions unit. That effort was thwarted, Daley said, when Wilson and his attorney, public defender Dale Coventry, declined to cooperate.

Coventry told me that he had indeed declined to cooperate. "The only thing I would expect from any investigation they did would be a total whitewash," Coventry said, "and anything they learned would be used by the prosecution against my client. I was on the Murder Task Force [in the public defender's office] for eight years with about fifteen attorneys, and we shared experiences and ideas, and I do not know anyone who worked on our side of the issue who didn't see things the same way. I was in court yesterday with someone who was thumped by the cops. It is just standard operating procedure. As the defense attorneys frequently say, the judges pretend to believe the police, and they don't, and the police get up there and tell their stories and nothing is ever done on these things."

IN CLOSING ARGUMENTS, Wilson's attorneys went back to their opening theme, reminding the jury that the case was not about the murder of the two policemen, that it was not about whether Andrew Wilson was a nice man, that it was about whether the prisoner had been tortured and deprived of his constitutional rights after his arrest. John Stainthorp pointed to some of the contradictions in the policemen's defense. Several cops had said the radiator in Interview Room Number 2 didn't work; Commander Milton Deas, Burge's supervisor, had said that the radiator worked just fine. Burge had maintained that he had never even entered the interview room where Wilson was held; another detective had said in a deposition that Burge had. Jeffrey Haas, summing up the case against the city, argued that the city had done nothing to investigate the brutality allegations. He pointed out that when the black community began to protest the police excesses, Superintendent Brzeczek had called a meeting, not of the white cops who were responsible for the excesses, but of the police department's black commanders, who might have been able to cool tempers in the community. Flint Taylor argued that "just because [a policeman] thinks Andrew Wilson deserves the electric chair doesn't mean [he] can start the process." He went on to ask why someone like Patricia Crossen, the white nurse who treated Wilson in the Mercy Hospital emergency room, would come in to testify for a convicted cop killer if she wasn't telling the truth, and why, if Wilson was going to make up a story to get his confession thrown out, he would concoct something as bizarre as a shock box and alligator clips—why wouldn't he simply say that he had been beaten up?

Wilson's defenders also raised a major question about the scenario presented by the police. Burge and his colleagues maintained that Wilson had given an oral statement of confession at 7:30 in the morning, shortly after his arrest; the implication was that from that point on there would have been no reason to torture him. But if Wilson did confess at 7:30 a.m., why had the police waited ten and a half hours to obtain a written and signed statement? A written and signed statement is an invaluable weapon in the hands of a prosecutor. Yet, even with a state's attorney present at Area 2 from 8:30 a.m., no one made any attempt to get Wilson to give a written statement until 6 p.m. Surely the police knew that each passing minute offered the possibility that Wilson might change his mind or that a lawyer might show up and advise him to remain silent.

James McCarthy, summing up for the city, argued that if the city had a policy of abusing people suspected of shooting policemen, then everyone would have abused Andrew Wilson. Yet the lockup keeper hadn't; he had first refused to accept Wilson until he had had medical treatment and then he had placed the prisoner in a front cell so he could be watched. If the city had such a policy, McCarthy said, then Superintendent Brzeczek would have done nothing upon receiving Dr. Raba's letter. Instead Brzeczek opened an OPS investigation and wrote to state's attorney Daley alerting him to the allegations and asking for direction.

Kunkle, closing for the individual policemen, said that the only thing he and the People's Law Office agreed on was that Andrew Wilson was entitled to the protection of the Constitution. With Wilson's guns on display, Kunkle went on to point out that Andrew Wilson didn't start getting concerned about constitutional rights until February 14, 1982, when "he didn't have his .38 anymore to make him seem like a big man," and after he had already deprived Officers Fahey and O'Brien of the basic human right to life. Kunkle asked where the black box was and why Wilson's first attorney hadn't asked the state's attorney for a search warrant to go find it. He argued that Wilson's attorneys had the burden of proving where Wilson's injuries had come from, that they hadn't done it, that the "scratches" (not burns) on Wilson's chest could have come from diving across the car to shoot O'Brien. Kunkle ridiculed Wilson's allegations, citing particularly the charge that one of the wagonmen had pulled on Wilson's penis, asking the jury to imagine the likelihood of a cop pulling on a prisoner's penis in front of six or eight other cops. Kunkle argued that Wilson was quite capable of dreaming up such a complicated story, that Wilson had all night to put it together, and that it was consistent with his nature as a plotter—look at the way he had approached Mrs. Downs disguised as a postman. Kunkle concluded that Wilson had a right to the protection of the Constitution, but no right to be believed.

After closing arguments were finished, Judge Duff instructed the jury in the law. Duff had dismissed the charges against Detective McKenna midway through the trial. The judge explained that the three remaining policemen—Burge, Yucaitis, and O'Hara—each faced two counts. The first count charged that they had abused Wilson, the second that they had engaged in a conspiracy to do so. Each policeman, Duff said, would be guilty under the first count if they participated in the physical abuse or if they were aware of it and did not assist or protect the plaintiff. On the second count, the three would be guilty if the jury decided there had been some common and unlawful plan to abuse Wilson. O'Hara, for example, would be guilty if the evidence showed that he understood that Wilson had been tortured and covered up the fact in his reports.

And so the jury retired. Afterward, individual members said that they were surprised to see that the people they had shared so much with for seven weeks could have such divergent opinions about the case. Four times they sent a message to the judge indicating that they were at an impasse. Ultimately, after ten hours of debate, they voted to clear O'Hara and Yucaitis on count one. On everything else, they remained deadlocked.

Assured that further debate would be useless, Judge Duff declared a mistrial on the unresolved charges, which meant that the whole proceeding would have to be done again. He thanked the jury members for their hard work and sent them home.

They left the federal building not knowing how much they didn't know about the case. They never learned, for example, that in the closing days of the trial, Wilson's lawyers had come into possession of evidence so compelling that Judge Duff referred to it as "a hand grenade."

{8}

Torturers

WHEN MOST PEOPLE imagine torture, they imagine themselves the victim. The perpetrator appears as a monster—someone inhuman, uncivilized, a sadist, most likely male, foreign in accent, diabolical in manner. Yet there is more than ample evidence that most torturers are normal people, that most of us could be the barbarian of our dreams as easily as we could be the victim, that for many perpetrators, torture is a job and nothing more.

Psychologists Mika Haritos-Fatouros and Janice Gibson have studied soldiers who served as torturers for the junta that ruled Greece during the years 1967–1974. In the *Journal of Applied Social Psychology, Psychology Today,* the *Journal of Humanistic Psychology,* and an unpublished paper, they have concluded that there was no evidence of sadistic, abusive, or authoritarian behavior in the Greek torturers before they entered the army, that there was nothing in their family or personal histories to differentiate them from the rest of the nation's male population of their age at that time, and that years after they stopped torturing, they lived what seemed to be normal lives.

The soldiers of the 11th Brigade in the American Division who murdered somewhere between 175 and 400 Vietnamese in the incidents known as the My Lai massacre were, according to the U.S. Army's commission of inquiry, "generally representative of the typical cross section of American youth assigned to most combat units throughout the Army." The soldiers, who dismembered, raped, and

88

tortured some of their victims, were ages eighteen to twenty-two; roughly half were white and half were black, and their educational level was slightly higher than the army's average.

In her article "Rorschach Records of the Nazi War Criminals: An Experimental Study after Thirty Years," psychologist Molly Harrower reported that ten experts could not distinguish the Rorschach test results of high-ranking Nazi war criminals from those of normal Americans. Douglas Kelly, the psychiatrist appointed to examine the Nuremberg defendants, had administered the tests in 1946 and had also concluded that "such personalities are not unique or insane . . . [and] could be duplicated in any country in the world today." Harrower agreed with Kelly and concluded that "well integrated, productive and secure personalities are no protection against being sucked into a vortex of myth and deception, which may ultimately erupt into the commitment of horror on a grand scale."

The German army's lower ranks were also filled with well-adjusted personalities. In his book *The Roots of Evil,* psychologist Ervin Staub points out that the Einsatzgruppen, who murdered Jews in territories overtaken by the Nazi advance, included highly qualified academics, civil servants, lawyers, a Protestant minister, and an opera singer.

Psychologists search for reasons, for some process of conversion that makes an ordinary man or woman—for there are women torturers also—into the monster of our imaginations. Some experts argue that the key is in the torturer's training, others that certain personalities are more capable. Some believe that the larger society serves as an incubator, while others contend that the situation alone dictates behavior, that what one believes goes out the window as soon as an authority figure calls for the opposite.

In January 1991, I went to Zimbabwe to meet Bruce Moore-King, a fellow writer, born in Rhodesia thirty-eight years earlier, who had recently been employed as an insurance company executive. He and his wife lived in what they called a "cottage"—a small cement-block house with a corrugated iron roof that sat off a dirt road on the grounds of a farm. They had five dogs, not much furniture, and no telephone. As I approached on a Saturday afternoon, Moore-King unlocked his gate and welcomed me. He was six feet, three inches tall, 220 pounds, his brown hair and beard were both long and bushy, and on his feet he wore a pair of rubber sandals, one red, the other blue.

We had much in common. We were the same height, roughly the same age, and some of our ancestors came from the same part of Ireland. As writers, we had both suffered at the hands of the same publisher years earlier. I had traveled a great distance to meet him because I wanted to learn how, as a young man, he had come to torture both adults and children.

He had given the question considerable thought, and he believed that the process had begun when he was sent to a British-style boarding school. "That whole boarding school system gears you for the colonial empire mentality," he said. "You have your duties, you have your position, and you have your obligations. The very rigid discipline gets you into the right frame of mind."

In the tradition of the school, Moore-King had to serve as a "fag," a sort of servant who shines the shoes and irons the shirts of upperclassmen as part of an initiation and hazing rite. "The upperclassmen had their own study rooms and they would wire up an old telephone dynamo or an old magneto from a motorbike to a door handle," Moore-King told me. "They would send someone to call a fag, the fag would knock on the door, and the guy would say, 'Come in.' And you would touch the handle and you were stuck there for a few seconds, being shocked."

While Moore-King was in secondary school, Rhodesia began to descend into civil war, a war generated by a system of white minority rule over a nation of blacks. As the country became more isolated internationally, the resident whites developed a siege mentality. "Everyone was against us," Moore-King recalled. "Everyone was an idiot, and we were the last bastion of civilization against the Communist threat."

Moore-King swallowed the propaganda whole. "I wanted to be an officer with a sword," he told me. He joined the army in 1972 at the age of nineteen and signed up for officer training school. His education as a torturer began when he took part in the school's escape and evasion course. During the course, he and seventeen other trainees acted as guerrillas, living rough in the bush and carrying out mock operations while being pursued by regular army troops. For five days the men had little to eat.

At about midnight on the fifth day, they were captured, hand-cuffed, hooded, and transported to a prison cell, a dark room flooded with ten inches of cold water. They remained handcuffed and hooded, and were ordered not to talk or touch a wall for support. Every half hour, a light was switched on and two soldiers armed with hoses sprayed the prisoners with cold water.

In the morning, Moore-King was taken out of the room and was made to kneel on rough cement. Protruding stones cut into his knees. After about an hour, an interrogator began asking him questions about the guerrillas' operations. Moore-King, who was still hooded, refused to answer. His interrogators then put a hose to the outside of the hood just at his forehead. Water covered his face.

"You can almost breathe," he recalled. "The bag goes into your mouth and nose and you can suck a bit of air through it, but not enough to keep you going. The feeling of asphyxiation, of drowning, builds up slowly, so it hits you quite hard. The main thing is the fear. I was scared, and deep down inside I knew it was an exercise, but for some guy who doesn't know if he is going to be killed or shot or what-ever, the fear must be tremendous."

Moore-King held out. When he was close to losing conscious-ness, he was allowed to breathe. Then the interrogation resumed. Again, Moore-King refused to answer. The hose went back to his forehead, and the near drowning was repeated.

Of eighteen men on the course, only six managed to maintain their resistance, Moore-King among them. He believes he was able to hold out because he was in excellent physical condition when he started the course and because he has a large nose, which he thinks made it easier to survive the water treatment.

After that training, Moore-King eventually joined the Grey's Scouts, a branch of the army set up to track guerrillas in the countryside, and he rose to the rank of sergeant. The Grey's Scouts were on horseback, the guerrillas were on foot, and Moore-King boasts that he and his men, starting with tracks eight hours old, could often surprise their quarry two hours later.

When the tracks led into a kraal, a small village in the bush, it would be impossible to separate the guerrillas' tracks from those of the local residents, and in that situation, Moore-King would pull a young man from the crowd and ask where the guerrillas had gone. If the man pled ignorance, Moore-King might pull a dynamo from his pack, attach alligator clips to the man's ears, and turn the crank.

Moore-King believes that the shocks he administered were minor, equivalent to ones he experienced in boarding school and when working on automobile engines, although he concedes that someone with a weak heart might perhaps have been killed. He thinks the real torture was not in the physical pain, but in the fear. "What does it feel like to someone who has no concept of electricity?" he asked. "What is the effect on a fairly simple black person in the middle of the bush who has never seen a light switch?"

As years passed and the conflict escalated, the Grey's Scouts often found themselves in villages populated only by women, children, and old men. The usual suspects—young males—were all away with the guerrillas. Moore-King would then search for the village elder. The most efficient method of questioning, he says, was not to torture the elder, but to find the elder's grandson. Once the grandson was in hand, Moore-King would order a soldier to hold the child by the ankles and lower his head into a bucket of water. The boy would be brought up for air just before he drowned and would be set on the ground, where he would spew water, writhe in pain, and weep from fear. The process would be repeated until the old man talked.

"Beating people up, physically assaulting people, that happened fairly irregularly," Moore-King told me. "Because that sort of thing requires anger, or a particular sort of mentality that could take someone and cold-bloodedly beat him to a pulp, and we didn't operate on anger or sadism or anything like that. And this is probably more horrific. It became a function. It became a part of the job. It became standard operating procedure."

Moore-King left the country in 1978 and wandered in exile for seven years. While he was abroad, Rhodesia became Zimbabwe and former guerrilla leader Robert Mugabe replaced Ian Smith as chief of state. Mugabe took a remarkably forgiving approach to his former enemies, assuring them that there would be no equivalent of the Nuremberg trials. As a result, Moore-King was in no danger of prosecution when he returned to the country in 1985.

During the course of his travels he had begun to question the beliefs that had fired the patriotism of his youth. He wrote a novelistic memoir, *White Man, Black War,* published in Zimbabwe in 1988. The book includes scenes of torture and atrocities witnessed by the author, and it lays the blame for the war and those incidents at the feet of Ian Smith and the elders of Rhodesian society. The book won him few friends and many enemies among Zimbabwean whites. When I met him, three years after publication, he seemed isolated and lonely, a stranger in his own land—not black, and yet not quite white either.

I asked him if he felt any guilt about his performance as a torturer. He acknowledged and showed none. There are two Bruce Moore-Kings, he told me, and the one who so casually tortured children and adults had been dead for a long time.

THE STORY of Moore-King's development as a torturer is not an unusual one. The combination of ideological indoctrination and severe training has produced similar results in other nations. In Greece during the years 1967 to 1974, the interrogation section of the Greek Military Police, known as EAT-ESA, became the torture squad for the junta that ruled the nation, and the severity of their training has been well documented by psychologists Mika Haritos-Fatouros and Janice Gibson. After the junta fell, Haritos-Fatouros, a professor of psychology at the University of Thessaloniki, was able to win the confidence of a single torturer, who ultimately introduced her to sixteen other members of the unit. As a result, the training and mindset of the Greek torturers has been more widely documented than most such units elsewhere.

Based on her sample, Haritos-Fatouros believes there was a method to the initial selection of the recruits, that commanders were looking for physically strong men from families with anti-Communist attitudes. All but one of the sixteen men came from a small village or a provincial town. Eleven were working class or lower middle class. Ten had not finished high school, five had completed high school and a technical school, and one was a university graduate. None seemed predisposed toward torture. Haritos-Fatouros and Gibson were both impressed by the cruelty of the training the men were put through and attributed the men's transformation into torturers largely to that process, a process so extreme that few of those recruited actually became working torturers. Haritos-Fatouros estimates that only 1.5 percent of those initially selected were finally chosen to torture.

Essential to the ESA men's training was a climate of fear established immediately upon arrival at the training camp. In an article published in the *Journal of Applied Social Psychology* in 1988, Haritos-Fatouros reported that almost all of her subjects reported part or complete retention of urine, sometimes up to four days, and retention of feces up to fifteen days at the beginning of their training. Yannis Maniateas, the sole university graduate in Haritos-Fatouros's sample, told me in 1990 that upon his arrival ESA instructors ripped the sideburns from the recruits' cheeks because sideburns were considered a sign of weakness. Maniateas, who was a high school history teacher when we met, recalled that an officer ordered the class to run around the training center "until the building felt dizzy. Of course, we were the ones who felt dizzy. Whenever somebody fell on the ground, he was hit with a belt."

The brutality did not diminish through the three months of training. "You were forbidden to walk," Maniateas said. "You had to run everywhere. You ate your meals while kneeling on pebbles, you had to eat in three minutes and one minute later be ready with your weapons. We would be awakened at three in the morning and would have to run in place with a bag of equipment around our necks." The men, clad only in their underwear, would be forced to wear their helmets without the customary protective padding so that as they ran, the helmet dug into their heads. The officer would not stop the exercise "until it rained from the ceiling"—until the room was so warm that moisture collected on the ceiling.

"If you got a letter from home, you couldn't reach for it with your hands because we were animals," Maniateas recalled. "We had to use our mouths. If you used your hands to reach for something like a letter from your parents, something which related to your past and your old self, you would be beaten for an hour."

The trainees were told repeatedly that they were not men. Maniateas recalled being forced to sit on his helmet and imitate a chicken hatching an egg, and others were ordered to simulate copulation with a kit bag. Maniateas was once beaten badly for breaking the rule that forbade laughing. Other punishments included being forced to inhale deeply in a toilet.

In an interview in June 1990, Vlasis Papoutsis, another of the sixteen ESA veterans studied by Haritos-Fatouros, told me that when his class of recruits arrived, they were obliged to tear off their infantry insignias and eat them. Everyone in Papoutsis's class went through the standing torture, being forced to stand for days, taking only water. Papoutsis recalled hallucinating about cold water and beautiful women and proudly told me that he had lasted for fourteen days, six days longer than anyone else in his class. He told me that he was driven to succeed in the training, as he had been in many other situations in his life, because he was the smallest man in the group. He said that he had never considered dropping out of the training. Those who did—and there were many—were kept around as waiters and lackeys and were humiliated at every turn, and Papoutsis believed that humiliation would be worse than his physical ordeals. "I did not have the psychological strength to fail," he said. "I wish that I had."

In an article published in the *Journal of Humanistic Psychology,* Janice Gibson, Haritos-Fatouros's research partner, concluded that certain elements of the Greek torturers' training assured its success. The initiation rites isolated the men from their families and other important relationships, bound them to each other, and perpetrated a belief that what they were going to do was morally correct. The enemies of the state were dehumanized, often called "worms." Various tortures were referred to euphemistically; a beating, for instance, was called a "tea party." The suffering the ESA men endured during their training helped to desensitize them and made later acts, which would ordinarily be repugnant, seem routine. The isolation of the recruits eliminated external points of view that might interfere with the indoctrination. Elitist and morally superior attitudes fostered by the trainers highlighted the differences between the torturers' unit and the rest of society. The men were told they would be the cornerstone of the regime, the guardians of the nation, and as such they could do whatever they wanted.

Upon graduation, the men found they had certain special privileges. They could wear civilian clothes, dispense with army haircuts, drive military cars on personal business, eat in restaurants for free, and take time off after forcing a confession. They tortured on demand, often beginning the process without knowing the person's name or what he or she was suspected of.

"Torturing became a job," chief torturer Michaelis Petrou told Haritos-Fatouros. "If the officers ordered you to beat, you beat. If they ordered you to stop, you stopped. You never thought you could do otherwise."

And yet despite the unquestioning obedience seemingly instilled in the ESA men during their training, they were not all automatons. One of the chief torturers later married one of the prisoners. Papoutsis took pity on a high-ranking air force officer who was tortured because he did not support the regime, and allowed him to sit during the standing torture. When I met Papoutsis more than fifteen years later, he and the officer were still friends and in regular contact. Papoutsis, who was a senior official of the postal workers union when I met him, felt particularly bad that the former air force officer still felt unsafe, that he often could not sleep in his own home and sometimes checked into a hotel in order to get a night's rest.

THE READER PERHAPS feels comfortable now, relieved by the assumption that as long as one avoids organizations with severe training processes, one cannot become a torturer. Yet there is good reason to question whether the Greeks' training was necessary for their transformation. A great deal of research suggests that most human beings, ordered to inflict pain on a stranger, will do so as long as the order comes from someone who seems to be in authority.

Landmark research in the field was done by Yale psychologist Stanley Milgram, who in 1960 designed an experiment to test the limits of obedience. He recruited students from the university to take part in a pilot study, and in individual sessions they were told that they were participating in an experiment that would measure the effects of punishment on learning. Each participant was then directed to inflict a series of electric shocks on a "learner," increasing the intensity of the shocks with each wrong answer given. Although the learner appeared to be just another volunteer, he was actually a confederate of Milgram's and received no shock at all. The setup, however, was very realistic. The instrument panel of the shock generator, for example, was engraved by precision industrial engravers and bore a label from the fictional "Dyson Instrument Company, Waltham, Mass." Each subject was given a sample shock of forty-five volts from the generator prior to beginning the test, a shock accomplished by depressing the third switch on the machine.

The students had no anger, no vindictiveness, and no hatred for the person they were shocking, nor would they have suffered any punishment for refusing to continue. Yet 60 percent of the students were fully obedient, applying shocks of 450 volts in spite of the label on the dial that said "Danger: Severe Shock." One of Milgram's colleagues immediately dismissed the results, arguing that Yale undergraduates were an unrepresentative sample of humanity, that they were highly aggressive and would step on each other's necks given the slightest provocation.

Milgram then began refining the experiment. He thought that the lack of protest from the "victim" in the pilot studies had enabled the subjects to go blithely on in spite of the designated shocks on the dial. And so he worked out a series of pleas that the victim would utter at different levels of shock. He used newspaper ads to recruit subjects from outside the Yale community. He varied the distance between the learner and the teacher. He changed the location and appearance of the testing site so that it did not carry the prestige of the university. And yet as long as an authority figure was present, people continued to obey. No severe training had taken place. No reward was in sight. No threat had been implied. No punishment was possible. The authority figure was a stranger and so was the victim.

In one variation of the experiment, the learner was placed in an adjacent room and began yelling at 120 volts: "Get me out of here. I told you I had heart trouble. My heart's starting to bother me now. Get me out of here please. My heart's starting to bother me. I refuse to go on. Let me out." The cries grew more desperate as the shocks went on. At 270 volts, there was an agonized scream. At 315 volts, the learner yelled, "I told you I refuse to answer! I'm no longer part of this experiment!" At 330 volts there were hysterical pleas and a prolonged, intense, and agonized scream. Yet as long as an experimenter in a lab coat ordered the volunteer to continue whenever he or she questioned the procedure, 62 percent of the subjects continued to give shocks all the way to the end of the scale.

In his book *Obedience to Authority,* Milgram profiles some of the people who took part in the experiment. He calls one of them "Elinor Rosenblum, Housewife." Mrs. Rosenblum had graduated from the University of Wisconsin twenty years before she participated in the study and was married to a film distributor who had attended Dartmouth. "She does volunteer work with juvenile delinquents once a week and has been active in the local Girl Scout organization and the PTA," Milgram wrote. "She is fluent and garrulous and projects herself strongly, with many references to her social achievements. She displays a pleasant though excessively talkative charm."

At 195 volts, the victim—a Yale actor—began screaming about his heart. After 300 volts, no noise at all came from the actor, and he did not answer any of the other questions, conveying the impression that he was no longer conscious. Mrs. Rosenblum was troubled, but she continued up the scale, eventually giving the learner the 450-volt shock three times. Milgram observed that although she was muttering to herself, "I'm shaking here," her communication with the learner continued in the officious tone she had taken from the start. "It is almost as if she were two women," Milgram wrote, "one giving a competent public performance, and the other an inner, distressed woman unable to refrain from anxious utterances."

At the end of the experiment, Mrs. Rosenblum was asked to assess the shocks. She said that she believed they were extremely painful. When asked what would be the highest shock she would be willing to accept as a sample, she said fifteen volts, and she was indignant at the idea that she would even have to endure that. She spontaneously began offering an account of her volunteer work, telling how she worked with "leather-jacket guys," teaching them "respect for people." After a few minutes she was told that she had not really been administering shocks and she was introduced to the actor who had played the learner.

"You're an actor, boy. You're marvelous!" she said. "Oh my God, what he [the experimenter] did to me. I'm exhausted. I didn't want to go on with it. You don't know what I went through here. A person like me hurting you, my God. I didn't want to do it to you. Forgive me, please. . . . I wouldn't hurt a fly. . . . I kept saying, 'For what reason am I hurting this poor man?' . . . I went through with it, much against my will. I was going through hell."

In a follow-up survey a few months later, Mrs. Rosenblum claimed that her "mature and well-educated brain" had not believed the learner was being shocked.

Other subjects made no such pretense. In his reply to the survey, a thirty-nine-year-old social worker who had been fully obedient reported his wife's reaction to his account of the experiment. She told him, "You can call yourself Eichmann."

Milgram's experiments showed virtually no difference in obedience rates between men and women. Aggressiveness did not seem to be a major factor: in one variation, subjects were given license to engage in unchecked aggression, being allowed to choose the shock levels to administer to the learner. Only two subjects administered more than 150 volts (one administered 375 volts, and the other delivered the maximum 450).

Obedience decreased as the subject came into close proximity with the victim, but still a stunning percentage were compliant. Milgram designed one variation so that the victim was shocked only when he had his hand on a shock plate. At 150 volts, the learner refused to place his hand on the plate, and the experimenter ordered the subject to hold the victim's hand on the plate. Twelve of forty subjects—30 percent—forcibly held the victim's hand in place and continued to administer shocks up to the maximum 450 volts.

More depressing still were the results achieved in a variation in which subjects read the questions while another person (a second confederate of the experimenter) had responsibility for depressing the shock levers: thirty-seven of forty adults from the New Haven area continued to the highest level on the shock generator. "Predictably, subjects excused their behavior by saying that the responsibility belonged to the man who actually pulled the switch," Milgram wrote. "It is psychologically easy to ignore responsibility when one is only an intermediate link in a chain of evil action but is far from the final consequences of the action. Even Eichmann was sickened when he toured the concentration camps, but to participate in mass murder he had only to sit at a desk and shuffle papers. At the same time the man in the camp who actually dropped Cyclon-B into the gas chambers was able to justify *his* behavior on the grounds that he was only following orders from above. . . . The person who assumes full responsibility for the act has evaporated."

Milgram observed his subjects deploying a variety of mechanisms to deal with the strain of what they were doing. Some withdrew their attention from the victim, becoming immersed in the procedures, reading the word pairs with exquisite articulation and pressing the switches with great care. Some raised their voices to drown out the victim's protests. Some turned away into awkward positions in order to avoid seeing the learner suffer. Some administered only the briefest of shocks, depressing the levers for 50 milliseconds, thereby "asserting their humanity." Others engaged in subtle subterfuge, trying to tip the learner off to the right answer by emphasizing it as they read. The learner, however, never picked up on the cue. "The subject is unable to act openly on his humane feelings, deflecting them into a trivial sub-terfuge of no real consequence," Milgram observed. "Yet 'doing something,' even if of only token significance, helps preserve his self-image as a benign man."

Milgram noted that some who expressed disagreement during the course of the experiment nonetheless continued, and it seemed to him that the dissent served different functions in different individuals. For some, it was the first step toward total refusal to continue. For others it was merely a way to reduce the strain of the experiment—they did not alter their course of action. Having established a positive self-image as one opposed to the continuation of the experiment, the person more comfortably continued shocking the victim.

Everyone who participated in the experiment was debriefed after-ward. Obedient subjects offered a variety of defenses before they were told that the learner had not actually been shocked. Some denied that the shocks they were giving were painful. Others blamed the victim for volunteering for the experiment. Many, Milgram wrote, harshly devalued the victim. "Such comments as, 'He was so stupid and stub-born he deserved to get shocked,' were common. Once having acted against the victim, these subjects found it necessary to view him as an unworthy individual whose punishment was made inevitable by his own deficiencies of intellect and character."

Other participants were completely aware that what they were doing was wrong, but could not bring themselves to disobey. Milgram reported that some of those took comfort from the idea that their thoughts were in the right place, feeling that "within themselves, at least—they had been on the side of the angels. What they failed to realize is that subjective feelings are largely irrelevant to the moral issue at hand so long as they are not transformed through action."

In the debriefing sessions, Milgram frequently heard subjects say, "If it were up to me, I would not have administered shocks to the learner." Because they did not have the inner resources to defy the authority figure, they attributed all responsibility to him. They were only following orders. They felt responsible to the authority but felt no responsibility for the acts the authority prescribed.

Those who did have the inner resources to disobey, Milgram said, paid a considerable psychic cost. "For most people, it is painful to renege on the promise of aid they made to the experimenter. While the obedient subject shifts responsibility for shocking the learner onto the experimenter, those who disobey accept responsibility for the destruction of the experiment. In disobeying, the subject believes he has ruined the experiment, thwarted the purposes of the scientist, and proved inadequate to the task assigned to him. . . . The price of disobedience is a gnawing sense that one has been faithless. Even though he has chosen the morally correct action, the subject remains troubled by the disruption of the social order he brought about, and cannot fully dispel the feeling that he deserted a cause to which he pledged support. It is he, and not the obedient subject, who experiences the burden of his action."

During the course of the variations of his experiment, Milgram saw several hundred participants. "With numbing regularity good people were seen to knuckle under to the demands of authority and perform actions that were callous and severe," he wrote. "Men who are in everyday life responsible and decent were seduced by the trappings of authority, by the control of their perceptions, and by the uncritical acceptance of the experiment's definition of the situation into performing harsh acts. . . .

"This is perhaps the most fundamental lesson of our study: ordinary people, simply doing their jobs, without any particular hostility on their part, can become agents in a terrible destructive process." Milgram went on to conclude that many people are unable to act on their values, that even when it is patently clear that they are inflicting harm, relatively few people have the resources to resist authority.

.   .   .

MILGRAM'S CONCLUSIONS—that people could inflict pain without any training at all—seem to be amply demonstrated in the case of Hugo Garcia, an Uruguayan torturer who came to his profession with none of the fierce training given Moore-King, Maniateas, and Papoutsis. When I met Garcia in Norway in 1991, he had difficulty estimating how many people he had tortured when he was on the job in the years 1976–1979. He could recall torturing one a day, sometimes two, though occasionally a week would pass during which he would torture no one. He told me that he came to the job quite simply. He had left school after nine years, the minimum required by law, and had enlisted in the army at age eighteen. His father was a bricklayer in the army's maintenance division and over the course of many years of service had risen to the rank of sergeant; Hugo was hired in part as a favor to his father. The young man was given no military training at all before being assigned to a job as a clerk in the same group of headquarters buildings that his father worked in. After two years, the younger Garcia was transferred to the Compania de Contra-informaciones, the Company of Counter-information. This was regarded as a major boost in status, so much so that the friends he had made as a clerk asked him to remember them once he got established in his new job.

Garcia believes that he might have received the promotion because friends of his father recommended him. His father didn't know exactly what the unit did, though he had friends in it. Garcia told me that he had seen members of the compania, "and they could sort of do what they wanted. They didn't have to wear the uniform and they could wear their hair as long as they wanted." He later came to believe that the compania was looking for people who didn't act like soldiers so they could more easily conduct surveillance without arousing suspicion. Garcia, with his complete lack of military training, thinks he was therefore an attractive candidate.

On his first day, a sergeant gave him a tour of the compania's headquarters, which had once been a house with a large garage attached. At one point, the sergeant opened a door and showed Garcia a room in which fifteen to twenty men were sitting on the floor, their hands tied, their heads encased in hoods, some of them shirtless. "I was really shocked," Garcia told me. "He just said that these were all Communists and they were trying to sell our country to the Russians and they wanted to send all our children to the Soviet Union. They were just our enemies."

When he reported to work the following day, he was told he would be attending an intelligence course along with other soldiers from all over Uruguay. It was a two-month course that covered a variety of topics, including surveillance, tracking suspects, the use of electronic listening devices, and staging attacks that could be blamed on terrorists. "The worst thing," Garcia said, "was that they tried to make us have a relaxed attitude about torture. They did it just by talking about it. It was an everyday matter, nothing to be ashamed of, something you just had to do. There was no question, you just had to do it. After a couple of weeks, they brought in a prisoner and the instructor said, 'Now we have to torture him to get the information we need.' It was like he was telling you that we were going for a walk."

The prisoner was brought in wearing a hood, which was never removed. "The hood is compulsory," Garcia told me. "It is always there so that he cannot recognize somebody if he is set free. Also, the hood makes them live inside the dark all the time and makes them eventually lose reality."

The torture equipment consisted of a plank of wood, which the prisoner would be strapped to, and a tub, made from an oil drum, which was filled with water. The plank was attached to the tub with hooks so that when the interrogators lifted the board, the prisoner's head would be submerged.

Garcia remembered the instructor very well. He gave me his name and described him as timid in appearance, lazy in manner, and captain in rank. Garcia said that the captain passed around a list of what the prisoner had allegedly done, then pointed to one of the dozen students in the room and told him to begin the interrogation. "It was up to us to find out what kind of pressure was the best," Garcia said, "whether to just start torturing at once or to ask questions first. The first person started asking questions and the prisoner said that he didn't know anything at all. Then he [the interrogator] signaled two of the other persons and they put the prisoner's head into the water."

The prisoner was pulled out of the water, allowed to recover his breath, and asked the question again, and then, when he produced no information, he was again submerged. Garcia recalls that that first torture session lasted four to five hours with the whole class taking turns as interrogators or manning the plank. No one obtained any information of significance. The session concluded when the captain told them to stop. According to Garcia, the instructor told the class that they had not been hard enough on the prisoner, but that even if they had been tougher, they still might not have learned anything. Sometimes, he said, people like this one have to go through this several times before they talk.

"I didn't feel anything at all," Garcia told me. "It was like being in a kind of intoxicated state. It was unreal because I would never have thought I could participate in anything like this and accept it. It was kind of like being brainwashed because for these two weeks we had been hearing all the evil things these people were going to do to us, that they would sell the country to the Soviet Union and to Cuba. You had the feeling that you did the right thing, that many other people would be grateful for the things you were doing."

Garcia was also instructed in other methods of torture. The class was shown an electrical device and instructed where the leads would cause the most distress, but Garcia says that in practice, the submarino—the near drowning—was considered more effective and was therefore the preferred technique. A method of hanging people by their arms was also taught, as was the use of a crossbar on which a prisoner would be forced to sit, one leg on each side, so that the captive's own weight caused the bar to dig into his or her genitals. "We talked about psychological torture," Garcia recalled. "Arranging a mock execution to make the prisoner believe you're going to shoot him, let him hear that you're loading your gun and feel you pressing the gun against his neck or his head. Or we said, 'Now we have picked up your brother or your sister or your mother.' That was used quite a lot."

And so Garcia came to torture on a regular basis. He found the job mentally tiring but not physically demanding. Two women torturers also served in the compania, one a sergeant, the other a private. One of the sergeant's duties was to make certain that the male torturers did not go soft when the victim was female. The sergeant, Garcia said, would tell the men to go harder.

"We had nothing personal against the prisoners," he told me. "It happened quite often that when we had finished the torture, we might buy them cigarettes and give them some extra food." Garcia indicated that the prisoners were very grateful for such kindnesses. He said that the men from the compania had not descended to the level that the Argentines had. The Argentines, he said, "were very sadistic. All we did was torture to get information. We never tortured to punish anyone."

In addition to torture, Garcia's duties included surveillance and arrest. He was also assigned the job of in-house photographer, and as such he took pictures of prisoners after they had been tortured. As care was taken not to mark the prisoners' faces, the photographs showed no obvious signs of a prisoner's ordeal. Sometimes prisoners, not realizing Garcia was part of the torture team, would plead with him to pass on a message to their families, but he refused.

Garcia eventually changed his mind about the virtue of what he was doing, and in explaining that change he cited the cases of three prisoners. When he had been with the compania for only a few months, he was involved in the arrest and torture of two union officials. One of them died as a result of the torture, uttering his last words ("I can't take it anymore") to Garcia, who was on guard duty. That haunted Garcia in later years when he came to suspect that the owners of the factory where the two worked had accused them of sabotage just to be rid of two union activists. Garcia now suspects that certain military officials were paid off in order to effect the arrests.

The incident that seemed to have truly undermined his loyalty, however, was the kidnapping of a woman in 1978. Garcia and other members of the compania traveled to Brazil in order to carry out the kidnapping, and they subsequently tortured their captive on both sides of the border.

At that point, Garcia had served three years in the compania and had told only one person—a cousin—what his real job was in the army. That cousin, an older woman named Alma, had advised him to quit. It also happened that Alma had gone to school with the woman Garcia had helped kidnap and torture. Alma told him that her former classmate was a strong woman but no Communist. When it came time to take the victim's photo, Garcia asked if she recalled his cousin from her school days. The victim said no. "Of course I understood that she thought I was trying to get more information out of her," Garcia told me. "I remember going home and I couldn't sleep. I was thinking about this all night. A couple of days later, I did something that could have cost me my life. I called the woman's mother and [anonymously] gave her the address of where her daughter was imprisoned."

Garcia spent a good part of 1979 assigned to a surveillance team watching that mother's house. That same year, Garcia says, he asked his superior officer if he could resign. The request was denied. A few months later, a new officer took over. Garcia approached again, armed with a doctor's statement that indicated the young torturer had psychological difficulties, and in December 1979, he was allowed to quit. He says that his resignation angered other officers, however, and that they killed his civilian job opportunities one by one. Garcia told me that he was eventually informed that it would be best if he came back to the compania. Garcia believes his commanders feared that a man who allegedly had psychological problems might stand in the middle of the street some day and start talking about what he had been doing with the unit.

At that point Garcia told his wife for the first time what the nature of his duties had been and the dilemma he now faced. They decided to flee the country. They went first to Brazil, where Garcia told his story to a lawyer, who then helped him get asylum in Norway. He has since told his story publicly to various journalists and human rights activists, freely giving the names of his superiors and fellow torturers and describing the torture of the union activists and the kidnapping in Brazil.

In Norway it took some time before he found work. His first job, he told me, was making wrenches in a factory where most of his co-workers were mentally and physically disabled. He eventually learned how to paint automobiles, and that was his trade when we met in 1991.

"I am a victim too," he told me. "I know that those I tortured, they hate me, but I also hate the officers, my superiors, those who got me into this. They made me do it. They told me things that were not true. . . . I never took the initiative to start torturing somebody. I was given the orders, and of course you can say I was a coward who did not say no. I think people see the difference because if I had been satisfied with what was going on, I would have stayed on. I could say I had a good job, good salary, a lot of fringe benefits—free taxis, free hotels if I wanted. I could get a lot of things for free, presents from businesses." Garcia said that in addition to his great regret that he had tortured at all, he regretted not being able to go to his victims and explain himself. "One day I will be back in Uruguay and I will look them up and I will talk to them," he said. "I believe I will be preoccupied with that for a long time."

Garcia also said that some of the blame must fall on the United States, which supported the Uruguayan government while it was torturing its citizens. Garcia said that many of his superiors had attended classes in the United States or on American military bases and that they came back enthused about the fight against Communism and well educated in torture techniques.

THE DAY AFTER I met Hugo Garcia, I flew to Sweden to meet another Uruguayan, Julio Cooper. Garcia had been a private in the army and has the air of someone who would follow orders, but Cooper had been a lieutenant and has the air of authority and strength about him. He too had been a torturer, but for a far shorter time than Garcia. He told me he could count his victims on one hand. Unlike Garcia, Cooper did have extensive military training, but he did not think it severe or abusive and made no complaint about it.

Cooper served in the Sixth Cavalry Regiment in Montevideo, where the methods deployed included beating, prolonged standing, deprivation of sleep, deprivation of access to a toilet, submarino, electric shock, and hanging by the limbs. Cooper said he thought that the electrical torture was the most painful, judging by the response of the victims. "I dreamt of those screams," he told me. "They were tremendous." While others in his unit used electrical devices, he said he shunned them, in part because he regarded submarino as more effective. There is something more terrifying than pain, he told me, and that is the inability to breathe.

He could recall the first man he tortured, a doctor. "I was aware of what I was doing and I did it voluntarily, but I was enraged that I had to do it. I thought at the time that the prisoner forced me to do it. He forced me to do it because he would not speak."

In Cooper's unit, lieutenants and captains did most of the torture.

There was a doctor present, as there was in Garcia's unit. Doctors who attend torture sessions typically help the perpetrators determine how far they can go with a prisoner before he or she dies. In addition, they lend a certain professional sanction to what goes on in the room.

"It was not possible to refuse [to torture] because they didn't ask you to do it until you had been indoctrinated," Cooper told me. Yet, unlike Garcia, Cooper found himself full of turmoil from the beginning. Two of the fourteen other officers in his unit, he said, declined to participate in torture and were eventually expelled from the military. Cooper says that he tortured his first subject in May 1972 and refused to torture again after September the same year. On November 29, 1972, he was ordered to torture a detainee whom he recognized as a childhood friend.

Cooper now thinks this situation was a trap. When he told his superiors he would not participate, he was arrested and subsequently tried by a military court. He served a short time in detention, but was allowed to remain in the army. He told me that he was harassed for five more years, transferred to sixteen different bases in that time, and was then dismissed. Like Garcia, he believes that his attempt to find work was thwarted by the military. He finally told his story to a foreign diplomat, who helped him get asylum in Sweden. He then told his story publicly to journalists and human rights activists.

He told representatives of Amnesty International that there was initially an urgency to the torture, that it was done to save the lives of military personnel who might be in danger of attack by revolutionaries, but that "subsequently the idea began to lose its force and changed into the application of torture for its own sake, as part of a routine, and also as an act of vengeance against the detainee."

He told me that he believed that anyone who participated in the violation of human rights should be put on trial, including himself. "There is no law that authorizes torture, therefore all have to be punished," he said. "All who tortured are responsible for what they did. They all say that they followed orders. To me that's a lie. All who tortured are responsible. Everything they did, they did consciously, knowing what they were doing, and because they wanted to."

Cooper thought that a prison sentence would be justified for anyone who was convicted of being responsible for torture, and in that population he included not only Uruguayans, but also officials from the United States who taught torture and the ideology that supported it throughout Latin America. "There isn't a prison big enough to contain all who should be punished," he said.

"What I did, I did with the intention of helping the country to solve the problem which was happening," he said. "At no time did I do it because I was a bad person. I never did it to see another person suffer. I began to change when I became conscious that it was wrong. I changed my way of thinking, my way of feeling, and my ideology. Those men which I previously hated, I came to love. I thought of them as my heroes. They symbolized good for me. Their ideas were mine."

Cooper told me he does not believe in churches, but he spoke of his transformation in religious terms. "Julio Cooper, soldier, conservative military man, fascist, is another person to me. Julio Cooper today is a different person. I was previously an atheist. Today, after the transformation, I feel God within me. I feel happy and at peace with myself."

Since leaving Uruguay in 1978, he said, he had not had contact with his eight siblings. While Sweden is home to other Uruguayans—Cooper estimated that a thousand lived there—he has no contact with them either. He told me that when he arrived, some Uruguayans thought he was a spy, an agent of the dictatorship, while others who believed his story wanted nothing to do with him because of what he had done. "I understand perfectly why they hate me—because I represent something that did a lot of harm to them," Cooper told me. "I am a representative of the regime that punished them, expelled them, killed their people, made them suffer in jail.

"This experience was very conflicting, very traumatic, and difficult to unravel. I had my friends within the military and the enemy were on the opposing side. Then I transformed, and all who were my friends became enemies. The rest continued being my enemies. I receive the hatred and scorn of both sides. It hurts me tremendously to not be able to have contact with friends, with people I love. It hurts me tremendously not to be able to return to my country. Not a day goes by that I don't think of this, but I have gotten used to living with that pain inside me.

"I don't have friends here," he said. "I have found people with whom I deal but not a friend."

When we met, Cooper was working as a laborer in a frozen-food processing plant in a city in which he thought he, his wife, and their four children represented the entire Uruguayan population. He would probably be living a far more pleasant life in Uruguay, perhaps as a career army officer, if he had simply followed orders and continued to torture. In 1989, the citizens of Uruguay voted to support a law that in effect granted immunity to the military for human rights violations committed during the "war against subversion."

Cooper told me he did not regret his change of heart. "If I had to do it all again," he said, "I would do exactly the same thing. I can't regret what I did because it makes me happy. It's a matter of conscience."

VARIOUS THEORETICIANS caution against placing too much emphasis on the obedience to authority so convincingly displayed in Milgram's experiments and in the work of other psychologists who have conducted similar experiments with similar results. In his book *The Roots of Evil: The Origins of Genocide and Other Group Violence,* Amherst professor Ervin Staub argues that obedience to authority is just one factor in the making of a torturer. Staub argues that a society can be an incubator for human rights abuse, that nations can march gradually along a continuum of destruction until the employment of torturers is no radical step and the men and women hired for the job merely reflect the attitudes of the larger society.

According to Staub, the process often begins when economic difficulties spread through the population. People then look for scapegoats and for a leader who promises a new day. Often those leaders point to a certain group that stands in the way of the nation's progress—the Left, the Right, the black, the Arab, the Jew, the criminal, the intellectual. The society gradually comes to accept various limitations on freedom, limitations imposed in order to isolate the scapegoated group. Initial acts that cause limited harm result in psychological changes that make further destructive actions possible. The scapegoated group is humiliated, ridiculed, dehumanized, and eventually finds itself beyond the compassion of the public at large. Torture, kidnapping, and execution follow. In Staub's analysis, the whole society learns by doing, and the torturer is part of the process.

The soldier who has been told that the enemies of the state are vermin has little difficulty rationalizing torture, particularly when more learned men than he—commanders, doctors, judges, government ministers—are aiding and abetting the torture, justifying it, or looking the other way. Analyzing the gross human rights violations that occurred in Argentina during the years 1976–1982, Staub argues that over time, "the many types of victims made it difficult [for perpetrators] to differentiate between more and less worthy human beings. It became acceptable to torture and murder teenage girls, nuns, and pregnant women. Learning by doing stifled the torturer's feelings of empathy and concern." Furthermore, the Argentine torturers could see that their actions were supported by the larger society. Their superior officers signed release forms for kidnappings, relieving the lower orders from responsibility for the acts they carried out. The judiciary commonly accepted the military's version of events. The press—threatened by prison terms for demeaning or subverting the military—largely accepted censorship and did not report on disappearances. Doctors were present in interrogation rooms. While the Catholic Church made official proclamations condemning torture, kidnapping, and murder, it did little else, and some priests visited secret detention centers, not on behalf of the victims but in solidarity with the perpetrators. The middle class, Staub says, was pleased by the junta's economic policy and was unmoved by the repression that accompanied it.

The pattern Staub outlines is by no means peculiar to Argentina, and in view of the positive reinforcement engendered by a largely satisfied society, it is not difficult to understand how a torturer can hold on to a positive self-image. The human conscience is flexible. Robert Jay Lifton, author of *The Nazi Doctors,* reports that the doctors at Auschwitz and other death camps felt sorry not for their victims but for themselves for being posted to such awful places and for being assigned to such unpleasant jobs. In his book *Ordinary Men,* a profile of the Germans who served in the Nazis' Reserve Police Battalion 101, Christopher R. Browning includes the rationalizations of men who shot thousands of Jews in Eastern Europe. One man, a metalworker from Bremerhaven, came to believe he was behaving humanely by killing only children. The families rounded up by the unit were often missing a father who had already been transported to a camp.

The metalworker, seeing his colleagues shooting mothers, concluded that it was an act of mercy to execute the children since they could not survive on their own.

Torturers who feel some pangs of guilt also seem to take some refuge in the idea that someone else has done or is doing something much worse. Bruce Moore-King told me that when he administered electrical torture he never attacked the genitals, as torturers elsewhere are wont to do, and that the tortures he administered were mild compared to what was done to people who were sent to Rhodesia's Special Branch. Hugo Garcia told me the Argentine torturers were far worse than the Uruguayan. Omri Kochva assured me that the men of the Natal battalion had not descended to the level of the Americans in Vietnam. A former U.S. Army interrogator who served and tortured in Vietnam told me how much worse the South Vietnamese National Police were. The unnamed soldier who narrates Jean-Pierre Vittori's *Confessions d'un professional de la torture* claimed that the Algerians he tortured while serving in the French army were much more frightened of being interrogated by a native Algerian.

The same defense is often deployed by nations that engage in torture. The British comforted themselves with the rationalization that their methods were nothing compared to the suffering created by the IRA. The Israelis regularly argue that their methods pale in comparison to the torture employed by Arab states.

Torturers and the governments that pay their salaries may also justify themselves because they can see results. Torture victims do provide information, some of which is often true. General Jacques Massu, who directed the battle against the Algerian FLN (Front de Liberation Nationale), has been credited by historians with winning the Battle of Algiers through the use of torture, the use of which he openly admitted and never apologized for. There seems little question that Massu destroyed the FLN's networks in the city, and yet some historians argue that he prolonged the war in so doing, that if Algiers had been lost, the peace negotiations that led to an independent Algeria would have occurred two years earlier.

On the other hand, there are many who believe that information received from someone tortured is tainted at best, and often sheer fabrication, produced by the victim in the belief that they can end their suffering if they give something, anything, to their tormentors. If a story doesn't stop the torture, the tale is embellished until the torturer puts down his tools. Asked about the efficacy of all of the torture he applied and witnessed, Bruce Moore-King could recall only two incidents in which anything significant was gained: both were locations of arms caches. More often, as the torture takes on a life of its own, the information sought is of less and less significance. Henri Alleg, editor of a Communist newspaper in Algiers, was tortured by the French in 1957 not to find weapons, or a ticking bomb, or the leaders of a guerrilla group, but simply to get the name of the person who had hid him. Had Alleg divulged the name, the sole result of the torture would have been the arrest of one more Communist. (Alleg survived to write *La question [The Question],* a powerful account of his treatment, which the French government seized and banned two weeks after publication.)

One of the bleakest views on the effectiveness of torture was given to me by Don Dzagulones, who served as an interrogator with the Americal Division of the United States Army in Vietnam and who witnessed and participated in torture.

In an interview in August 1995, he told me that he could not recall a single incident in which torture was used to a positive end. "If it happened, I am certainly not aware of it. Like prisoner X comes in, you beat the living snot out of him. He tells you about a Viet Cong ambush that is going to happen tomorrow, you relay this information to the infantry guys, and they counter-ambush and the good guys win and the bad guys lose, all because you tortured a prisoner. Never happened. Not to my knowledge. And you don't get any more functional as an interrogator than I was. I mean I was the bottom rung, you don't get any lower, this is it, this is the front line for interrogators, that's where I was. So my experiences aren't universal, but they were at the nitty-gritty level, down at the base. We started the ball rolling."

Dzagulones believes that torture did generate reports, and reports pleased the chain of command. "They can say, look what we've got. We developed information about a Viet Cong political school and we are going to go in there and bomb the piss out of it. So you go in there and you bomb the piss out of it and you don't know if anybody is there or not. You don't know if the information is accurate, but there was information and there was an action based on it, so everybody is happy. You had a reason to go drop all these bombs instead of just dropping them on empty jungle. You had a target. That is what they looked for—body counts and hard targets. Show them a Viet Cong stronghold—God damn, that was great, because here we have all this military might and we are spinning our tires, we are pissing in the wind. Give us a hard target. Give us something to go after. It doesn't matter how you get it, just give us that information and we will go after it full bore."

Like Hugo Garcia, Dzagulones came to his position seemingly through coincidence. He had grown up the oldest of eight children in a working-class Catholic family in Detroit, and when he entered grammar school he spoke more Polish than English. His father had served in the American army during World War II and came home suffering from malaria and what was probably post-traumatic stress disorder. Dzagulones describes an upbringing shaped by his mother's strict Catholicism and his father's alcoholism and violence. He told me that the last time his father punched him was at Christmas 1987, the blow a by-product of an argument about the Vietnam War. Dzagulones was then forty years old.

Dzagulones was drafted into the army in October 1967. During basic training he was an enthusiastic soldier; he still owns a trophy he received for being the outstanding trainee in his company at Fort Knox. While at Fort Knox, he received a call from the Pentagon, most unusual for a draftee. On the basis of his scores on an aptitude test, he had been selected for the first class of a new intelligence school at Fort Meade. "The people that they used to start that school were the cream of the crop," he told me. "I was the only non-college-graduate, the only nonprofessional person, and [I was there] only because I scored well on the tests. The other guys were teachers and a journalist and a guy that owned a printing shop and a high school biology teacher. I was the shlump in the group. They were all-American boys, all of them, all of us were." At Fort Meade, Dzagulones was again chosen outstanding trainee.

At Fort Meade, torture was not part of the training, but techniques were mentioned casually when the class was turned over to some guest lecturers, Vietnam veterans who had served as interrogators. "I think they felt somewhat guilty," Dzagulones told me. "They seemed to be constrained. They did discuss theoretical tortures, the stuff that you see in all the movies, like kicking a guy out of a helicopter, the field phone, beatings, the fundamental stuff, but we were never instructed directly that we would use torture."

Dzagulones recognizes now that throughout his training, the Vietnamese were being dehumanized. "Even in the training at Fort Meade, they were referred to as dinks or gooks. It was ironic because the interpreters that we worked with in Vietnam would refer to the Viet Cong or any prisoner as a dink or a gook. They thought it meant a prisoner, not realizing that they were also dinks and gooks but they just happened to be our dink or our gook."

Dzagulones came out of the school certified as a Polish linguist, certain that he would therefore be sent to Europe. He was in Vietnam by January 1969. He was sent to work as an interrogator for the 11th Brigade of the Americal Division, stationed in Duc Pho, in Quang Nai province. One of the first interrogations he witnessed as part of his training was the questioning of a prisoner whose leg had been blown off by an artillery shell. A team of interrogators hovered over the man while they waited for a helicopter to evacuate him. According to Dzagulones, the prisoner was going into shock from loss of blood. The brigade intelligence officer, a major, became frustrated at the interrogators' lack of progress and took over, prodding the man's wounds with a pencil as he posed his questions. "This is a major," Dzagulones told me, "and he was surrounded by captains, lieutenants, MPs, doctors, nurses. It is not like this was done on the QT. There was no subtlety involved; it was open and nobody gave a shit. Torturing prisoners was wholesale, rampant, at every level."

By the time Dzagulones began witnessing interrogations in Duc Pho, every American soldier who served in Vietnam was supposed to be carrying a "pocket card" entitled "The Enemy in Your Hands." The card instructed soldiers to handle the enemy "firmly, promptly, but humanely. . . . He must not be tortured, killed, mutilated, or degraded, even if he refuses to talk. . . . Mistreatment of any captive is a criminal offense. Every soldier is personally responsible for the enemy in his hands. It is both dishonorable and foolish to mistreat a captive. . . . Not even a beaten enemy will surrender if he knows his captors will torture or kill him. He will resist and make his capture more costly. Fair treatment of captives encourages the enemy to surrender. . . . Treat the sick and wounded captive as best you can. The captive saved may be an intelligence source. In any case he is a human being and must be treated like one. The soldier who ignores the sick and wounded degrades his uniform."

At Dzagulones's base at Duc Pho, the POW compound was on the perimeter and was guarded by military policemen. It was not meant to be a permanent holding area. Typically, prisoners were held for no more than a week before being released or sent elsewhere for further questioning. When an interrogation was to take place, an MP would escort the suspect to the interrogation bunker, remain with him or her throughout the interview, and then return the prisoner to the compound. Dzagulones told me that he and other interrogators could make arrangements with the military police to prepare prisoners so they would be ready to talk by the time they were interviewed. One of the favored techniques was dehydration.

Dzagulones described the method at a 1971 hearing conducted in Detroit by Vietnam Veterans against the War, and his testimony was later inserted into the *Congressional Record* of April 6, 1971. "Our main objective in getting a prisoner to talk was to make sure we left no marks, nothing that was traceable. So the MPs were very cooperative with us. We'd get a prisoner and we'd keep him on a diet of crackers and peanut butter, which comes in C rations. The prisoner was kept out in the sun for three or four days eating crackers and peanut butter and occasionally they'd make him do a little physical labor. If the guy wasn't suffering enough, they'd make him fill sandbags and carry them around. They did this until it was obvious that the prisoner wasn't going to talk, or the prisoner broke. No steps were ever taken to prevent these actions. . . . If people did find out about it, they just let it go because it was an accepted practice. It was common. They were after the information, and since the Vietnamese were treated and held as less than human, anything that we did was perfectly all right."

"The MPs were supposed to be there during all interrogations and were supposed to be sure that we adhered to the Geneva conventions, that there was no brutality, that there was no torture," Dzagulones told me. "As a rule, if I wanted to torture a prisoner, I didn't have to do it myself. The MPs were more than willing to. I know of no occasion when an MP stopped an interrogation because there had been a violation of the Geneva convention. We are not supposed to touch these prisoners, let alone beat them, or stab them, or wire them with a field phone, or set their pubic hair on fire, or any of a number of things that happened."

Dzagulones says that he witnessed the use of the field telephone as a torture device many times, that one old man died of a heart attack during a field telephone interrogation. He claims that he used the device only "three or four" times himself. One of those times was when a suspect was brought into custody who seemed to be a high-ranking member of the Viet Cong. Dzagulones recalls discovering that the man's alibi was false and then finding a single-edged razor blade taped to the man's thigh.

"As soon as I saw that, I went off," Dzagulones told me, "because I figured, 'What is the purpose of that razor blade? It is not there for him to shave.' And I hit him a few times and I didn't feel the least bit bad about doing it. And I still don't." The suspect, who had seemed cooperative until his cover story was shaken, went silent. Dzagulones then instructed the MPs to make sure their prisoner didn't sleep, to activate the dehydration routine, and to "put him out on the sand." When daylight arrived, the man was made to kneel in the sand while holding sandbags in his arms. If he lowered or dropped them, he was kicked in the ribs until he resumed the required posture.

In spite of the ordeal, the prisoner continued his defiance. Dzagulones decided to use the field telephone. "I knew it was wrong. I really didn't want to do it, and I didn't think he was going to crack either, but I figured, 'What the fuck, why not? It's worth a try.'

"I really wanted to crack this guy, this was my personal mission. I wanted this guy big time because I knew he knew some shit. The area that he had been in was in the vicinity of what we believed was a POW camp with Americans in it. Winning the war never entered my consciousness, the possibility of it. How the hell do you win the war? You kill everybody, that is the only way you could win the Vietnam War. [But] if there was a possibility of saving American lives, then I would go nuts. If I felt that information that I could develop from a prisoner could be helpful in saving American lives, then I would do whatever I felt was necessary. In this case I thought the guy had information and it was real possible that he knew where some POWs were located.

"We brought him into a hootch, it was right in the MPs' cage area, and sat him on a metal folding chair and put his feet into a container of water, soaked him with water, doused him with water so that he was in contact with the metal chair all the time, and—from what I remember—put one of the electrodes to his earlobe and I think on the inside of his thigh. I don't remember—the MPs did all that. As long as I didn't care, they would have killed the guy if I had let them.

"The harder and faster you crank the field phone, the more electrical current it generates. So it was like watching somebody have a seizure. The faster the phone was cranked, the more involuntary movement took place. People would literally dance. This guy danced. Didn't make a noise, didn't utter a peep, didn't say shit. I am not kidding you, I was amazed at what this guy went through. And there was more than one interrogation session at which he was tortured. I was the primary interrogator, but everybody took a crack at this guy—a few of the other guys wanted to see if they could crack this tough nut. But he never did crack."

Not long after that interrogation, Dzagulones decided, "as a goof, as a joke," to try a new technique on some recent arrivals. "When they put them on a helicopter, they would put sandbags over their heads so they couldn't see anything, and they would tie their hands behind their backs. Right away they feel helpless, and you want to maintain that feeling of helplessness. There was a group of women or a bunch of people from this hamlet, so I told my interpreter to tell them that they were in the United States. These people have no concept of what the United States is, how far it is. They land, they see Americans around, they see a lot of vehicles, stuff that they have never seen in the hamlet, and God, it was amazing how many of them would break down and cry, how many of them actually believed that they were no longer in Vietnam. It was the most amazing thing, a half-hour helicopter flight.

"And it worked. I learned more by just fucking around. That is when I realized you don't have to torture people. You can trick them. Especially these people. Now someone that is a sophisticated Viet Cong fighter, it is not going to work with. But if you are looking for information about infrastructure, about when the tax collectors come, when the Viet Cong are moving through the area, the kind of stuff that we were supposed to develop, it wasn't hard. That would have been one of the things that I would have told the guys in the interrogation school if I had gone back. 'Hey look, these are culturally advanced people, but technologically they are not and you have to use that against them if you can.'

"But by the time I had made that discovery I was so disenchanted with the whole situation that I just stopped interrogating. I just said, 'Fuck you, I am not interrogating any more prisoners.' "

Dzagulones's enthusiasm for the military had begun to fade even before he arrived in Vietnam. In the year he spent in basic training and in intelligence school, Martin Luther King Jr. and Robert Kennedy had been assassinated. Dzagulones had admired both men (a picture of Dr. King adorned the wall of the former interrogator's apartment when I visited him in 1995), and their deaths made him re-examine his gung-ho attitude toward the military. He was also influenced by another member of his unit, an African American from Oakland who regarded the conflict as a "white man's war" and who refused to carry out any interrogations. When Dzagulones, after interrogating hundreds of suspects, made the same refusal, he was given the job of trying to find jobs for former members of the Viet Cong who had allegedly changed sides. The turncoats were supposed to serve various U.S. Army units as scouts, but were often regarded as untrustworthy, a position Dzagulones sympathized with. "My career was over as far as I was concerned," he told me. "I just realized how senseless and futile everything was. For my last two or three months in country, I treaded water, I marked time. Didn't do much of anything."

Dzagulones returned to Detroit. His re-entry into normal society was difficult. The next several years were marked by insomnia, nightmares, many fistfights, serious consideration of suicide, and a certain paranoia, a feeling that "Armageddon was about to happen" and that therefore the best thing he could do for himself and his family was to remain in top physical condition. He married, had three children, and, after working in construction, in an auto plant, and as an insurance salesman, settled in with the *Detroit News*. His first job was loading newspapers on trucks, then he drove the trucks, and eventually he was overseeing the operation as a circulation manager, a position he had held for twelve years when I met him in 1995. At that point he had been separated from his wife for three years and was living in an apartment he had chosen to furnish sparsely. He ate only when he was hungry, with the result that he often had one meal a day and sometimes none, but he was physically imposing nonetheless. He told me he had found great peace in the practice of aikido, that he had not been in a "real fight" since he had taken up the martial art ten years earlier. He was fiercely proud of being a Vietnam veteran, and his license plate and baseball cap proclaimed that accomplishment, but he said he would never allow his son to serve in such a conflict, and he was angry that his father, a war veteran, had not encouraged him to travel the few miles to Canada to evade the draft.

He told me that he did not care what readers of this book might think of him, that the only opinions he cared about were those of his children. I asked what he would want them to understand about what he had done. "I would want them to understand that it was an ugly time in American history, that I was in a situation over which I had no control, and that according to the way I was trained and what I was told, I did what I felt was appropriate, not necessarily right, not necessarily the best thing to be done, but the appropriate thing, and if any veteran reads that, he'll understand what I mean. A veteran of any war. But as far as somebody being an apologist for me, frankly I don't give a shit. I really don't. I don't care. I've got real strong principles and morals, believe it or not. They were tempered through my Vietnam experience because I was compelled or coerced to do things that I knew were wrong. I mean, it wouldn't bother me if I didn't know that it was wrong. But I let myself be pushed into doing it. I don't let anybody push me into doing anything now. I mean, I will die before I will give up my principles. It happened to me once when I was a kid, but I will be damned if it is going to happen to me as an adult. And that is the way I have been ever since."

Dzagulones believes that responsibility for the torture he administered and the atrocities he witnessed is difficult to assign because the whole society was mentally ill. "War is psychopathic behavior on a grand scale," he told me. "It is a society behaving psychopathically. At least that is the way I have put it all to rest for myself. [I was] a little tiny bit of a psychopath in this big old sea of psychopaths, and I did my bit of psychopathic behavior and everybody did a whole bunch of psychopathic behavior. I am not holding them responsible, and I hope they don't hold me responsible.

"But above all I don't want my kids to hold me responsible. I don't want my kids to think that I was an evil, villainous, wicked person. I saw a movie [*The Music Box,* starring Jessica Lange] a couple of weeks ago, and a woman, middle-aged, with little kids, found out that her dad was a Nazi in the Second World War and that he was responsible for executing some people, and when she found out, she kicked the old guy out of the house. She couldn't stand being around him or living with him with the knowledge that her father had done this fifty years before. And I could kind of identify with the old coot, you know what I mean? It is conceivable—I mean, it is a real stretch, but I could understand something like that happening. I don't understand him wantonly killing civilians, like the Nazis did, but who is to say, if I had been pushed any further, that I wouldn't have. A lot of GIs did."

CERTAIN FLAWS are inherent in research on torture. Former torturers who consent to be interviewed usually do so at a time when society has roundly condemned them, not when they are in their full glory. Their rationalizations may well be different when their careers are over than when they are fully employed, and it is certainly possible that recollections of their service to the state may be tailored for an audience primed for condemnation. Those who consent to be interviewed are not enthusiastic proponents of the old ways but dissidents, soldiers who have recognized that they took the wrong course. It seems unlikely that such men could be called a representative sample. I say this to caution the reader that I cannot claim to have achieved a scientifically valid survey here, though I think there is nonetheless great truth in what I have set down.

I confess also that some part of me hopes that the men I have interviewed are not representative of the whole, because for several of these men I have a certain respect. Whatever their misdeeds, and they are awful, I cannot shake the impression that some have shown a certain honor since committing them. Thousands more have done the same, thousands more have done worse, and never speak a word of it. In talking to me, these men had little to gain but a reputation of the worst sort.

And I must confess that in a few I could see myself. Don Dzagulones and I were both raised obedient Catholics, we were both teenage patriots, and but for a high number in the draft lottery, I might have found myself faced with similar choices. Bruce Moore-King and I share the same profession and the same ethnic heritage, and when he recalled his naïveté as a teenager—his fantasies of carrying a sword—I could easily recall my own lack of political awareness at the same age. The worst part of these interviews was that they were not difficult. Finding the men was not easy, convincing them to talk to me was hard work, but invariably our meetings went well. I never met the monster I anticipated.

{9}

BELFAST

Ireland vs. the U.K.

W HEN THE INITIAL euphoria wore off among the hooded men in
the Crumlin Road Jail, they began to show some stark symptoms. Almost to a man, the survivors I interviewed in 1991 mentioned
Sean McKenna's transformation. "His hair was as black as your boot,"
Kevin Hannaway told me. "He was in the cell across the way, and
somehow everyone always ended up in our cell, and I remember
someone came in and said, 'McKenna's gone white overnight.' And I
thought he was kidding, and I looked out and I could see Sean's hair
was all white. We kidded around, saying he'd gone off for a haircut
and had his hair colored."

At forty-two, Sean McKenna was the oldest of the hooded men.
During one of the interrogation sessions he had forgotten the names of
his children. At Crumlin Road, his cellmate was Jim Auld, who recalls
that McKenna "looked as if he was somebody mad. He had staring,
glaring, wide-open eyes, he was in a rush to get talking, he was not
able to stand steady, not able to concentrate, and he had no control
over his temper. Anybody that disturbed his wee space, he would have
flown off the handle at them. He was continually weeping—I remember some flowers dying and he broke into tears. At night in the cell he
would continually talk about what had happened and end up crying.
He hadn't any control over it."

In mid-October, the men were transferred from the Crumlin Road
Jail to the internment camp in Long Kesh, where inmates were

housed not in cells but in huts made of corrugated iron, referred to by the internees as "cages." Forty men were assigned to each hut. Auld likens the atmosphere of the camp to that of "a twenty-four-hour-a-day supermarket" because "there was no peace and quiet, no privacy, no personal space for somebody to reflect or to think about themselves or to collect their thoughts. There were always people there."

In that atmosphere, McKenna deteriorated quickly. Other hooded men recall that he started to believe that he was receiving messages over the television advising him how the camp should be run and that he was being persecuted by fellow prisoners who were doing nothing to him at all. Hannaway recalls that an older internee would sit on McKenna's chest at night "to stop him from having fits." In May 1972, *The Guardian,* the British daily newspaper, reported that McKenna shook continually, that he found it hard to articulate sentences, that he had severe headaches, and that he suffered from recurring nightmares about being surrounded and attacked by groups of men.

By that time, forty-year-old Pat Shivers, the second oldest of the hooded men, had already been released from custody. Shivers had had a facial tic before he was arrested; it seemed to have been aggravated by the torture. "He couldn't control his facial expression," Auld recalls. "His head shook and his eyelids were twitching. He was the most stunning to look at." In the Crumlin Road Jail, Shivers found himself overtaken by a crushing feeling when he lay down in the bottom bunk. In the middle of the night, his cellmate heard moaning and awoke to find Shivers standing against the wall in the torture position.

And Jim Auld himself was not well. After a few months in Long Kesh, he began having sudden blackouts. "I just went boom, out, gone," he told me. "I was only unconscious for a minute, a half minute, two minutes. My mind was just shutting down." By spring, the blackouts were becoming frequent, he was shuddering spasmodically, and he was experiencing violent headaches, insomnia, and nightmares. In its article on McKenna's condition in May 1972, *The Guardian* also reported that Auld had collapsed in his hut and had been admitted to the camp hospital. Three weeks after being admitted, the twenty-one-year-old dental technician was released to a mental hospital in Armagh in the company of a psychiatrist.

"I remember I was walking into another area of the camp and I had seen Jim five minutes before," Kevin Hannaway recalls. "He was right as rain when I left the cage. And I looked over and I saw a medic—he wasn't a medic really, he was just a screw in a white coat—leading him away by the hand.

"I remember afterward I was joking with Joe Clarke. First Mc-Kenna went off, then Shivers, and you thought, 'Well, those are the older guys.' But then there was Jim, and you started to think, 'Wait a minute, this is going to happen to all of us.' And me and Joe would point at each other and say, 'You're next.' And we were only joking, but there was part of you that wondered about it."

THE CONSTITUTION OF the Republic of Ireland claims the entire island of Ireland as its own, and citizens of Northern Ireland are enti-tled to carry an Irish passport even though they are governed from London. The Irish government has considerable allegiance to its northern constituents, and after internment was introduced in 1971, civil servants in Dublin were sympathetic to the accounts of torture and abuse told by men who had been picked up in the initial intern-ment sweep.

On December 16, 1971, the Irish government filed a complaint with the European Commission of Human Rights, alleging that dur-ing the course of the introduction of internment, Britain had violated the European Convention on Human Rights and Fundamental Free-doms on several counts, chief among them the prohibition against sub-jecting prisoners to torture and inhuman and degrading treatment. The complaint was a very bold step by the Irish government, which was economically and politically dependent upon the maintenance of stable relations with the United Kingdom. In London, the govern-ment of Prime Minister Edward Heath was infuriated by the Irish complaint.

The commission hearings, closed to the press and the public, began in the Human Rights Building in Strasbourg on October 25, 1973. In January, the British legal team announced that, for security reasons, they would not allow their witnesses—soldiers, policemen, and civil servants—to testify at either the Strasbourg site or at any site any-where in the United Kingdom. The government had never had any difficulty before in allowing similar witnesses to testify before various tribunals and commissions investigating events in Northern Ireland.

After much negotiation, arrangements were made for the British witnesses to appear at a remote air force base near Stavanger, Norway. Even there, the British insisted upon a screen being installed so that their witnesses would not be seen by anyone from the Irish legal team except the leading counsel. The British also instructed their witnesses not to disclose their names or anything that might lead to their identification. They appeared before the commission delegates identified only by letters and numbers.

The commission delegates ultimately heard testimony from 119 witnesses. The transcript ran to fourteen volumes and 4,500 pages.

That transcript has never been made public, and the members of the Irish and British legal teams were sworn to secrecy about the proceedings, and it is therefore impossible to present anything like a comprehensive picture of what went on in the hearing rooms. A Northern Irish solicitor who represented one of the hooded men, however, was able to provide me with transcripts of some of the psychiatric testimony.

The Irish legal team had recruited the psychiatrist Dr. Robert Daly to advise them and to serve as an expert witness. Daly had been born and raised in England, the son of Irish emigrants. Daly's father had worked in airfield construction and had raised his family on two air bases in Cornwall. As a child, Daly had once been in a building that was strafed by a German fighter plane, and he also was present in London during the Blitz. He went to Dublin for medical school and did his psychiatric internship at the University of North Carolina at Chapel Hill, where two of his colleagues had advised the United States government on brainwashing. The department of psychiatry at Chapel Hill had also conducted research on the effects of sensory deprivation, and Daly had done some work in the sleep laboratory. He had written his dissertation on dialysis patients, men and women who are faced with the prospect of sudden death and who have been exposed to some sensory deprivation. From Chapel Hill, Daly moved to the faculty at the University of Edinburgh, and while there he began treating pilots from the Royal Air Force who suffered from flying phobias; some of those men suffered from what was later to be labeled post-traumatic stress disorder. He moved to Cork, Ireland, in 1971, and had been resident in the country only a few months when he was hired by the Irish legal team to serve as their psychiatric adviser.

He had never been politically involved with any side in the Northern Ireland controversy and was recruited largely because he was considered an expert on stress. The Irish government only learned later that Daly also knew something about interrogation as a result of his work with RAF pilots.

On the witness stand at Strasbourg, Daly testified that the five techniques used by the British were refinements of a system of torture developed by the KGB. He cited the work of Doctors Lawrence Hinkle and Harold Wolff, former consultants to the United States Defense Department, who had studied the interrogation methods of both the KGB and the Chinese and had reported their conclusions in "Communist Interrogation and Indoctrination of 'Enemies of the States,'" an article published in 1956 in the American Medical Association's *Archives of Neurology and Psychiatry*. In that article, Hinkle and Wolff alleged that the Soviet Union had devised a system of deprivation and isolation in order to conform, "in a typical legalistic manner, to overt Communist principles, which demand that 'no force or torture be used in extracting information from prisoners.'"

Hinkle and Wolff reported that the KGB usually made its arrests in the middle of the night and then placed its prisoner in an isolation cell. The prisoners were not told what laws they had allegedly broken, and for an indefinite period they were totally isolated from human contact. "[The prisoner] has nothing to do, nothing to read, and no one to talk to," Hinkle and Wolff wrote. "Under the strictest regimen, he may have to sit or stand in his cell in a fixed position all day. He may sleep only at hours prescribed for sleep. Then he must go to bed promptly when told, and must lie in a fixed position upon his back with his hands outside the blanket. If he deviates from this position, the guard outside will awaken him and make him resume it. The light in his cell burns constantly. He must sleep with his face constantly toward it. . . .

"The prisoner becomes increasingly dejected and dependent. He gradually gives up all spontaneous activity within his cell and ceases to care about his personal appearance and actions. Finally, he sits and stares with a vacant expression, perhaps endlessly twisting a button on his coat. He allows himself to become dirty and disheveled. . . . He no longer bothers with the niceties of eating. He may mix [his food] into a mush and stuff it into his mouth like an animal. He goes through the motions of his prison routine automatically, as if he were in a daze. The slop jar is no longer offensive to him. Ultimately he seems to lose many of the restraints of ordinary behavior. He may soil himself. He weeps; he mutters, and he prays aloud in his cell. . . . It usually takes from four to six weeks to produce this phenomenon in a newly imprisoned man."

Hinkle and Wolff went on to outline the course of the feelings and attitudes of the prisoner during the isolation regime. "Some prisoners may become delirious and have visual hallucinations. God may seem to appear to such a prisoner and tell him to cooperate with his interrogator. He may see his wife standing beside him, or a servant bringing him a large meal. In nearly all cases the prisoner's need for human companionship and his desire to talk to anyone about anything becomes a gnawing appetite, which may be as insistent as the hunger of a starving man. If he is given an opportunity to talk, he may say anything which seems to be appropriate, or to be desired by his listener, for in his confused and befuddled state he may be unable to tell what is 'actually true' from what 'might be' or 'should be' true. He may be highly suggestible, and he may 'confabulate' the details of any story suggested to him. . . .

"Yet another method of creating pressure is to reduce the food ration to the point at which the prisoner is constantly hungry. . . . Chronically hungry people can sometimes be induced to overcome a surprising number of their inhibitions in order to relieve their hunger. The effects of isolation, anxiety, fatigue, lack of sleep, uncomfortable temperatures, and chronic hunger produce disturbances of mood, attitudes, and behavior in nearly all prisoners. The living organism cannot entirely withstand such assaults. . . . All of them . . . lead to serious disturbances of many bodily processes; there is no reason to differentiate them from any other form of torture.

"Another form which is widely used is that of requiring the prisoner to stand throughout the interrogation session or to maintain some other physical position which becomes painful. This, like other features of the KGB procedure, is a form of physical torture, in spite of the fact that the prisoners and KGB officers alike do not ordinarily perceive it as such. Any fixed position which is maintained over a long period of time ultimately produces excruciating pain. Certain positions, of which the standing position is one, also produce impairment of the circulation. Many men can withstand the pain of long standing, but sooner or later all men succumb to the circulatory failure it produces. After 18 to 24 hours of continuous standing, there is an accumulation of fluid in the tissues of the legs. This dependent edema is produced by the extravasation of fluid from the blood vessels. The ankles and feet of the prisoner swell to twice their normal circumference. The edema may rise up the legs as high as the middle of the thighs. The skin becomes tense and intensely painful. Large blisters develop, which break and exude watery serum. The accumulation of the body fluid in the legs produces impairment of the circulation. The heart rate increases, and fainting may occur. Eventually there is renal shutdown, and urine production ceases. Urea and other metabolites accumulate in the blood. The prisoner becomes thirsty. . . . Men have been known to remain standing for periods as long as several days. Ultimately they usually develop a delirious state, characterized by disorientation, fear, delusions, and visual hallucinations. This psychosis is produced by a combination of circulatory impairment, lack of sleep, and uremia."

On the witness stand Daly also cited research performed on Americans who had been subjected to "brainwashing" by the North Koreans during the Korean War. "I think the important point to remember," Daly said, "is that the actual processes of inducing marked anxiety, or extreme coercive pressures through the use of, for example, sensory deprivation techniques, are common, and the only difference between the techniques by, say, the people in North Korea and the hooding procedures [used by the British] is that the hooding procedures are much more severe. . . . From the torturer's point of view [the British methods] would be an advancement in the technique in that they can speed up the process. . . . In this case the experience was much more intense than it had ever been for any other group described in brainwashing procedures."

Daly and the other members of the Irish legal team submitted written evidence and medical reports relating to 228 individuals arrested during the internment sweeps. Of those 228, the commission chose to investigate sixteen "illustrative cases." Those sixteen included two of the men subjected to the five techniques: Pat Shivers, whose facial tic had been aggravated and who had seen his dead son during the torture, and Paddy Joe McClean, the schoolteacher from Beragh, County Tyrone, who had lost more than forty pounds in his time at the wall.

Shivers, a forty-year-old plasterer, lived in Toomebridge, a small town northwest of Belfast, where he had been active in the civil rights movement. He had told Daly that he felt short of breath from the instant that the hood was pulled over his head, and he had also said that after three days on the wall, he felt he was going insane.

"I do not think I need to point out to anybody the significance of the fear of insanity," Daly told the assembled delegates. "It is one of the greatest and most traumatic fears. . . . He [Shivers] began to injure himself by tearing off his fingernails against the wall. This is not an uncommon finding in schizophrenia where individual patients report that the sensation of pain brings back reality in some way. It was about this time that, you will recall, he began to have the hallucinations of seeing his dead son and the vision of hundreds of glasses of sparkling lemonade—a wish fulfillment. . . . He recalls sweating excessively. One might presume that the temperature of the room was high. . . . I think it is important to remember that there are episodes of extreme clarity in victims undergoing this procedure when the E.G. returns to normal so that people can in fact remember things. . . . He also told me about difficulty in going to the bathroom, disurea, and he described clearly that he had offensive odor from the urine, which suggests that he was having very much concentrated urine, a sign of dehydration.

"After that, he was brought to Crumlin Road Jail. . . . He has described to me the attacks of what must have been hyperventilation, or rapid breathing, which occurred at night. These are characteristic of patients with marked anxiety. The anxiety perhaps contributed to his being released in October 1971." Shivers was released after only two months of internment. Some of the other hooded men remained interned for more than three years.

Daly went on to say that after being released, Shivers relived his experience when he was "alone with his thoughts," particularly when he attended mass and when he sat in the bathtub; in the bath, he would shout "You bastard" at his chief interrogator. Daly testified that Shivers had said that he felt the need to meet his interrogator again, not to inflict injury, but for some reason he could not define. During their first meeting, Shivers told Daly that if police or soldiers came to arrest him again, he would run away—he preferred being shot to being taken back to the wall. Shivers's house was subsequently raided by a helicopter patrol; when they left, he had a fit of uncontrollable weeping.

Daly also testified that Shivers had become hyperacousive, a state in which a person finds noise extremely irritating. The ex-internee was disturbed by the sound of a comb placed on a shelf in his bathroom. He could not tolerate the sound of the engine of a car running outside his house, and when he heard an engine idling he would ask the driver to turn it off. Shivers had also admitted that he sometimes lost his way while driving to work, and his wife told Daly that her husband's driving had become erratic, that he was suspicious of other cars on the road, that the two were having many arguments, that Shivers was irritable and impatient with his children and that one of them had suggested that life would be better if Dad went back to jail. Mrs. Shivers also reported that her husband acted strangely when he saw policemen: he had, for example, followed a constable into a pub on one occasion. She feared that this would arouse their suspicions and that he would be shot.

Daly's portrait of Paddy Joe McClean was quite different. McClean, the thirty-nine-year-old schoolteacher from a small town in the middle of Northern Ireland, had had a more stable upbringing than Shivers, whose father had left the house when he was eleven and whose mother had been treated by a psychiatrist (then a rare occurrence in Northern Ireland). McClean had grown up on a farm as the oldest of eight children. He acquired nationalistic sentiments along the way, and joined Fianna Uladh (Gaelic for "Warriors of Ulster"), a legal but militant political organization that had a secret military arm called Saor Uladh ("Free Ulster"). McClean insists that he never was part of the military wing. He was interned in 1956, and in 1957 his organization was declared illegal. McClean was never charged with any crime, but he was not released until 1960. During that internment, he was kept in a wing of the Crumlin Road Jail where the men, housed two to a cell, had free movement within their section, prepared their own food, and did their own housekeeping. In the years after his release, he was active in the civil rights movement in Northern Ireland, often addressing rallies. When he was interned a second time on August 9, 1971, his wife was eight months pregnant with their eighth child and he had been spending his nights sitting up with his sick mother-in-law, who died within hours of his arrest.

McClean arrived at the secret interrogation center on August 11. He was put in a boilersuit that chafed his armpits and his crotch and eventually drew blood. After some time on the wall, he heard a firing squad, and subsequently he heard hymns and saw his own funeral, with his children walking behind the casket. He thought at one point that he was drowning in the sea. He became confused about his identity, and for a time thought he was a farmer from Enniskillen. He tried to vomit his tongue; it was so swollen that he feared he would choke on it. He came to the conclusion that he was going to be executed and adopted a mode of passive resistance, refusing his place on the wall and being kicked and beaten as a result. During one of the periods when he lay on the ground, he believed he was examined by a doctor or a medical orderly; he had a vivid memory of hearing the man say, "If I am needed to dispatch him, you'll find me at the country club." When his ordeal ended on the seventh day, he could not walk unaided to the helicopter that was to take him away, and at the jail, prison guards had to help him to the entrance. He was sent immediately to the prison hospital and was the last of the original dozen victims to learn that others had also been through the ordeal.

When the survivors were moved from the Crumlin Road Jail to Long Kesh in October, McClean refused to be moved by helicopter. A special convoy was arranged so he could be moved overland. He had a constant buzzing in his head. He found the noise in the forty-man cages unbearable, and so he tried to spend as much time as he could outside. His stomach ulcers, which predated the torture, began to flare up, but in the camp he had difficulty getting treatment for them. As the months passed, he became more concerned with a developing growth on his leg. He was released in May 1972, having served nine months without being charged, and two months later, a specialist removed the growth, found it malignant, and ordered him to undergo radiotherapy treatment.

At home, his wife found him short-tempered and impatient. He could not stand noise of any kind; he left social gatherings, he could not go to a concert or a movie, and friends stopped inviting him over. At home, he sometimes demanded complete silence.

In his testimony before the European Commission of Human

Rights, Dr. Daly said that schoolteacher McClean, unlike Shivers, was a very controlled personality, that he was very anxious that he be perceived as normal and not mentally disturbed, and that as a result, he was inclined to minimize his experience. As an example, Daly cited his third and final session with McClean, which occurred in November 1973, two years after the torture. At that session, McClean told Daly that he had "no damage" anymore, that the psychiatrist who examined him from the British legal team had indicated that he was "as sound as a bell." Daly then had McClean respond to a prepared questionnaire, which brought out that McClean had trouble sleeping, that he was still having nightmares, that he was afraid to travel, that he suffered from periodic depression, that he was afraid of the army and the police, that he feared assassination, and that he had frequent headaches and stomach trouble. Daly noted that after admitting to a symptom McClean often said, "But it is not too bad."

Daly concluded that McClean was "a very courageous individual . . . [who] was handling what would have caused most people extreme anger by rationalization. He had formed a new philosophy of life so that he could tolerate other people doing such things."

Daly said, "It did not matter so much to him whether he now lived or died. The experience had made him realize how unimportant he was. . . . He felt he was just a pebble on the seashore." He had also, Daly said, lost all fear of dying, and he claimed no continuing resentment of his torturers. In his first session with Daly, McClean said, "I wouldn't want anyone to suffer for this."

In addition to calling Dr. Daly to testify, the Irish government also called Dr. Jan Bastiaans, a Dutch psychiatrist, fifty-six years old, who was well known for his work with survivors of German and Japanese concentration camps. During World War II, Bastiaans had worked in the resistance, and afterward was named a member of the British Royal Air Force Escape Society in recognition of his service during the war.

Bastiaans agreed with Daly's diagnosis of both Shivers and McClean. He thought that Shivers had a more idealistic personality, was predisposed to see what happened to him as an expression of mental cruelty, and was unable to prevent sudden outbursts of grief, anger, and protest. McClean, he said, had a more balanced personality, was better able to tolerate frustration and deal with conflict, was more likely to see the torture as physical rather than mental cruelty, and, because he had been interned once before, was perhaps better able to deal with the confinement a second time around. Bastiaans also suggested, however, that McClean might develop more symptoms as time went on. The Dutch psychiatrist told the delegates that survivors of concentration camps often lived seemingly normal lives only to suffer from symptoms that surfaced as many as twenty years after their traumatic experience.

The British legal team took some comfort from the appearance of Dr. Padraig Pearse O'Malley, a Belfast psychiatrist who examined McClean and Shivers within two weeks of their emergence from the secret interrogation center, long before Daly or Bastiaans did their examinations. O'Malley said that he had examined McClean on August 26, nine days after the interrogation ended, and came to the clinical conclusion that the schoolteacher "had suffered from some form of confusional state . . . but that he had recovered." O'Malley had examined Shivers on September 1, 1971, and concluded that he was "showing signs of some active psychiatric symptoms. . . . The symptoms were not severe, they were what I regard as mild. . . . A year later I felt that he was much better although some tension and anxiety symptoms were still evident." O'Malley did say, however, that he had attempted to organize a study of all of the men who had been subjected to the hooding, and that he and two well-known London psychiatrists had been denied access by the British government.

The British legal team also had their own psychiatric expert witness, Dr. Denis Leigh, a prominent psychiatrist affiliated with London's Maudsley Hospital. Leigh said that during the interrogation, Shivers developed a number of acute psychiatric symptoms, but that they had largely subsided when the interrogation ceased and he was left with a number of minor psychiatric symptoms. Regarding Paddy Joe McClean, Leigh said that some of the symptoms the schoolteacher suffered from in 1972 had also been present after his release from internment in 1960, and that those earlier symptoms had disappeared within a year. The source for that statement, however, could only have been McClean himself, since no psychiatrist had examined McClean after his release in 1960.

The British legal team claimed that the symptoms experienced by McClean and Shivers after the interrogation were minor, that they were not a by-product of the five techniques but rather the result of the strain of everyday life in Northern Ireland, strain that was greater for ex-internees like Shivers and McClean who had to travel to different areas to do their jobs. There was a certain irony in the argument; the men who had been interned had never been convicted of any crime and were in many cases picked up because of faulty intelligence, but the fact that they had been interned marked them forever as suspect in the eyes of both Protestant paramilitaries and the Northern Irish security forces. As a result, all ex-internees became targets for assassination and harassment, and particularly the survivors of the hooded treatment, who had achieved considerable fame as a result of the torture. No other group of internees, for example, had been denounced as "thugs and murderers" on national television by Defense Minister Carrington. Paddy Joe McClean had received threatening letters, and on June 10, 1972, a month after his release from Long Kesh, shots were fired at his house. The British defense that lingering symptoms were due not to torture but to the fact that the men were ex-internees seemed to include no acknowledgment that detainee status had also been inflicted by the government.

In cross-examination of Daly and Bastiaans, British attorney J. B. R. Hazan argued that the symptoms shown by McClean and Shivers might be self-inflicted. The argument was based on an assumption that McClean and Shivers might have been members of the IRA, and that they might feel guilty for having betrayed comrades during interrogation, or they might live in fear that that betrayal would be discovered and they would be punished for it.

Hazan also questioned the scientific basis of the two doctors' conclusions, arguing that there was no reason to attribute McClean's and Shivers's symptoms to the five techniques, that any traumatic shock could have caused them, that psychiatry was an inexact and subjective science, and that it was mere speculation and conjecture for a psychiatrist to say that the sudden emergence of a certain symptom was directly attributable to an event that occurred years before.

Hazan also accused both Bastiaans and Daly of having lost their objectivity. The British attorney accused Daly of having become "emotionally involved on the side of the patient" and asked Bastiaans if he was identifying with the hooded men because he thought they might "have gone through the same sort of ordeal as your countrymen were exposed to during the war." Daly's prognosis of Shivers—that the ex-detainee would suffer considerably for some time—was obviously wrong, Hazan argued, because Shivers by his own admission was working steadily. Hazan also attempted to cast doubt on the accounts by Shivers and McClean of their time on the wall by pointing out that a government that uses torture and physical beatings to get information at short notice will not receive very accurate information, "because the victim may say anything in terror."

IN GENERAL, the British government seemed to have adopted a general policy of obstruction and obfuscation. Where the Greek government, accused of torture in 1967, had allowed delegates from the European Commission of Human Rights to visit three of the sites where the alleged abuses had taken place, the British denied all such access. The British legal team repeatedly missed or ignored deadlines for providing documents, and they refused to provide interrogation records, which would have indicated which police officers had questioned particular witnesses. The British government instructed policemen and soldiers to refuse to answer questions about the five techniques; the government justified its position by saying that the use of the techniques had been discontinued and that there were "security considerations involved." Britain also declined to allow the commission to question the government officials who had ordered the use of the techniques, sending instead civil servants who read statements and then refused to be cross-examined. The Irish government's witnesses, on the other hand, had been cross-examined thoroughly.

The last oral submissions by the two sides were made in March 1975, and the commission delegates held their final deliberations in December. On September 3, 1976, they released their report. In a unanimous decision, they ruled that the use of the five techniques amounted to torture and inhuman and degrading treatment. The judges also noted that the British had failed to "accord the Commission full assistance, as required by Article 28" of the European Convention on Human Rights.

In Britain, the newspaper response was largely forgiving of the government. The *Daily Mail* said "this kind of interrogation was not pleasant, but it was necessary and nothing to be ashamed of." The

Daily Express said that no serious physical or mental injury had been inflicted, and that it must be understood that the security forces were "not dealing with normally law-abiding citizens, but with fanatics." The *Daily Telegraph* said that the word "torture" had been misapplied to what had happened to the hooded men; describing a situation in which a captured terrorist knew where a bomb had been planted in a school filled with children, the paper said, "Many people who are neither callous nor fascist might reluctantly accept the use of the Compton methods, whereas very few would endorse outright brutality." The *Times* thought it important to draw a distinction between the five techniques and "the rack, water torture, electric torture, beating and such brutality." The five techniques were less evil, the paper said, because they were designed to induce a state of mental disorientation so that the victim's will to resist would be lost, while the less scientific methods induced terror and pain in order to get the victim to submit.

In Ireland, the government thought the commission decision was incomplete, since no one was held responsible for the torture and there was no legal sanction to prevent the five techniques from being used in the future. The Irish decided to press for prosecution of the torturers and the soldiers and politicians who gave the orders, and to that end, the Irish took their suit to the European Court of Human Rights, where commission rulings can be appealed.

In London, the *Guardian,* the voice of liberal Britain, argued that in so doing, the Irish were "torturing Northern Ireland" by "force feeding the IRA with propaganda."

The same day's newspapers carried accounts that British military personnel were still being trained to use and resist the five techniques. William Rodgers, minister of state for defense, was quoted defending the practice, saying that it was designed to prepare servicemen for what might be done to them by "an unscrupulous enemy."

{10}

ISRAEL

The Court-Martial

In THEORY, soldiers in the Israel Defense Forces understand, as do their counterparts in other nations, the concept of a manifestly illegal order. When such an order is given, the correct response is disobedience, and failure to disobey can result in a court-martial.

In Israel, the definition of a manifestly illegal order was spelled out in strong terms after an incident that took place in 1956 at Kfar Kassem, a small Arab village that sat on the Israeli side of what was then the Israel-Jordan border. At the time, Israel's borders were being crossed by Palestinian guerrillas who attacked civilians, mined roads, and carried out acts of sabotage, and to thwart such raids, curfews were sometimes imposed in border areas. On October 29, 1956, Major Shmuel Malinki of the Israeli border police ordered his subordinates to institute and enforce a curfew at Kfar Kassem and several other villages to start at 5 p.m. Anyone who violated the curfew, he said, was to be shot. When asked about the citizens who would be returning to the village in the late afternoon, people who had jobs elsewhere and who would be unaware of the curfew, Malinki was said to have replied, "May Allah have mercy on their souls." Malinki reportedly said that a few deaths would impress upon the villagers the seriousness of the situation.

Malinki's men carried out the order without protest. A truckload of women begged for their lives. They were shot dead. Fifteen people on bicycles were told to dismount. Upon doing so, they were riddled with bullets. The cyclists were followed by a series of trucks and a wagon, all of them carrying workers. One corporal repeatedly used the command, "Mow them down," and his men obeyed. In the course of a few hours, Malinki's border policemen executed forty-seven men, women, and children.

Malinki and some of the policemen who participated in the incident were tried and convicted and sentenced to relatively long terms in prison. Over the course of the next few years, however, the perpetrators' sentences were significantly reduced, and they ultimately served little time. The presiding judge's opinion in the case, however, provided a benchmark for all subsequent cases regarding manifestly illegal orders. Judge Benjamin Halevi concluded that there had been no reason to fire at the citizens of Kfar Kassem and that every soldier should have understood that the order was manifestly illegal, "a clear-cut violation of the law, clearly criminal in nature, an illegality which pierces the eye and enrages the heart, if the eye is not blind and the heart is not sealed or corrupt." A manifestly illegal order, he said, "is one which should have a black flag flying above it, like a warning which says 'Forbidden!' It is not a formal illegality, hidden or partly hidden, known only to the legal experts, but an illegality striking to the eye and repugnant."

And so it was that as Colonel Yehuda Meir's court-martial began, thirty years after Judge Halevi's opinion, the Beita and Hawara orders were said to have been marked with a black flag. The incidents, once revealed to the Israeli public, aroused a certain revulsion, a revulsion that was somewhat surprising given that the breaking of arms and legs was a common occurrence throughout the occupied territories. By January 27, 1988, less than two weeks after Defense Minister Yitzhak Rabin had instituted his "force, might, and beatings" policy, two members of the Israeli parliament returned from a trip to the Gaza Strip with the news that they had seen two hundred Arabs whose limbs had been broken by Israeli troops.

On February 25, 1988, a CBS film crew secretly filmed a group of Israeli soldiers beating two Palestinian youths near a wall in Nablus. The beating lasted for more than forty-five minutes and showed the soldiers using rocks as clubs. Segments of the tape were broadcast in Israel and around the world.

At the end of March 1988, the Boston-based group Physicians for

Human Rights filed a report documenting "an essentially uncontrolled epidemic of violence by soldiers and police in the West Bank and Gaza Strip," a policy of "brutalization, indiscriminate in choice of victim but precise in choice of injury, adhered to quite consistently. . . . The word 'beating' does not properly convey the literal pounding and mauling with clubs and other weapons used to produce the injuries we saw." The PHR team noted that they had seen multiple fractures on various individuals as well as an absence of the sort of injuries that usually occurred in the course of resisting arrest. The doctors also noticed that the hand and arm fractures followed a certain pattern: people who favored their right hand had bones broken on the right, those who were left-handed had bones broken on the left.

The beatings continued throughout the year. In February 1989, eleven months after the PHR report, the U.S. State Department's human rights report on Israel said that at least thirteen Arabs had died from beatings in the previous calendar year.

One of the dead was Hani al-Shami, forty-three years old, a resident of the Jabaliya refugee camp in the Gaza Strip. On August 22, 1988, during the course of fierce clashes with stone throwers in the camp, four soldiers from the Givati Brigade entered al-Shami's house while pursuing his son. Al-Shami tried to block their entry, but the soldiers forced open the door. They then beat al-Shami for ten to fifteen minutes, after which they arrested him and transported him to a local military post, where he was subsequently beaten by different soldiers. Within hours, al-Shami was dead.

The four Givati soldiers were charged with manslaughter, and their court-martial began two months later. In testimony given in court and to the military police investigator assigned to the case, the defendants admitted that once inside the house, they had beaten two children about six or eight years old, a teenage boy about thirteen or fourteen, and Hani al-Shami. The soldiers said that they had beaten the teenager and his father around the head with their hands and around the legs and kneecaps with rifle butts and a broomstick, and one soldier said that he had jumped off a bed onto the older man's body. The soldiers admitted that al-Shami had offered no resistance once the beating had started. One of the defendants testified that he had continued to club al-Shami and his teenage son even when the beating was finished and the two were motionless. "Every now and then he got a blow to the leg," the soldier said, "so that no thought goes up to his head."

The four soldiers defended themselves by saying that they had been acting according to orders that dictated that they should break bones or beat so hard that those beaten could not walk. A sign from the base's bulletin board was produced in court, startling in its frankness: "The battalion will observe and detain and beat rioters, day and night." The MP who investigated the case said that the beating orders had come from high up the chain of command, naming a colonel and a brigadier general as possible culprits.

On the witness stand Captain Oz Noy, the four defendants' commanding officer, verified that the men had acted in accordance with standing orders and said that he had also beaten Arabs who were showing no resistance. He went on to say that when he went into a house to beat someone, he was careful that he did not damage the furniture, because that would not help him toward his goal. In response to the prosecutor's questions, Captain Noy said, "It's not easy to beat a person, and it isn't easy to beat a woman and a child. . . . Beating a person is unpleasant. But if I see one of my soldiers beating a local who hadn't resisted, I would not prosecute him." The judge asked Noy if he would expect to be beaten if he was a suspect of the police and had shown no resistance. "This is a different population," Noy said. "This is a different kind of citizen."

In the end, the judges ruled that it could not be proven that Mr. al-Shami had died as a result of the beating by the four Givati soldiers. The fatal blows, the judges said, could well have been inflicted by the unidentified soldiers who beat al-Shami once he had arrived at the military camp. But while acquitting the defendants of manslaughter, the judges announced that they were guilty of brutality, that their defense of following orders would not wash because the orders were manifestly illegal. The presiding judge expressed great outrage at the crime and bewilderment at the attitudes that prevailed throughout the brigade, but his strong words seemed incongruous with the sentences he handed out. Three of the soldiers were sentenced to nine months, one was sentenced to six.

Even those minimal sentences, however, caused some uproar. The newspaper *Ha'aretz* reported that army morale was suffering, that there was a sense that the Givati soldiers had taken the fall for the senior command. The newspaper *Ma'ariv* reported that Defense Minister Rabin, the author of the beatings policy, wanted the soldiers to be pardoned. In the end, three of the prisoners were pardoned after six months and one was released after five.

THE COURT-MARTIAL of Yehuda Meir began ten months after the Givati case ended. Although the Givati beatings had ended in a death, many in Israel viewed the Hawara and Beita incidents with more horror. The Givati beatings had been done during the course of a civil disturbance, when passions were inflamed, and Mr. al-Shami had been beaten before he was technically under arrest. The beatings ordered by Yehuda Meir were different. In both Beita and Hawara the victims were under arrest. They were also bound with plastic handcuffs, gagged, and left unconscious in a muddy field on a winter night. In Hawara, the victims had not only put up no resistance—they had, in the words of one of the soldiers, "arrested themselves," reporting dutifully to the Israelis when summoned by the mukhtar. In Hawara, soldiers had beaten their prisoners coolly, dispassionately, never having seen them before, having no idea who they were or why they were being beaten. All they knew was that the Arabs whom they were smashing with clubs had turned up on a list provided by the General Security Service.

Chief military prosecutor Finklestein saw the Yehuda Meir case as a chance to refute the common belief that only the lowly would be punished, that high-ranking officers were immune from prosecution. Here was a colonel who was being held solely responsible, who had been designated, by no less an authority than the judge advocate general, as "the father of all sin" in the two incidents.

Yehuda Meir, however, saw it differently. He had received an order to beat from his superiors, he had passed it down the chain of command, and he could not understand why he was being singled out when hundreds—perhaps thousands—of arms and legs were being broken at the time. In Meir's mind, beating prisoners was not manifestly illegal—it was standard operating procedure throughout the territories, and if there was anyone who was the father of all sin, it was Defense Minister Yitzhak Rabin.

MEIR'S COURT-MARTIAL began in April 1990, in a military compound in Tel Aviv. The three officers who sat in judgment did so for only a few days each month, and as a result the proceedings dragged on for more than a year. I attended sessions in late June, and given the importance of the case, I was surprised at the frugality and informality of the setting. The courtroom was small (about thirty feet by twenty-five) and almost bare of adornment. A single ceiling fan buzzed overhead. The stenographer's keyboard clacked loudly, and she sipped from a can of soda during the sessions. The audience sat not on formal courtroom pews but on hard wooden benches, unanchored to the floor, that seemed more appropriate for a mess hall, and spectators and reporters rested their feet on the benches in front of them and held private conversations during the proceedings without fear of reprimand. Soldiers came and went throughout the sessions, giving wilted, halfhearted salutes in the vague direction of the judges. Amnon Goldenberg and Boaz Okon, Meir's two attorneys, were the only men in the compound wearing neckties. No provision was made for the witnesses' comfort; they stood through their testimony at a podium in the middle of the room, the prosecution five feet to the left, Colonel Meir and his defenders five feet to the right, the judges and the stenographer straight ahead, the press and spectators behind.

On the first day of the trial, prosecutor Finklestein called Omri Kochva to the stand and asked the young lieutenant from Na'an kibbutz a series of questions about the incident at Beita. Kochva, trim, athletic, and straightforward, described the battle that had taken place between the villagers and the Nahal troops, the former throwing stones, the latter growing more and more frustrated with the rules of engagement, which forbade the shooting of stone throwers. Kochva said that the GSS list arrived some time after the battle was finished, that the soldiers then began rounding up the villagers whose names were provided, and that Colonel Meir gave his notorious order when the bus full of prisoners reached the crossroads a few minutes later.

"Had you never heard such an order before?" Finklestein asked.

"No," Kochva said. "It was something irregular. . . . I remember Eldad [Ben-Moshe] saying that because there were a few pacifist soldiers in the company, he wanted to choose the soldiers and not force anyone to carry out the order because it was irregular."

Kochva went on to say that there were "two or three soldiers for every prisoner. . . . [The] officers—Ilan [Shani], myself, and Eldad [Ben-Moshe] . . . directly supervised what was going on. There was a problem of controlling the soldiers that day. People were inflamed beyond what we could control. . . . Those that volunteered for the mission were very hot. I remember the soldiers going wild, hitting mainly with batons. I remember that some batons broke. Those beaten were lying on the ground, on their backs. They were bound, with something stuffed in their mouths so that they could not shout—with scarves, cotton, whatever we could find. It was very quick. The strength was immense. The soldiers went wild in a way that it was very difficult for us to control them. I am not sure we had control."

Finklestein then asked Kochva to describe the visit to Hawara the following night.

"In this case, too, a few soldiers were chosen," he said. "Soldiers who didn't want to do it were not forced to get off the bus. We left Hawara [with the prisoners] but there were a few houses outside of the village and we covered their mouths in order not to arouse provocation. We wanted to break limbs as quickly as possible and as quietly as possible. The beatings were given with batons and this time it was quieter. . . . They did it in an orderly way. They were laid together. The officer gave orders. I told them they had one and a half to two minutes to carry out the mission, to give a few blows and to do nothing unnecessary. There were four soldiers for every prisoner. Here, too, some batons broke.

"After a few seconds of beating most of them stopped screaming. After a half minute of beating they were no longer conscious. We took the scarves out of their mouths, broke the handcuffs, and left the field."

In the ensuing weeks, Finklestein questioned other soldiers who had carried out Meir's orders. Amiram Avirash, one of the beaters in Beita, said that he had "let loose," that he had beaten out of rage and frustration. "We left them on the ground," he said. "They shouted, moaned, and cried. . . . To this day I cannot absorb the fact that I carried out these terrible things. It just doesn't fit."

Shmuel Shefi admitted that he was also one of the volunteers at

Beita. "Eldad [Ben-Moshe] told us to beat them on their arms and legs," Shefi said. "I lost track of time. This was my first action in the intifada. . . . Arms and clubs were broken. There were soldiers who beat with their guns. There were screams and they pleaded and fainted. . . . The next day there was a similar thing in Hawara. I didn't get off the bus."

"You didn't ask yourself questions?" Finklestein asked.

"I am not an individual," Shefi said. "I passed through a process in Nablus. I came into contact with violence as a way of life. You have no time to ask yourself questions. I didn't think it would be wise on my part to go on a Don Quixote war."

ON APRIL 12, 1990, Finklestein called Eldad Ben-Moshe to the witness stand. Ben-Moshe, a short, thin, pleasant man of dark complexion, was by then twenty-five years old and a student of accounting at Tel Aviv University, having left the army two years earlier. He described Yehuda Meir's order to break arms and legs as being something new, something that he did not know quite how to digest. "It was not detached from the daily reality of the time," he said, "but it was detached from normal reality."

Ben-Moshe told the court that in Beita, he had chosen to stay at the bus until the end of the mission, when he ran first to one side of the road and then to the other, ordering his men to stop, to give the victims their ID cards, and to return to the bus. When the soldiers returned to their base, Ben-Moshe had given a speech instructing his men that they were not to be breaking arms and legs every day. The following morning, he mentioned his misgivings to Meir and Brigadier General Ze'ev Livne, commander of the Nablus region. Ben-Moshe could not recall the specifics of his conversation with Livne, but he did remember that he had walked out of the Nablus headquarters with the firm belief that Livne had endorsed both the Beita operation and its repetition in Hawara.

In describing the Hawara incident, Ben-Moshe said that he had left the bus only for a brief period when he told one group of soldiers to stop beating. He admitted that he had ordered the bus driver to accelerate the engine to drown out the screams, but he assured the court that the acceleration only lasted for a few seconds.

On the morning after the Hawara beatings, Ben-Moshe said, Brigadier General Livne gave his talk to the Nahal company, never mentioning the words "Hawara" and "Beita." Ben-Moshe was infuriated, but said nothing. He told the court that he had not thought it proper to disagree with the division commander in front of the assembled troops.

He decided instead to take his qualms to the commander of the Nahal battalion, Israel Ziv, who was "shocked by the whole story. It is not that he did not understand what is taking place in the territories," Ben-Moshe said, "but Ziv was disconnected from the territories for a month or two, so when he got back it was normal that what he had just heard would sound crazy."

Ben-Moshe said that Ziv phoned Major General Amram Mitzna, then the commander of all troops in the West Bank and superior officer to both Livne and Meir. Ben-Moshe said that he could hear only Ziv's portion of the conversation, but from that he understood that Mitzna was aware of the matter. At that point, Ben-Moshe felt he had done all he could, having questioned the order at the highest levels of the army.

Amnon Goldenberg, Meir's attorney, began cross-examination by asking if Ben-Moshe had objected when he heard the order to break arms and legs. Ben-Moshe said he hadn't. Goldenberg asked if the orders were unclear. Ben-Moshe said that, at the time, the written orders given to the troops were always being changed, but that "the order I received regarding Beita and Hawara was specific and clear. Yehuda's words were unequivocally to break arms and legs. Not to beat—to break." Ben-Moshe went on to say that the soldiers under his command had not asked where the order came from.

"Did you not think you should refuse the order?" one of the judges asked. "Did you not think that this was clearly an illegal order?"

"At that time," Ben-Moshe said, "I did not realize that even though there are orders, there are also orders one should not carry out. Today it is very popular to talk about orders that are clearly illegal. At the time, this was not a concept talked about at all. The idea of an illegal order never came up."

.   .   .

BEN-MOSHE'S VERSION of the events implicated the highest levels of the army. If Brigadier General Livne endorsed the Hawara mission before it took place, he as well as Meir should have been in the dock. If Major General Mitzna had been informed about both sets of beatings within twenty-four hours of the incident at Hawara, as Ben-Moshe claimed, he seemed to have chosen to look the other way; he initiated no investigation and within months promoted Meir from lieutenant colonel to colonel.

But the senior command's version of the story differed considerably from Eldad Ben-Moshe's. When Brigadier General Livne was called to the witness stand in early May, he said that the young captain had never mentioned breaking arms and legs. "I am surprised," the general said, "since one sentence from Eldad could have perhaps prevented this entire trial. I would have prevented the Hawara incident."

Livne said that the two talked only in general about beatings: "I told him that the issue bothered everyone, but it was more ethical than shooting and killing. He appeared to me to be in distress and in need of help. I asked him if a talk with the company would help. He said yes, and I sensed his relief. Before he left he asked me: 'So I understand that we are carrying out the mission as planned?' I said: 'Certainly.' "

Livne said he did not learn about the Beita incident until September 1988, eight months after it occurred. He learned about the Hawara beating the day after it occurred, he said, because a General Security Service officer from Nablus told him that the mukhtar from Hawara had complained. Livne said that he had understood only that a regular arrest operation had taken place and that the soldiers had gotten out of hand. Although he had an obligation to report the incident to Major General Mitzna, he admitted that he had let a week go by before he did so. He testified that he raised the matter with Mitzna a second time at the end of February 1988, in the wake of the beating incident filmed by CBS in Nablus. Livne testified that Mitzna had replied by saying, "That happened in the first stage of the uprising, and we are not opening it up."

MAJOR GENERAL MITZNA took the stand with a dark and full beard and a reputation as a liberal, a reputation derived in part from his attempt to resign his military post in 1982 as a protest against the war in Lebanon and from his more recent willingness to denounce violence by Jewish settlers against Palestinians. As a witness in Meir's trial, he contradicted both Livne and Ben-Moshe. He denied that Livne had told him anything about the incidents in January or February and said that he had first heard about them in November, eleven months after they occurred and seven months after he promoted Meir to the rank of colonel.

Mitzna admitted that he had heard the term "break arms and legs" among soldiers and in the media, but he said he had always emphasized that he found it unfit. He said that the rules he had laid down forbade the use of beating as punishment, allowing beating only to subdue a rioter or demonstrator. Mitzna admitted that there were gray areas in that rule—the definition of the precise moment that someone ceased being eligible for beating and qualified as someone under arrest seemed to be in the eye of the arrester—but at Beita and Hawara, he said, there were no gray areas. "There was no question of security. No one was under fire and there was no reason to fulfill this order. I think that this kind of order should have lit the warning lights. . . . Here the area was not gray but blacker than black. . . . In this case they went on their own initiative to collect people from their houses without them being connected to any incident, took them out, and broke their arms and legs. This is an infinite distance from that gray area."

Various members of the press had a field day with the contradictions between the testimony of the two generals. Writing in *Hadashot,* columnist Yehuda Meltzer said, "One of them is lying or should be released from the army immediately for severe hearing or speaking disabilities." *Ha Ir,* a Tel Aviv weekly, suggested three possible explanations for the conflicting testimony: Mitzna and Livne were liars; Mitzna and Livne were senile; or Mitzna and Livne did not control the forces at their disposal at the start of the intifada.

Yossi Sarid, the member of the Knesset who had written the pivotal newspaper article about Hawara and Beita after reading the file given him by Yehuda Meir, denounced Mitzna for being "smart after the fact." Writing in *Ha'aretz,* Sarid pointed out that Mitzna had no trouble denouncing Eldad Ben-Moshe for carrying out an order that was "blacker than black," but that same Mitzna had done nothing to reprimand Meir once he did know about the incident. Even if one believed that Mitzna had initially learned about the beatings only in November 1988, eleven months after they occurred, Sarid wrote, the general had remained silent thereafter and had participated in the cover-up. Mitzna, Sarid wrote, "took the black flag, put it in the central command's flag closet, and locked the door. It would have been left there, folded and hidden, until today, had the affair not been exposed in this column at the beginning of May 1989."

Sarid also asked why no one had been court-martialed for events similar to, and in some cases worse than, the beatings at Beita and Hawara. Sarid cited four incidents in particular: at the village of Kafr a-Dikh, residents were taken from their homes and were beaten with iron bars; at the Halhul garbage dump, fifteen Arabs were left with broken bones; at Kalkilya, residents had their bones broken in an orchard; and in Ramallah, a Golani battalion had broken bones near a wall that became known as "the wall of beatings."

"Yehuda Meir should not be sitting on the accused bench by himself," Sarid wrote. "Yitzhak Rabin, accused number one, should be sitting beside him. There was not one citizen, not one soldier in the country during those dark days at the beginning of the intifada who failed to understand Yitzhak Rabin's blushing shock and loss of wits as none other than a license to beat and break bones. . . . I have sworn: when Yehuda Meir's trial comes to an end, the courtroom doors will not close."

Though Rabin was not called as a witness, he was often alluded to in the courtroom and in discussions about the case. In interviews, he claimed that while he had told soldiers to beat, he had never told anyone to "break bones."

THE FORMER DEFENSE minister's refusal to acknowledge any responsibility and the fact that one or both of the generals seemed to be lying made Meir seem a much more sympathetic character when he stood to testify in late June 1990. Sympathy had initially been in short supply.

In reviewing Colonel Meir's army career, the press had portrayed him as no stranger to controversy. He had been court-martialed once before. Meir was commander of a Nahal battalion in Lebanon in 1982 when eight soldiers were kidnapped by Islamic fundamentalists, and although he had been in charge for only two months and had been on

leave on the day of the kidnapping, he had been held responsible for
lax discipline, lax levels of alert, and lax attention to regulations. Meir
took the fall for the whole command—no one else was blamed for the
incident. After a decent interval he was given command of the Nablus
region. In the years before the intifada, it was not a prestigious assignment, but it offered great power over the inhabitants, and in exercising
that power, Meir became known as "the sheriff of Nablus." He was
everywhere. He was at all the major demonstrations and riots. He
could be seen jogging through the streets of the city in order to stay in
shape. He was considered right-wing, perhaps too close to the settlers
(being a settler himself), and yet even the left-wing soldiers liked him,
including some from the Nahal battalion who would later testify
against him on the Beita and Hawara charges. He was charismatic,
they said, devoted to the army, and he worked very hard.

With the start of the intifada came chaos, and in reacting to that
chaos, troops in the Nablus region committed some heinous acts. In
addition to Beita and Hawara, there was the beating filmed by CBS
and a well-publicized incident in the village of Salem in which soldiers
used a bulldozer to bury four Palestinians alive (the four survived).
While Meir was not present when the various beatings or the burial
took place, they did occur on his watch. In assessing his former commander, a Nahal soldier told me, "Meir had no luck."

In court, he did not seem the sort of man who was prone to accident. He was handsome, trim, and at ease with reporters, even those
who had portrayed him in an unfavorable light. When he was called
to the witness stand, he told the court that he had been born in Roma-
nia in 1952, that he had come to Israel at the age of nine, that his
mother had died when he was fifteen, and that he had joined the
Nahal Brigade at eighteen. After sketching in his army career, he
was asked his current status. "Today," he said, "I am unemployed."
Throughout his days on the stand, it was that unemployment that
baffled him. How could he, who had always been a loyal soldier, who
had risen to the rank of colonel, who was only following government
policy, now be purged from the ranks? He was immensely sad, he
said, to be fighting the very organization that had given him the best
years of his life.

Meir's troubles seemed to stem from a meeting that took place in
mid-January 1988, when the intifada was only a few weeks old. Meir,

Livne, and about ten other officers from the Nablus region assembled at the headquarters of the civil administration to talk with Defense Minister Rabin. Meir testified that Rabin told those assembled, "Go in and break their bones. If they are beaten, it will hurt them, and the demonstrations will stop."

Meir told the court that he had expressed reservations about what the media and military prosecutors would say, whereupon Rabin reportedly said, "You do the work, I'll take care of the media and the lawyers." In an interview with Israel Radio, Rabin later confirmed that he had said whoever carried out his orders would not be prosecuted, but he claimed he had said that soldiers should beat demonstrators only while riots were under way. "I didn't use the phrase 'break bones,'" he said.

Meir also testified that in a separate discussion with Major General Mitzna about a particularly troublesome refugee camp, the general had said, "Go in hard. Break heads."

Meir claimed he was opposed to the beating policy at first but later "saw that it bore fruit."

To refute Meir's claims about the army's policy, prosecutor Finklestein produced written orders from both Mitzna and Livne that explicitly limited beatings, orders that allowed soldiers to beat during the course of subduing a rioter or stone thrower but that forbade the use of beating as punishment. The orders had been issued weeks before the Beita and Hawara incidents. Meir did not contest the existence of those orders but said that the army practiced "dual bookkeeping": the higher ranks were very careful about what they said in large forums and to the press, but in the field they said something else.

The chief judge asked, "You mean that clearly there was an instruction to beat in order to punish?"

"This was the intention of the beatings—for punishment," Meir said. "This was said clearly, they intended it, and they did it. Afterwards they didn't know how to stop it. This was the big catastrophe. . . . They allowed beating until you achieve control. What is achieving control? There were cases where they achieved control only after the person died."

Once beatings became policy, Meir said, soldiers "began to behave like hooligans. The distance between them and the Phalangists was nil. . . . The soldiers used rifle butts, metal rods, and other gadgets."

"What was the approach of the division commander, Brigadier General Livne?" defense attorney Goldenberg asked.

"For a month he would ask me at the end of the day—merrily— 'How many people had their bones broken today?' "

"[Major General] Mitzna testified before us that it is forbidden to beat for punishment, that there were many limits on beating," Goldenberg said.

"I say that he did not tell the truth here in this court," Meir replied.

When asked what had happened at Beita, Meir explained that he had thought that the men on the GSS list were terrorists (not the graffiti writers and singers of nationalist songs they turned out to be), and that he had given Captain Ben-Moshe an order to beat those men on the limbs and release them. While praising Ben-Moshe as an excellent commander, Meir explained that he had not told the young captain to break arms and legs, to bind and gag the victims, or to leave them in the field with one man physically able to get help for the others. When Ben-Moshe came to see him the day after the Beita beatings and said he was not prepared to repeat the operation at Hawara, Meir said he told the young captain, "Eldad, my friend, I understand you. As one Nahal soldier to another, maybe it is harder for us in this situation. Maybe for Golani, it would be easier. We cry and they laugh, but this is what we must do."

"Was it difficult for you to give that command [to beat]?" Goldenberg asked.

"Very difficult," Meir said. "It is very difficult to be party to such a thing. To be at the place when it happens is impossible from my point of view. The entire situation was more difficult than opening fire."

Meir said that every night he reported to Livne on what had taken place during the day. On the night of the Beita beatings, Meir said he told Livne that Ben-Moshe had beaten the people on the GSS list and that he hoped that the village would straighten out as a result.

"Livne wasn't shocked?" Goldenberg asked.

"It was the norm," Meir replied. "There was nothing out of the ordinary for Livne to be shocked about." Meir went on to cite as an example the assault at Kafr a-Dikh, which he said had taken place either the day of the Beita operation or the day before it. Meir said that a special unit had visited the village and had beaten six people with pipes, leaving four of them in critical condition. Meir also mentioned a system of regular beatings at a three-story lookout on Prophets Street in Nablus, where people were taken for "a short treatment." "We called it the beatings operation," Meir said.

Meir said that those who were hit during disturbances were not the inciters, but those who could not run fast enough to get away, people Meir characterized as "women and twelve-year-olds." In Meir's mind it therefore made sense to beat people from a GSS list rather than people who were simply slow runners, and he said he had been told by various members of the civil administration who dealt daily with Arabs that the Arabs preferred being beaten to being shot at with live ammunition. In the case of Beita, he indicated that he did not expect tremendous casualties because he told his officers to do it quickly and because, in his mind, the soldiers were "cold." He also told the court that Major General Mitzna had visited the region in the middle of February, and Meir said that at that time, in the course of talking about the problematic areas of the region, he had told Mitzna about the actions at Beita and Hawara.

Defense attorney Goldenberg then asked Meir how he felt as he sat in the courtroom listening to the testimony of Mitzna and Livne.

"I feel they've abandoned me and thrown me to the dogs," Meir said. He began to cry.

"What did you expect from these officers?" Goldenberg asked.

"I of course believed that all of those same commanders, starting from the minister of defense [Yitzhak Rabin], the chief of staff [Dan Shomron], Mitzna, and Livne, gave explicit orders. It was possible to expect that those same commanders would testify that that was how things happened—orders were given, it was a difficult period—and that we would not reach this state of degradation, of newspaper articles and nonstop television, of standing in front of the court, a colonel in the army, who for nineteen years gave his all to the army. You expect that when they send you out to the battlefield, they will not leave you in the field. They won't abandon you."

When prosecutor Finklestein took over the questioning, he asked Meir why he had not let Ben-Moshe off the hook when the young captain said he didn't want to carry out another beating mission. Meir replied that he was not commander of the district, that Livne was. As soon as Ben-Moshe raised objections, Meir said, "I made it possible for him to see the division commander [Livne]."

"You left [Beita] immediately after giving the order," Finklestein said. "Why?"

"Because it was very difficult for me to give instructions like that," Meir said. "Eldad also found it difficult to do something like that."

"How can you, a military commander, let nineteen- and twenty-year-old youngsters do things that you found difficult yourself?"

"This matter is very difficult for me," Meir said. "I have no smart explanation for it." After further grilling on the matter, Meir pointed out that his behavior had been no different than that of other officers. Mitzna, he said, had issued the order, and had stayed where he was, not carrying it out himself. Livne passed on the order, Meir said, and didn't venture into the field much. Meir said that he too had issued the order and had then "stepped back," and so had Eldad Ben-Moshe, who had given the command to break arms and legs and had then stayed at the bus. "Each one of us stepped back a bit," Meir said.

"You claim that you told all this to Livne that night."

"I had no doubt that the division commander was aware of the operation at Beita before it was carried out."

"Why, in your opinion, didn't Livne make a big deal out of the Beita operation?"

"Because the operation at Beita pales in comparison to the operation in the village of a-Dikh that was carried out that night. According to my information, Livne approved the a-Dikh operation."

AMONG THE WITNESSES who were called by Meir's attorneys was Lieutenant Colonel Zvi Barkai, a commander in the Golani Brigade who had been stationed in Ramallah at the time of the Beita and Hawara beatings. Barkai testified that on the day before the Beita incident, Defense Minister Rabin had visited Ramallah, accompanied by journalists. Barkai said that in a private conversation he had with Rabin, the defense minister had said that the Arabs must be beaten.

"Did you hear reservations regarding beatings from the minister?" Goldenberg asked.

"When he talked about giving beatings, he did not have any reservations and he did not say when it was prohibited or anything like that," Barkai said. "All the other senior commanders got hold of my company commanders and talked to them at the same time and gave them orders to beat. When the minister's entourage left, the locals started to go wild and the soldiers beat them. All the soldiers wanted was to be able to sock it to them. Things went out of control, and I quickly issued restraints that the beatings should be 'dry' beatings. We don't want to kill or maim anyone but we have to deter. A local who gets beaten up should feel some pain."

Barkai went on to say that he had also taken people from their homes at night and beaten them, that this was the norm throughout the district, and that from conversations with commanders stationed in the Gaza Strip he knew it was the norm there as well. Barkai said that he had tried to show some consideration for the man being beaten, taking care that the beating did not occur in front of his family. After rumblings about the procedure began to be heard from the press, he said, Rabin and chief of staff Shomron arrived and ordered him to stop.

"They said something that wasn't clear," Barkai said, "that beatings were allowed, but not for punitive or deterrent reasons. I really didn't understand, but I felt embarrassed to ask him about it in front of the press. So I approached the chief of staff on the side. He told me that beatings were not allowed except in cases of stone throwers, and that the offenders must be beaten while throwing stones. I told him I didn't understand him, that those who are caught are not throwing stones at that exact moment. The chief of staff told me that when you catch someone who was throwing stones you can give him a few strikes with the baton and then release him. That was a big restraint compared to what had been going on, but it also wasn't clear."

Asked if he had ever given an order to break arms and legs, Barkai said no. "The purpose," he said, "was to cause pain, not to break bones."

MEIR'S LAWYERS ALSO called chief superintendent Mose Viltzig of the border patrol to testify. Viltzig had been commander of a border patrol company in Nablus at the start of the intifada, and in response to defense attorney Goldenberg's questions, he described a meeting that had taken place in Nablus at which Rabin, Mitzna, and Livne were present. "The problem of dealing with demonstrations was raised because the army was not prepared," Viltzig said. "And then I remember that the defense minister said they must be caught, that their arms and legs must be broken and that then they must be released. To apprehend, break legs, release or arrest."

"Did you understand that the beatings were for punishment?"

"Yes."

"Did any of the participants at the meeting have any reservations regarding the minister's order?"

"No, neither Mitzna nor Brigadier General Livne."

"Major General Mitzna testified here that no orders were ever given to anyone to beat for punitive reasons."

"I tell you that he is lying because he personally sat next to the defense minister."

MOST TORTURE TRIALS are dominated by testimony of the victims, or testimony about them if they are dead. The Meir case was unusual in that the victims were hardly seen at all. The prosecution found it difficult to get the men from Beita and Hawara to testify. Some had gone to Jordan or other Arab countries to find work. Some were too frightened, some had no expectation that it would do any good, and some could not be found. In the end, only two of the twenty victims appeared.

The first was Samir Hamous, a twenty-year-old from Hawara who had commuted daily to work in a Tel Aviv restaurant until the night of the beating. He told the court that he had been awakened by his mother at about 10:30 p.m., that the mukhtar had come by to report that the Israelis wanted him, and that he had gotten dressed and had gone down to the mukhtar's gas station. He was handcuffed, he said, a cloth was stuffed in his mouth, and after a short bus ride, he was taken off the bus and led about two hundred meters into the field. He said that he was made to lie on his stomach, that soldiers put their feet on his back, and that they then began to beat his arms, legs, and back. He lost consciousness, he said, and woke up in a car that was taking him to a hospital in Nablus. His leg was broken and was put in a cast. He said he fled the hospital after two days because it was common for soldiers to come and arrest patients.

The second witness was Muhammad Beni Mufala of Beita, twenty-eight, a short man in a dark beard who testified on one of the days I was in court. He seemed a man who was easily confused but too proud to admit it. His testimony about the severity of the damage the soldiers had done to his left arm was unclear; the arm may have been broken, or it may not. Under cross-examination by defense attorney Goldenberg, Mufala said that the army had not been in Beita on the morning before the beatings took place, that there had been no stone throwing, that there had been nothing like the battle that all of the soldiers testifying against Meir had described. (It may be that Mufala was speaking from his limited perspective. When I interviewed him in 1993, he insisted he had been in the mosque on the morning of the beatings. If so, he might have known nothing of the stone throwing and the battle that followed.) He rolled up his pants leg to display the remnants of his leg wounds, but only the judges, lawyers, and Meir could have seen the display. Given the confusion of his testimony, I had the feeling he was not a very convincing witness.

Prosecutor Finklestein was not overly concerned, however, as he was confident that he could get a conviction based on the testimony of the Nahal troops. In Finklestein's view, it did not matter much that the victims formed no resounding chorus because the perpetrators of the assault—Ben-Moshe, Kochva, and the other Nahal soldiers—admitted the beatings.

In November, after all the testimony had been completed, Meir stood up and, without retracting anything he had said, admitted some guilt. He said that with the passage of time, he could see that issuing orders to give beatings was illegal. He pointed out that other orders from the senior command produced in court—written orders permitting the beating of those who violated curfews or refused to dismantle a roadblock—were also illegal. But, he said, the acts of the high command and their lack of support of him were not at issue. He went on to say that at Beita he had been a party to beating those on the GSS list, though he had not given any order to tie them up, to cover their mouths, or to beat them with clubs. At Hawara, he said, he had passed on an order, it had been objected to, and at that point he had absented himself from the picture. "The technique which was finally adopted," he said, "that the mukhtar gather the people, that mouths be covered, was never dictated or stated by me."

The judges heard closing arguments in the next session, and then retired to deliberate.

$\left\{ 11 \right\}$

CHICAGO

Informants

N OT LONG AFTER Andrew Wilson's trial began in Judge Duff's courtroom, the People's Law Office received the first of what was to be a series of anonymous letters written by someone who seemed to be a policeman with inside knowledge of Area 2. The letter alleged that in the wake of the shootings of Fahey and O'Brien, several men picked up by the police were beaten up in police headquarters in the presence of an assistant state's attorney and two of the highest ranking policemen in the department. A second letter arrived in a police department envelope; it said that Detectives O'Hara and McKenna had had nothing to do with the beating of Andrew Wilson, that the prisoner was beaten after he confessed, not before, and that he had been given the rough treatment "because Burge and company were showing off."

It was the third letter, however, that produced what Judge Duff would refer to as "the hand grenade." "I advise you to immediately interview a Melvin Jones who is in the Cook County Jail on a murder charge," the anonymous officer wrote.

Wilson's attorneys found Jones, and he told them that he had been arrested on a murder charge on February 5, 1982, four days before Fahey and O'Brien were shot and nine days before Andrew Wilson met Jon Burge. Jones said that in an attempt to get him to confess, Lieutenant Burge shocked him with an electrical device on the foot, penis, and thigh. Jones said he had told the story seven years earlier at a hearing on a motion to suppress his confession, and Wilson's lawyers located a copy of the transcript:

> Q. Have a seat, Mr. Jones. What if anything happened after he placed the electrical device on you, or on your foot?
> A. When he put it on my foot, I started hollering, I made a statement to him, "You ain't supposed to be doing this to me."
> Q. And what happened then?
> A. He told me that he ain't got no proof, you know to this, and that's when he looked over to [another officer].
> Q. When he looked at [that officer], did he say anything to [him]?
> A. Yes, he did. . . . He said, "Do you see anything?" And [the other officer] looked up at the ceiling and told him he didn't see nothing. . . . Then he said, "You see, it's just me and you," you know. He says, "No court and no state are going to take your word against a Lieutenant's word."

Later in the transcript, Jones says that Burge asked him if he knew two men with the nicknames Satan and Cochise:

> A. I told him I have heard of them; I didn't know them personally.
> Q. What if anything did he say to you at that time?
> A. He said, they both had the same treatment, you know. He was telling me what kind of guys they was as far as supposed to be being, you know, kind of tough or something. They crawled all over the floor.

Armed with the Jones revelations, Wilson's lawyers came to court hoping to break the case wide open but knowing that they had a time problem. The letter naming Melvin Jones arrived about a week after the People's Law Office attorneys had finished presenting their evidence, so in order to get Jones's allegations aired in court the PLO, would have to convince Judge Duff to let them reopen their case or present the new evidence in the rebuttal portion of the trial.

Duff conceded that the evidence was "awesome." He also felt, however, that it required substantial investigation and development. The trial was already running well over its allotted time (it had been scheduled for three weeks and would run seven), and Duff, who prided himself on his case management, blamed much of the delay on Taylor, Haas, and Stainthorp. Ultimately the judge refused to allow them to reopen their case, and so the jury retired with no knowledge of Jones, Cochise, or Satan.

I report this as if it were simply a legal decision, made in a calm moment after weighing various arguments, and perhaps that is indeed how Judge Duff came to his decision. It is difficult to imagine, however, how the judge could divorce himself from the emotional heat in the courtroom. The relationship between the judge and Wilson's lawyers had been deteriorating almost from the first day of the trial. That deterioration escalated when the judge began to suspect that the People's Law Office was disobeying his orders not to talk to the press about the case, a suspicion that arose after the appearance of a *Chicago Lawyer* article that contained photographs of Wilson's injuries and a portion of Dr. Kirschner's deposition. By sheer coincidence, the article appeared in the same issue that carried the survey results that rated Duff as the worst judge on the federal bench. From that point on, Duff seemed very concerned with his press coverage.

The concern became part of the court record in the trial's third week, when, with the jury out of the courtroom, Wilson's attorneys alleged that Duff had referred to their client as "the scum of the earth." The lawyers maintained that, in an off-the-record conference, the judge had said, "This is a case where it will be determined whether the Constitution will protect the scum of the earth against governmental misconduct." The judge was horrified and claimed that he had said, "Each of you feels that the other is the scum of the earth. I'm going to let the jury decide."

"I can tell you that tonight on the ten o'clock news there will be a news piece that says the judge called the plaintiff the scum of the earth," Duff said; ". . . you're going to have a headline in the paper today, maybe not a front page headline, maybe not a banner headline, but you're going to have big news stories that say that Mr. Haas said that the judge called the plaintiff the scum of the earth. . . . Now you have done it. . . . You all know that I have very recently been characterized as dumber than a box of rocks and prejudicial and a lot of things . . . what you have just done is attack the integrity of this trial and attack the integrity of this court in public, and it's very, very serious. It's heartbreaking, as a matter of fact. . . . I feel like I have been bludgeoned. . . . It is disgraceful, an injury from which I doubt this Court will recover."

Duff's nightmare—a "scum of the earth" headline and story—never materialized, but his irritation with Haas, Taylor, and Stainthorp surfaced daily. By the time Duff declared a mistrial on March 30, 1989, he had chastised them for shuffling their feet, for their facial expressions, for having their hands in their pockets, for leaning on the lectern. The judge's irritation continued to surface. By April 12, he had held Taylor in contempt four times and Haas once.

It came as no surprise then when the People's Law Office filed a motion arguing that they could not possibly get a fair trial from Judge Duff the second time around. The motion for recusal charged that Duff had suggested that Wilson was under the influence of drugs when he broke down while describing his experience at Area 2; that the judge had incorrectly assumed Wilson was a gang member; that he had repeatedly referred to Wilson, the plaintiff, as the defendant; and that he had called the prisoner "the scum of the earth." Wilson's attorneys also argued that the judge's rulings showed extreme prejudice in favor of Kunkle's clients. The lawyers cited several examples, among them an occasion when Taylor used a document that Kunkle contended had been declared off-limits by the judge in an earlier ruling. The judge agreed with Kunkle, said that he had even issued a written ruling on the matter, and indicated that because of Taylor's error he would entertain Kunkle's motion for a mistrial. Later it became apparent that Duff had never ruled on the matter and that during pretrial negotiations, all parties in the case had agreed that the document was admissible.

On April 11, 1989, after a rambling, emotional morning session that seemed more like a family argument than a legal proceeding, the judge said that he was not in any way biased against Andrew Wilson and ruled that he would not step down. The retrial was scheduled for mid-June.

. . .

IN PREPARING FOR the second trial, Wilson's attorneys began to follow up their Melvin Jones leads. Jones's attorney, Cassandra Watson, led the PLO to other men who had made claims of torture. Wilson's attorneys found the man called Satan in Stateville penitentiary in Joliet. His real name was Anthony Holmes, and ironically, his arrest had been cited in one of Burge's police department commendations, a commendation that cited Burge for "skillful questioning." Holmes claimed that Burge had used the black box on him in 1973, nine years before Wilson made similar allegations.

Wilson's attorneys found a man named George Powell, resident in Danville penitentiary, who said that Burge had shocked him in the genitals and stomach with a cattle prod. Lawrence Poree, an inmate in Pontiac, told the attorneys that Burge had shocked him in the arm, armpits, and testicles; on another occasion years later, Poree said, Burge began another electroshock session with the words "Fun time again."

Other men told of brutal treatment, naming not Burge but men he supervised. Gregory Banks, convicted of murder and armed robbery, claimed that three detectives from Area 2 Violent Crimes had beaten him with a flashlight, stuck a gun in his mouth, and, saying they had something special reserved for "niggers," put a plastic bag over his head. Darrell Cannon, who had been arrested five days after Banks by the same three officers, claimed that the policemen had addressed him as "nigger" when they put a shotgun into his mouth; that he had been handcuffed behind his back and then lifted by his handcuffs in an attempt to cause excruciating pain in his arms; that they had pulled his pants down to his ankles and shocked his testicles with a cattle prod; and that they had also put the cattle prod in his mouth. Cannon had drawn pictures to illustrate his story, and the detail was striking; in one illustration in which Cannon is being shocked on the genitals, he shows two policemen standing on his feet in order to keep him from moving.

The graphic stories of Banks and Cannon, however, were of little use to Wilson's attorneys. Given the limits of their lawsuit, they had to concentrate on the cases involving Commander Burge. Those cases, which included the names of five other Area 2 detectives, covered the years 1968 to 1982.

And Wilson's lawyers had two significant legal obstacles to over-come before they could use even those cases. First, Wilson's complaint had alleged that Burge and his colleagues had abused people suspected of shooting policemen, and that the city had a policy of allowing such abuse. All of the victims the People's Law Office had located had been charged with felonies, but only one, a man named Willie Porch, had been arrested in connection with the shooting of a cop. So Wilson's lawyers moved to amend their complaint. Judge Duff, however, ruled against them. He believed that if he allowed the new evidence to be heard, the proceeding would become a series of trials within a trial and that the whole process could easily take a year. "In my opinion," Judge Duff said, "the allegations that have been made about Commander Burge are extremely serious. If true, they might very well require an investigation on the part of the U.S. Attorney and/or the FBI." Duff said that he had in fact informed the U.S. attorney of the allegations, saying that if they were true, a federal investigation was warranted, and if they were false, then federal authorities should investigate whether Wilson's lawyers or those they had spoken to had engaged in a conspiracy "to suborn perjury and/or interfere with the process of this court."

Wilson's attorneys did not give up hope, however, because they thought they might be able to work Melvin Jones into their case even though he had not been arrested for the murder of a policeman. To do so they would have to surmount the obstacles posed by the federal rules of evidence, which usually forbid the introduction of evidence of prior crimes or actions to sully the character of the accused; the reasoning is that a man on trial for bank robbery should not be con-victed of the robbery at hand simply because he has been convicted of some crime in the past. However, the rules allow such evidence to be introduced if it tends to prove facts at issue in the case, in-cluding motive, opportunity, intent, preparation, plan, knowledge, or identity.

Wilson's lawyers claimed that the Jones material did exactly what the rules of evidence require—demonstrated that Burge's intent was to obtain confessions by torture; that his motive was to punish suspects; that his plan was to torture people until they confessed; that he was prepared or equipped to torture people and that he knew how to do it;

that he had the opportunity to do it; and that the similarities between the Jones and Wilson claims were so pronounced that they amounted to a trademark, a signature, an identification of the perpetrator.

On May 19, four weeks before the start of the second trial, Judge Duff ruled that the Jones evidence was not admissible. His ruling was made orally, not in writing, and from the transcript it is difficult to follow his reasoning. He states that the Jones evidence does not show intent, but he does not explain why. He states that the Jones evidence does not show motive because Jones's case had no connection to Wilson's. He goes on to say that the evidence could not be used to prove identity because no one was contesting Burge's identity, and he finds that the Jones testimony did not show that Burge had the opportunity to torture Wilson, or that he was prepared or equipped to do so, because the device used against Jones was "dissimilar to the two devices used against Wilson." (Jones had testified that the wires on the device used against him were connected to a couple of objects that resembled tweezers; Wilson had described them as alligator clips.) The judge did rule that the Jones testimony was "possibly relevant" to the issue of punitive damages, and so he ordered that the issue of punitive damages would be separated from the trial. If the second jury came back with a verdict in Wilson's favor, the judge might then allow Jones to testify in order to help the jury decide what damages should be assessed against Burge.

THE SECOND TRIAL opened on June 19, 1989, with little fanfare. None of the courthouse reporters stopped in to hear opening arguments. Over the next seven weeks, many of the witnesses from the first trial came back and told their stories a second time. Wilson's lawyers added a few new voices as policy witnesses against the city, among them Willie Porch, the only man uncovered during the interval between trials whose allegations of abuse involved an incident in which someone had shot at a policeman. Porch, who was serving thirty years for armed robbery and attempted murder, said that he was handcuffed behind his back and that a Sergeant X had stood on his testicles, hit him on the head repeatedly with a gun, and tried to hang him by his handcuffs to a hook on a closet door. Judge Duff's interpretation of the rules of evidence concerning prior crimes prevented Porch from telling the jury that Sergeant X was Jon Burge.

The detectives revamped their defense for the second trial. They dumped Dr. Warpeha, who had argued that Wilson had not been burned, and instead argued that Wilson's wounds were indeed burns and that they were self-inflicted.

In the first trial, the police had maintained that Wilson had been kept in Interview Room Number Two, and several detectives had claimed that the radiator in that room didn't work. In the second trial, it was suggested that Wilson was kept in Interview Room Number One, where the radiator did work, and that Wilson had burned himself on it. The man brought forward to support this contention was a jailhouse informant named William Coleman.

Coleman, born in Liverpool in 1948, has also been known as Mark Krammer, Paul Roberts, Richard Hallaran, R. W. Stevenson, Doctor Roberts, W. Van der Vim, Peter Karl William, John Simmons, and William Clarkson. He has served time in prisons in England, Ireland, Germany, Holland, Monaco, Hong Kong, and the United States. He has been convicted of manslaughter, blackmail, theft, fraud, perjury, and making false statements to obtain a passport. On March 13, 1987, he was arrested in a Chicago suburb and charged with possession of cocaine with intent to deliver. He eventually ended up in Cook County Jail on the same tier as Andrew Wilson, who was at that point awaiting the retrial on his murder case.

Coleman, who is white, claimed that within a few days of meeting Wilson, the black convict made two amazing admissions: he said that he had indeed killed the two police officers (a particularly stupid admission given that he was maintaining his innocence in his impending retrial), and he said that he had burned himself on the radiator in the interview room in order to make it appear as though his confession had been coerced. (Coleman offered no explanation for the pattern of scabs on Wilson's ears and nose.)

Coleman was an unbelievable witness to those who knew his record. The jury, however, did not know most of it, as in most circumstances legal precedent precludes the mention of convictions more than ten years old. In order to convey to the jury that Coleman was always willing to make up a story, the People's Law Office paid for journalist Gregory Miskiw to be flown in from England. Miskiw was prepared to testify that in 1986, he was working in London as a reporter for the *Daily Mirror* when he received a call from Coleman, who was then living in Washington, D.C., under the name Clarkson. Coleman told Miskiw that he could prove that Lord Litchfield, a cousin of Queen Elizabeth, had been arrested for possession of cocaine on a visit to Washington the previous October. Miskiw flew to Washington and waited for Coleman to connect him with the police officer who would provide the documentation. The policeman never materialized. In the meantime, Coleman offered information about the sex life of British tennis star Kevin Curran. Miskiw investigated William Coleman instead and ultimately filed a story under the headline "AMAZING ROYAL SMEAR OF BILLY LIAR."

Wilson's attorneys were gambling, however, when they imported Miskiw. Kunkle and James McCarthy, the city's lawyer, seemed gleeful at the prospect of questioning a reporter who worked for a tabloid that regularly carried photos of bare-breasted women on page 3 (the copy that was passed around the defense table had the front-page headline "FURY OVER DOLLY WHOPPERS—SEX SLUR ROCKS BUSTY QUEEN OF COUNTRY MUSIC"). Judge Duff excused the jury, heard Miskiw's story, and allowed Kunkle some cross-examination. Kunkle asked if Miskiw had any personal knowledge of Lord Litchfield or his habits; Miskiw said no. Kunkle asked if Miskiw had any personal knowledge about the sex life of Kevin Curran; Miskiw said no. Kunkle successfully argued that the contents of Miskiw's "Billy Liar" story amounted to hearsay, not evidence. The reporter left the city the following day, never having faced the jury.

In the meantime, the trial's bitter atmosphere continued. Wilson's attorneys helped organize an anti-Burge demonstration outside the federal building, risking a mistrial by doing so. Judge Duff cited them for contempt at least four times, and they told him that he was running "an Alice in Wonderland proceeding." In a sidebar on July 28, corporation counsel McCarthy suggested that he and Taylor should settle their differences with their fists. Taylor accused Judge Duff of lying. Duff held Taylor in contempt and said it would cost him $500. The following day, Taylor said, "I've had enough of this horseshit." Duff fined him another $500. (In the end, however, although Duff had held

Wilson's attorneys in contempt at least eight times in the two trials, he delivered only three formal charges.)

The second trial came to an end after eight weeks. To everyone's surprise, the jury of six suburbanites debated for three days. When they ultimately emerged, they carried a strange verdict. In deciding whether the city had had a policy of abusing people suspected of shooting policemen, the jury had been directed to answer three questions, and for Wilson to win a judgment against the city, the three questions had to be answered affirmatively. (1) Were Andrew Wilson's constitutional rights violated on February 14, 1982? The jury said yes. (2) Do you find that in 1982 the city had a de facto policy, practice, or custom whereby the police were allowed to abuse those suspected of killing policemen? Again, the jury said yes. (3) Do you find that Wilson was subjected to excessive force due to this policy? The jury said no.

The jury went on to clear Burge and his comrades of all charges.

On its face, the verdict makes no sense. The jurors seemed to be saying that Wilson's rights were violated, but not by these policemen, that the city did indeed have a policy of abusing people suspected of shooting policemen, but that Wilson escaped that policy, although he was abused.

After the trial I called jury foreman Allen Gall for an explanation. The twenty-eight-year-old lithographer said that the jury had been deadlocked, "almost hung," but that the outcome was pretty much what he wanted. He said that he believed the witnesses who testified that the police had run amok in their search for the killers of Fahey and O'Brien, and as a result, he believed that there had been a policy of abuse. He did not, however, believe that Wilson was injured under that policy. "If anything, I believe it was an emotional outburst by them," Gall said, "and that was the reason why he suffered his injuries. I don't think it necessarily had to be done under this policy."

Gall went on to say that he did not believe that Burge and his colleagues had tortured Wilson. "We believe that he did sustain these injuries from the police, some of the injuries, but there wasn't enough evidence to show that he got all of the injuries from the police. As to whether or not he was actually tortured, there is not enough evidence either. . . . It just seemed to me they were just really mad at this guy for shooting one of their buddies, and you know a couple of these guys took the liberty of letting their emotional attitude toward this guy show. They were just acting out of their anger toward this guy. That is something that we agreed upon. . . . [But] it is kind of hard to find someone responsible for something so serious without an actual witness coming forward, a neutral witness coming forward and saying, 'I seen him do it.' . . . We did agree that he got those injuries from someone, but as far as being specific as to who actually did the damage, there just wasn't enough evidence. . . . You know convicts, a lot of these guys are streetwise and they're pretty good at bullshitting."

Gall told me he had been surprised that he was chosen for the jury because he had admitted to having a criminal record. He said that he had committed a burglary in 1980, that the charges had ultimately been reduced to criminal trespass, and that he had been sentenced to a year of supervision.

$$\left\{ 12 \right\}$$

Victims

A PRISONER WHO is forced to stand for days on end, or who is made to assume painful body positions, or who is denied food, sleep, or a toilet, does battle with his or her own body. The prisoner can come to see the pain as self-inflicted; it continues when no oppressor is present. The body cries for relief, begging its owner to give in, while the mind may urge the prisoner to resist, to endure more pain. When the mind gives up, the body does not relent. The prisoner, already degraded and humiliated, is betrayed by his own muscles.

Hope is impossible, as the very people who in a normal society might stage a rescue are the ones who are staging the assault. No solace may be taken in the belief that one day justice will be done: the government will deny all allegations, blindfolded victims may not be able to identify their assailants, and those who would provide justice will almost certainly take the word of the policeman or soldier over that of the black, the Jew, the Arab, the Irish, the Communist, the counter-revolutionary, the subversive, the heretic, the criminal. Prisoners who would take refuge in reason, in trying to understand their persecutors, often find only additional torment; the torture so often seems senseless. The experience of the hooded men in Northern Ireland, none of whom were interrogated before being tortured, is far from unique. In *A Miracle, a Universe,* Lawrence Weschler quotes Dr. Liber Mandressi, a plastic surgeon, on his torture in Uruguay: "All of us were hooded all of the time. . . . And all of us were tortured for days on end, without even being interrogated at first. There must have been a hundred and fifty, two hundred people there; you could hear breathing, coughing, moaning—we weren't allowed to talk to each other. . . . At one point they kept us standing, our hands tied behind our backs, for four full days. . . . Eventually, they'd take us in for their interrogations—beatings, shocks, submarino immersions. They weren't really after any information—they knew everything already, had everybody's name. It was all just part of the process."

A survey of two hundred torture victims conducted by Dr. Ole Vedel Rasmussen ("Medical Aspects of Torture," *Danish Medical Bulletin,* January 1990) found that when survivors were asked to indicate what they thought was the worst part of their detention, they often cited the periods between torture sessions, when they were frightened of what was going to happen. For the torturer, each session may last for only a few minutes. For the victim, there is often no break, the mental anguish filling the void between sessions. Prisoners confess not only to stop the pain, but also to assert some control over a situation that seems to lack reason and therefore any sign of termination. (Due to an interrogator's confusion about code names, one man tortured by the African National Congress confessed to murdering himself, while another confessed to murdering several people who were still very much alive.) When, as often happens, the confession does not stop the torture, the victim is likely to come to the belief that he or she has absolutely no control over what happens, and that sense of unpredictability further undermines psychological stability.

Irena Martinez, now a doctor in Chicago, was tortured in Argentina in 1977, and hers was a painful but not uncommon odyssey through a regime designed to assure prisoners that nothing was in their control. In an interview eight years after her arrest, she told me that she had been a student activist, an advocate of a democratic government, when she was arrested at her parents' house. She was immediately blindfolded. Her first torture session was in a basement full of soldiers, where she was stripped naked, tied, and beaten. "They slapped my face, pinched my breasts. 'You have to talk, this is your last opportunity, and this is your salvation.' And then they just put me on a table. And I thought, 'Well, if they are going to kill me, I hope they kill me pretty soon.' They pushed my head underwater, so I could not breathe. They take you out, ask you things, they put you in, they take you out—so you cannot breathe all the time. 'Who did you receive this from? Who do you know?' Who can control anything when you cannot breathe? They pull you out, you try to grab for air, so they put you back in so you swallow water, and it is winter and you are very cold and very scared and they do that for a long time. Even if you are a good swimmer you cannot stand it anymore. . . .

"They give me part of my clothes later. Other women were kidnapped when they were sleeping, so a lot of people spend months just with their nightgown. Or they give you the clothes of other prisoners, people who have been killed."

Between interrogations, Martinez spent her time blindfolded, in solitary confinement, in a dark cell. When she wanted to go to the bathroom, she had to call the guards. She was brought to the toilet and back, blindfolded all the while. "You know that you are in a detention center. You have been tortured, but you don't know what is going on, you don't know if they are going to kill you right now or if they are going to kill you tomorrow, you don't know what else they want from you. You don't even know where you are.

"There was a guy who talked with a very soft voice. 'In this moment you are nobody. You don't have any rights, you don't have any voice, you are neither alive nor dead, you are *desaparecido*.' Basically they want you to feel that your life depends on them, that they are omnipotent, and that every nice thing that you do for them will have some influence on their decision about your life or death."

"I slept all the time," Martinez said. "Almost 50 percent of the people did that. They come to the cell and say, 'What is your name? Why are you here?' and you go to sleep for the rest of the day."

After about ten days of interrogations and torture, Martinez was transferred from her cell to a room with about ten other women, age twenty to sixty-five, all blindfolded. "It was very cold, and we had one towel and one piece of soap for all of us. This was the first time I was allowed to take a shower or clean myself. I smelled like a pig. I couldn't eat because I would lean over and my own smell would come up."

The torture continued. "The interrogators always came at night. We called them the vampires. We could tell when they arrived—

everybody started to have diarrhea at the same time. They called us one by one. One night they took us out, stood us in front of a wall, and cocked their weapons to shoot us. Then they didn't. . . .

"After three or four months I was sent to a prison. I met a lot of women there who had been raped. I lived with one woman for a year, she had been raped almost every night. The rules there changed all the time. One day they say, 'Why are your shoes like that? Wear them this way.' And the next day, 'That is not how to wear your shoes.' And you can be punished for that, or punished for smiling, or sometimes punished for talking."

Martinez was released after nearly three years. "When I got out, boom, I broke. Emotionally, physically. I had a rash all over. My lips swelled up. I couldn't sleep. I couldn't eat for three months. One of the guys who tortured me called me on the phone and tried to make me afraid. I was afraid to walk in the streets by myself. You don't want them to see you. When I went back to university, my father took me to the door and my cousin picked me up and I came straight to my house.

"But on the other hand, I have been very lucky. They didn't kill me. I used to think it was part of the torture not to kill you, but I am living better now. Other people are not working, their lives have been destroyed, their marriages have been destroyed. I am eating, I am sleeping, and I've got a job. And I start to feel again that I might be worth it, that life might be worth it."

THE COPING MECHANISMS of torture victims are many. Some rely on complete defiance, using their beliefs as a bedrock, seeing their torture as a battle in a war. That, however, often results in death.

Other torture survivors have coped by retreating from the world around them. Some, like Irena Martinez, have used sleep, while others have used fantasy. In his book *A Miracle, a Universe,* Lawrence Weschler reports that Uruguayan playwright Mauricio Rosencof survived twelve years of solitary confinement by carrying out elaborate fantasies in which he might stretch out on a beach, buy himself a soda, and then face the dilemma of hiding the soda bottle in his prison cell, which guards searched daily. "Hiding objects I acquired in my fantasies," Rosencof said, "became quite a chore."

Dr. Hugo Sacchi, an Uruguayan doctor who believed he might

be arrested and tortured, prepared himself for that eventuality, and in an article published in the Montevideo journal *Estudias* (volume 84, October–December, 1982) he wrote that such preparation enabled him to reduce the fear, and therefore the suffering, when he was tortured. Sacchi claimed that by seeing his physical pain as a normal reaction taking place in his brain as a result of messages transmitted by nerves, he was able to meditate and control his anxiety both while being tortured and in between torture sessions.

In their 1947 article "Reactions among Allied Prisoners of War Subjected to Three Years of Imprisonment and Torture by the Japanese" (*American Journal of Psychiatry,* volume 104), Major Stewart Wolf and Lieutenant Colonel Herbert Ripley reported seeing a similar ability to dissociate from pain among the thirty-five prisoners they studied immediately after their release from captivity. The prisoners had been tortured and starved (weight loss varied from 29 to 110 pounds), and many had been overworked. "Many were successful in making adverse situations less unpleasant by conscious or unconscious suppression of their feelings," Wolf and Ripley wrote. "Some eventually became unable to laugh or cry. . . . Somatic sensations were suppressed as well as emotional feelings. Several survivors said that they were enabled better to withstand the tortures by learning to 'turn off the pain.' " Wolf and Ripley went on to describe one man who suppressed his feeling for pain so well that he was eventually able to withstand the beatings without any sensations whatever, but the man then began to have hallucinatory episodes in which he relived the tortures inflicted on him, episodes during which "he could see and hear his tormentors and feel the pains that had been inflicted a day or two earlier. To these experiences he reacted volubly, crying and shouting and writhing in pain." After his repatriation, army doctors gave him a detailed examination and found that although he showed no neurological problems, he demonstrated "a complete insensitivity to all sensations except on the cornea."

Wolf and Ripley noted that the suppression of certain emotions may have been a crucial survival technique for many: "The testimony of survivors is practically unanimous that prisoners who became depressed or allowed themselves to become agitated by thoughts of home developed distaste for food and died."

Concentration camp survivors and survivors of more recent torture also believe that the formation of self-protective groups of prisoners was crucial for survival. Other torture survivors have seemed to benefit from being in a position that allowed them to make decisions or to retain and act on their values (imprisoned doctors and nurses have, for example, tried to relieve pain in others, and in so doing have eased their own strife).

Throughout history prisoners have survived by collaboration and conversion. Sometimes prisoners, facing torture, take on the values and behavior of their captors and become torturers themselves. The narrator of Jean-Pierre Vittori's *Confessions d'un professional de la torture,* analyzing the enthusiasm of the convert, says, "These men must constantly give proof of their sincerity and devotion to the cause which they have just embraced. Furthermore, they feel terribly guilty compared to the militants who are faithful to their ideal. Their cruelty, their knowledge of the Algerian mentality, renders precious services. We quickly learn that the prisoners prefer an interrogation led by a Frenchman and we use the menace of an Algerian interrogator as a means of bringing pressure to bear on them."

Some torture victims have come to feel some attachment to their tormentors, a thought process that is not so difficult to understand. It may be that food or drink are supplied by the same person who turns the crank on the electrical device, so the prisoner's sole source of support is the interrogator. The torturer may offer a cigarette or coffee during a break in the ordeal, and that act may be perceived as kindness. After being subjected to the five techniques, Jim Auld sincerely believed that the man who spoon-fed him was his friend, though he now recognizes that the man was just another cog in the torture apparatus, perhaps even one of the torturers.

In their article, "Communist Interrogation and Indoctrination of 'Enemies of the States' " (*Archives of Neurology and Psychiatry,* volume 76, 1956), Lawrence Hinkle and Harold Wolff describe a process in which a prisoner comes to believe that his interrogator is not torturing him, that instead the system is to blame. "There are instances of prisoners who signed depositions largely out of sympathy for their interrogators, because they felt that these men would be punished if a proper deposition were not forthcoming. . . . Not infrequently, the prisoner develops a feeling that the interrogator is the only warm and sympathetic person in the hostile and threatening world in which he exists. His need for human companionship and acceptance is such that he overlooks the pressures which the interrogator puts upon him and ascribes them to the necessities of the system rather than to the willful activity of his friend. If the interrogator rejects the prisoner or implies that he disapproves of him, the prisoner may feel bereft." In such a situation, it may be that perpetrator and victim are both distancing themselves from the act, each believing that it is a job, performed not out of anger but out of duty, that what is happening is, as the torturer Hugo García told me, "nothing personal."

After many interviews with survivors and perpetrators and after reading many studies of torture, Hinkle and Wolff's depiction of a bond forming between torturer and victim does not seem so peculiar to me. I suspect that such relationships are rare and that the reasons for them vary with the individuals involved, but I do not doubt that such relationships develop. Wolf and Ripley, writing of American POWs in World War II, observed that some Americans who had been starved, tortured, and brutally abused by their Japanese captors were observed giving cigarettes to their former guards after liberation, and those whom Wolf and Ripley interviewed not long thereafter directed their resentment toward fellow Americans, not toward the Japanese. (It had been, of course, safer to resent American officers, who often were forced to administer the cruel regime of the prison camp, because any sign of resentment toward the Japanese was punished severely.) The French torturer featured in Vittori's *Confessions d'un professionnel de la torture* tells of Algerians who, after being tortured and released, returned to visit their interrogators, and the torturer-narrator describes his own deep friendship with one of the victims. An Argentine victim told me of a fellow survivor who became the girlfriend of one of her torturers.

In an interview with British journalist Iain Guest ("Portrait of a Torturer," *The Guardian,* December 7, 1989), the former Chilean torturer Andres Valenzuela recounted his interaction with Miguel Rodriguez Gallardo, a Young Communist leader, who aroused Valenzuela's admiration by resisting the most strenuous torture. Valenzuela described finding Gallardo hanging by his handcuffs one day, in obvious pain. Valenzuela was about to let Gallardo down when the prisoner told him not to, saying he was afraid Valenzuela would thereby earn the wrath of the chief of the torture section. Gallardo was executed not long after.

In an interview with me in June 1990, Chrones Missios, tortured in 1947 during the Greek civil war, described meeting his persecutor twenty-five years later. At the time, Missios was working as director of production at a factory, and the former torturer walked into his office. The man explained that his son was unemployed and he asked Missios to give the young man a job. Missios agreed to do so, and told me that he and the former interrogator then went to a taverna, had a few drinks, and danced together. I asked if they had talked about the torture. "No," Missios said. "We were both ashamed."

Emmerson Mnangagwa, tortured in Rhodesia, also met his former torturers years after the experience. As a young man, he had been a guerrilla fighting the Rhodesian government, and he was captured after blowing up a locomotive. Members of the Special Branch hung him upside-down on a meat hook that moved in a track on the ceiling of the room of a police station. They then beat him, sending him caroming from one side of the room to the other with each blow. He lost hearing in one ear as a result. Tacks were also pounded into the soles of his feet, and when I met him in January 1991, he took off his shoes to show me a constellation of purple marks still present twenty-eight years after the torture.

In 1980, when Robert Mugabe and fellow guerrillas became rulers of the newly created Zimbabwe, Mnangagwa was appointed minister of security. As such, he found that two of the men who had tortured him worked on his staff. Mnangagwa told me that he called them into his office, asked them their rank, and promoted them.

"If we had taken over and decided that we should punish certain people, there would have been no end," he told me. "The majority of our people, the blacks, had grievances against the white community. They would all want revenge. On the other side, there are also white families who have lost their sons, killed in the war, and they would want revenge for their dead fathers and dead sons. So where would it end?"

And in some peculiar way, Mnangagwa felt he had had his revenge. The best way to punish a torturer, he told me, is not with hatred. If you want to torture a torturer, he said, you do it with love.

Torture in Zimbabwe did not cease once Mugabe and Mnangagwa took over. Their personal responsibility for that sad truth is difficult to determine. Four years after Mugabe and his comrades took power, the police and the Central Intelligence Organization were accused of beating people on the soles of their feet with sjamboks, truncheons, and hoses; using hand-cranked dynamos to shock people during interrogation; and half-drowning victims in canvas bags full of water. According to Africa Watch, some people died under torture. When Amnesty International voiced its concerns, Mugabe denounced the organization as "Amnesty Lies International" and an "enemy of Zimbabwe," a peculiar position for someone who had once been one of Amnesty's prisoners of conscience.

WHAT BECOMES OF a torture victim in the years after the experience has become something of a medical specialty in the last twenty years, and lessons have been drawn from studies of survivors of Nazi concentration camps and Americans held as prisoners of war by the Japanese and the Koreans. The conclusions drawn by various experts differ enormously. Some have concluded that committed dissidents who are tortured will fare better in the long run, that their beliefs give some meaning to their pain, while someone swept up in a mass internment or a random police raid may be paralyzed by what seems to be a senseless turn of events. Some experts have claimed that strength of character is a strong predictor of who will survive more successfully, that stronger personalities will do better than weaker ones. In their study of thirty-five Allied prisoners of war tortured by the Japanese, Wolf and Ripley said that two personality types seemed to predominate: "personalities of the highest order of adjustment" and "those with features of a psychopathic personality." Wolf and Ripley speculated that, at least in those particular POW camps, psychopathic characteristics might have been an aid to survival, that, lacking the restraints of conscience—a well-known trait of psychopaths—some of the prisoners were able to "seize every opportunity to satisfy their own personal needs without consideration for the group as a whole," and their shallowness of feelings "may have protected them from sustained depression or anxiety associated with anorexia which proved fatal to other prisoners."

A study of American POWs held captive in Vietnam ("Psychiat-ric Illness in U.S. Air Force Viet Nam Prisoners of War: A Five-year Follow-up," *American Journal of Psychiatry,* March 1981) asserts that severity of stress is a far better predictor of subsequent psychiatric disturbances than personality factors. The study, by Robert Ursano, James Boydstun, and Richard Wheatley, used data compiled from a sample of 253 ex-POWs and concluded that the more severe the stress, the more severe the reaction, regardless of the underlying personality. A study of sixty-two former World War II POWs ("Posttraumatic Stress Disorder as a Consequence of the POW Experience," *Journal of Mental and Nervous Disease,* volume 177, no. 3, 1989) found that pre-service psychological status—even evidence of unusual trauma like child abuse or parental death—had little impact on whether a par-ticular former prisoner would be suffering from post-traumatic stress disorder forty years after captivity. The best predictors of PTSD turned out to be severe weight loss during captivity and the experience of torture.

There are significant problems in trying to study torture victims. Because of the variety of tortures imposed by torturers, the varying lengths of time of captivity, and the varying intervals after torture in any sample of survivors, the effect of torture on individuals is not chartable in the way that, for example, the progression of heart dis-ease, or diabetes, or breast cancer can be predicted. A woman raped by her torturers, for example, shows much different sequelae than a woman subjected to near drowning. The cultural background of the survivor can also affect the reaction to torture. In some cultures, a woman raped is considered unclean or unsuitable for marriage, and that has a severe psychological effect that might not be present in a woman who lives in a more forgiving society. Torture victims who are forced to flee their country and live elsewhere, where they may not speak the language, where they may not be employable in their old professions, where they may live as illegal aliens, fearing arrest and deportation, may show symptoms that are difficult to isolate. Is their depression a by-product of the torture or of their status as refugees? Similarly, a psychologist or doctor selecting a group of torture victims to study may examine those who have found their way to clinics, which may not be a representative sample. A better sample would include those who have such severe effects that they are dead or soon will be, those who are already housed in mental institutions, and those who are doing perfectly well and are in no need of medical or psychological help. Several studies have noted that there can be a delay of many years in the onset of symptoms, and that also can skew results.

Other studies indicate that some people seem to escape psychologically unscathed. The *Journal of Mental and Nervous Disease* study of sixty-two American POWs noted that seven had suffered torture and deprivation as intense as that experienced by the other fifty-five men in the sample, yet did not suffer any significant aftereffects. Other torture survivors, though they may be suffering privately, show remarkable resilience and demonstrate outward signs of success. A study of Holocaust survivors conducted by Zev Harel, Boaz Kahana, and Eva Kahana compared a sample of Holocaust survivors with European Jews of the same age who emigrated to the United States before World War II. Although the survivors had less education, their incomes were greater, they were more likely to do volunteer work in their communities, and they were more likely to have an altruistic outlook. A study by City University of New York sociologist William Helmreich comparing survivors with a sample of American-born Jews (*Against All Odds: Holocaust Survivors and the Successful Lives They Made in America*) found the survivors had far more stable marriages than the Americans.

It is altogether safe to conclude, however, that mental and psychological problems affect a great majority of torture survivors, no matter how successful they appear to be after their experience. Nightmares and other sleep disturbances are very common. (In an article in the October 6, 1992, edition of the *New York Times,* author and cartoonist Art Spiegelman, the son of Holocaust survivors, was quoted saying, "My parents woke up howling almost every night. For a long time as a child, I thought all parents did.") When Doctors Finn Somnier and Inge Genefke examined twenty-four torture survivors an average of 9.5 years after their torture (see "Psychotherapy for Victims of Torture," *British Journal of Psychiatry,* 1986, volume 149) they found 71 percent had nightmares, 79 percent complained of headaches, 79 percent had impaired memory, 75 percent had impaired concentration, 75 percent experienced fatigue, 50 percent suffered from persistent fear and anxiety, 38 percent had impaired hearing, 38 percent had withdrawn socially, 33 percent experienced vertigo, 21 percent reported sexual problems, and 13 percent had tremors or shaking. Other research has found common psychological symptoms to be depression, paranoid ideas, a certain self-centered regression, and an inability to connect with others, even with family members. Dr. Rasmussen's survey of two hundred victims (examined three days to twelve years after their torture) found that the incidence of mental symptoms at the time of examination was significantly higher among those who had been subjected to a mock execution. Rasmussen's *Danish Medical Bulletin* article noted that 83 percent of those who experienced mock executions exhibited mental symptoms, about 20 percent more than those who had not been subjected to that particular torture.

A range of chronic physical symptoms are also common in torture survivors. Gastroenteritis, respiratory infections, skin eruptions, and peptic ulcers are common. Aside from those more general symptoms, localized sequelae remain from various specific tortures. Falanga, for instance, the beating of the soles of the feet, often results in permanent difficulties in walking. A beating about the head can leave its mark in organic brain damage. Sexual torture often results in sexual dysfunction.

Doctors have also observed a certain impairment of vision among those who have been tortured. Wolf and Ripley reported that a medical officer interviewed during the course of their study described an episode of "mass hysteria" at Bilibid prison in Manila, during which there was widespread impairment of vision among the Allied prisoners of war held there. Several other survivors whom Wolf and Ripley examined complained of partial blindness and hearing loss. "Some of them indicated that their deafness and visual impairment may have partially protected them from witnessing the tortures inflicted on their fellows," Wolf and Ripley wrote. The two physicians went on to say that in most instances, a medically induced narcotic state readily dispelled the symptoms.

A similar problem with eyesight has been observed more recently in Cambodian women who live in and around Long Beach, California. Using the most sophisticated technology, researchers examined more than one hundred women between the ages of fifty and seventy who had spent from one to five years at forced labor in Cambodia. All of the women claimed to be sightless, yet all of the machinery indicated that the women could see, that their brains were receiving messages from their eyes. Some of the women indicated that they first lost their vision after a relative was killed by the Khmer Rouge, or after being forced to watch someone else be tortured and executed. Doctors have diagnosed the women as having hysterical or psychosomatic blindness, but cures have proved elusive.

A possible explanation for the Cambodian women's symptoms lies in the theory of conversion disorders. Psychologists believe that victims of trauma, suffering from great anxiety, sometimes transfer their inner conflict onto the offending body part. While there are other examples of psychosomatic blindness in the annals of medicine, usually those are brief episodes, while the Cambodian women's symptoms seem more permanent. That would not, however, be so different from the reactions of other torture victims, who have sometimes come to the conclusion that their entire body is the enemy.

Though the symptoms of the Cambodian women may be unique, the persistence of them is not. Richard Juma Oketch, tortured during the reign of Idi Amin in Uganda, testified before Congress in 1996 and described how his torture dominated his life for fifteen years. "Physically, you portray a mask of who you are," he said, "while mentally you are like a furnace." Oketch, a teacher of the deaf and a nephew of a former member of the Ugandan parliament, said that while residing in the United States in 1991, he was still "living the realities of those endless nights. Relentless nightmares, sleeplessness due to fear, anxiety attacks, distrust of people including family members, antisocial behavior, reclusiveness, difficult and hardened personality traits and mood swings, were the invincible scars I lived with. My life remained a total mystery since I allowed no one to penetrate my psyche. I was at most robotic and became workaholic and a perpetual student, as I would fill my time and reduce flashbacks. I made sure I stayed awake past 2:00 a.m. to reduce the hours of the night for fear of persistent nightmares. I had lost most of my sensible emotions. . . . By 1990 I was tired and getting serious injuries as a result of the nightmares. I had lost interest in living." After undergoing treatment at the Center for Victims of Torture in Minneapolis, Oketch said, his ability to relate to people started to return and his reclusiveness abated. He reconnected with his children, still in Uganda, whom he had not seen in fifteen years.

Fifteen years is actually not so long a time to be suffering from torture. It is not uncommon for the effects of torture to last decades or even to surface decades after the experience. One study of Americans held as prisoners of war by the Japanese during World War II and by North Korea or China during the Korean War found that some effects were "essentially permanent." Gilbert Beebe conducted follow-up studies on those former POWs and in 1975 published a study ("Follow-up Studies of World War II and Korean War Prisoners," *American Journal of Epidemiology,* volume 101, no. 5, page 400) that concluded that many carried a "variable loss of ego strength . . . essentially permanent . . . marked by lowered thresholds for both physical and psychologic complaints. . . . The most common impairment is psychiatric." Among other things, Beebe noted higher admissions to hospital for psychoneuroses and schizophrenia in his groups than in veterans who had fought against Japanese and Koreans but not been prisoners of war. Specialists working with concentration camp survivors have also noted long-term damage, some of it similar to that found by Beebe.

Some torture survivors don't live long enough to qualify for such studies. One study of Americans held as POWs during World War II and the Korean War ("Follow-up Studies of World War II and Korean War Prisoners," *American Journal of Epidemiology,* volume 92, no. 2, 1970) noted that in the first three years after their repatriation, POWs who had been held in Japan showed a 50 percent increase in deaths over what would be typical of a similar group of white American males. Accidents, tuberculosis, and cirrhosis of the liver were the primary causes of those excess deaths. Suicides, though few in number, were about 30 percent more frequent than in control groups. Deaths from homicide were also three to four times higher in Pacific and Korean War POWs than in control groups. (American POWs held in Europe, who were not systematically abused, as those in the Pacific and in Korea were, had a lower mortality rate for all disease than that of white U.S. males of the same age.)

Torture can also have severe effects on the families of survivors. Living with someone who may be irritable, paranoid, distrustful, and unable to connect with other human beings also takes a significant toll. A study of eighty-five children whose parents had been tortured in Chile ("A Study of Chilean Refugee Children in Denmark," by Jorgen Cohn et al., *The Lancet,* August 24, 1985) showed 68 percent had emotional disorders, physical symptoms, or both. Thirty-four of the 85 children had insomnia and nightmares, 34 suffered from anxiety, 5 had tics, 12 complained of chronic stomach aches and 13 of headaches, 15 wet their bed, 13 suffered from anorexia, 4 had impaired memories, and 16 demonstrated "behavior difficulties."

Studies of the children of torture victims from Chile, Argentina, and Mexico have found "chronic fear, depressive mood, clinging and overdependent behavior, sleep disorders, somatic complaints and an arrest or regression of social habits and school performance."

Studies of Holocaust survivors have found that their children and even their grandchildren have higher rates of clinical depression and suicide than the population at large.

Thus the forces unleashed by a man only doing his job, a man simply following orders, a man who may not know even the name of his victim, are extraordinarily powerful. Long after the torturer and his or her prey are dead, the acts committed in a hidden place—perhaps in a matter of a few minutes or hours—live on. The man who feels "nothing personal" against his victim, who takes comfort in the belief that he is not as bad as some other torturer, who believes that he was not so bad because his victim did not die, never sees the extent of his damage, never considers that he has assaulted generations yet unborn.

{ 13 }

BELFAST

Life Sentences

JIM AULD'S blackouts did not stop when he was taken to the camp hospital at Long Kesh. He was kept for three weeks and was released in May 1972 in the company of a psychiatrist, who brought him to a mental hospital in Armagh. "I stayed there for about a week," Auld told me. "And it was just flipping my head, I couldn't settle in the place." He asked the psychiatrist if he was legally compelled to be there, and upon being told that he was not, he walked out.

He returned to Belfast, where friends offered him work as a dental technician. "It's very precise work," he said, "and I just couldn't settle. It was too slow, too laborious, too methodical for me to be able to concentrate."

He moved to Dublin, and for two years he wandered from job to job. He worked as a bricklayer on building sites, as a laborer in the Guinness brewery, and as a truck driver. The blackouts he had experienced in Long Kesh—which he described as momentary shutdowns of his mind—continued, and he went down to Cork, where Dr. Robert Daly, the psychiatrist from the Irish legal team, had volunteered to help him. Auld left the hospital within a fortnight, however, again because he "couldn't settle." "After that there were anxiety attacks," he recalls. "When things started getting too much for me, I just blacked out. And I had no control over it."

He got a job on the Dublin ferry, and was pleased because the work changed every day. "You were always busy," he recalls. "One day you were a bar man, the next day you were emptying rubbish, the next day you were serving biscuits and tea, the next day you were making beds."

He got married in September 1973 and returned to Belfast the following summer. He got a job driving a bread truck, and later he drove a lorry for a bottling company. The blackouts stopped, and by November 1974, he had not had one for almost a year.

On November 28, 1974, he was arrested. He was taken to the Castlereagh police station. It happened that Joe Clarke, another of the hooded men, was arrested the same day, and Auld sees it as no coincidence: the day after their arrests, compensation checks from the government arrived in the mail. Clarke's was £12,500, and Auld's was £16,000, which at that point was the highest amount paid to a survivor of the treatment. At Castlereagh the two men were never interrogated. They were released after about forty-eight hours. On the way out they joked of the celebration they would have that evening with their newfound fortunes. The celebration, however, did not take place. The two men were re-arrested as they left the police station, served with internment notices, and sent back to Long Kesh.

Auld's blackouts returned. Two days after his return to Long Kesh, his wife, pregnant for the first time, suffered a miscarriage. Auld was released five months later.

He returned to west Belfast. Over the course of the next few years, he and his wife had three children. He resumed his old hobby of tinkering with cars, and he and his brother raced a stock car for a while. When John DeLorean opened his auto factory outside Belfast in 1979, Auld was hired to work on the production line.

WHILE AULD WAS getting his life back together, the Irish government's appeal of the case of the hooded men was heard in the European Court of Human Rights.

In its written submission to the court, the British defense team announced that the government would not contest the charge that the five techniques amounted to torture. In so doing, however, British Attorney General Sam Silkin let it be known that the British were not admitting that the techniques were in fact torture; they were merely saying that "no beneficial interest would be served" in contesting that particular finding of the European Commission of Human Rights. To repeat the torture allegations, Silkin argued, would serve only the IRA, handing them another propaganda weapon.

Journalists covering the case, however, speculated that the British government was pleading no contest in order to avoid having to produce the politicians who ordered the torture and the police and soldiers who carried it out.

In the course of its presentation to the court, Silkin and his colleagues argued that the techniques were "a mistake" and that such mistakes were likely in circumstances of great violence. Silkin pledged that the techniques would never be used again and pointed out that the victims had been compensated (an average of £14,000, roughly $28,000, had been paid to each of the fourteen men). Silkin also claimed that prosecutions of those responsible for the ill-treatment would be impossible because of a lack of evidence and because such prosecution would be destructive in efforts to beat the terrorists in Northern Ireland. Silkin urged the court to conclude that the British had done all that they could in response to the commission's ruling and that no further action was necessary.

Declan Costello, the Irish attorney general, had fierce objections. He argued that the British had previously waffled on the question of whether the techniques would ever be used again, and that therefore prosecutions were necessary so there would be some legal sanction against those who would resort to the high-tech torture. Costello also argued that if the court decided that the Irish case was moot because Britain was no longer contesting the torture charge, then any other government in the future could avoid legally binding decisions of the court simply by not contesting charges. The Irish wanted the techniques formally outlawed so that no nation within the court's jurisdiction could put them to use. Finally, Costello could not accept the British excuse that the techniques had been "a mistake." They were not mistakes, Costello argued, but deliberate and well-planned acts of brutality.

The British and Irish arguments were heard over the course of three days in February 1977. The judges of the court heard no witnesses. They deliberated for four days in April, four days in July, and eight days in December, reaching their decision on December 13,

1977, more than six years after black hoods were fastened around those fourteen individual necks.

By a vote of thirteen to four, they ruled that the five techniques constituted inhuman and degrading treatment, but not torture.

"They did not occasion suffering of the particular intensity and cruelty implied by the word 'torture' as so understood," said the court. The majority seemed to have agreed with the position laid out by Sir Gerald Fitzmaurice, the British judge on the court, who argued that if having one's fingernails torn out, being impaled on a stake through the rectum, or being roasted on an electric grid is torture, then the five techniques were something less. Fitzmaurice believed that the techniques should not even be labeled inhuman and degrading treatment, but he held that view by himself.

The seventeen judges of the court also declined to order that anyone be prosecuted, arguing that they did not have the power to order a state to institute criminal or disciplinary proceedings in accordance with its domestic law.

The ruling, which stunned the Irish government, was made public on January 18, 1978. In Britain, the *Daily Telegraph* hailed it as a "triumph." Admitting that the country had been found to employ inhuman and degrading methods, the paper said, "Can a state threatened by anarchy be properly and realistically expected not to employ such methods?" The *Daily Express* said that British people from Berwick to Belfast were amazed that the case should have been brought at all.

Amnesty International said that despite the judges' decision, it still considered the five techniques to be torture.

THE PERPETRATORS, instigators, and defenders of the five techniques thus escaped unscathed, their reputations untarnished. Northern Ireland Prime Minister Brian Faulkner, who had personally signed all of the hooded men's detention orders and who had claimed that "no brutality of any kind had occurred," was killed in a hunting accident in 1977; in the wake of the European Commission's ruling the previous year, Faulkner had claimed that he had not known the details of the interrogation procedures, and John Taylor, Faulkner's minister of state for home affairs when internment was introduced, stated that the only politicians who had known the details of the five techniques were Prime Minister Heath and Defense Minister Carrington. Heath and Lord Carrington declined to answer a list of questions I submitted to their offices as I did the research for this book. In Britain and abroad, both men have solid reputations as elder statesmen who often demonstrate great concern with tragedies in other parts of the world.

Lord Balniel, the minister of state for defense at the time of the torture, also declined to be interviewed. In the wake of the Compton Report, issued in November 1971, Balniel claimed that no evidence of torture or ill-treatment had been produced. He was made a life peer in 1975 and is now the Earl of Crawford and Balcarres.

General Harry Tuzo, who was knighted in July 1971, also declined comment. Tuzo, the Oxford-educated commander of the army in Northern Ireland at the time of the torture, did grant an interview to the Canadian Broadcasting Corporation for a program broadcast in 1982: "To my mind," he said, "you have to choose between inflicting acute discomfort and humiliation, because it is that of course, on a few people in order possibly to save life and safeguard the well-being of perhaps a million people. . . . It sounds terribly utilitarian and terribly heartless to say that they were very well compensated and looked after. I cannot of course say what permanent scars have been left, and if there are any, I can sympathize with the people concerned, but I personally would have thought that they had got over it by now."

JIM AULD'S FORMER CELLMATE, white-haired Sean McKenna, the oldest of the hooded men, missed both the European Commission and the European Court rulings. He had been released from Long Kesh in 1973, two years after his arrest, and was subsequently treated in psychiatric hospitals. He was examined by Dr. Daly in February 1975, three and a half years after the hooding treatment. Daly recorded that McKenna "had a feeling of impending fatal illness (a 'brain tumor' or a 'heart attack') and had gross symptoms of anxiety." Hospital tests, however, gave no indication that anything serious was impending. Four months after being examined, on June 5, 1975, Sean McKenna died of a heart attack. He was forty-five.

· · ·

Pat Shivers, the second oldest of the hooded men, whose dead son appeared to him during the ordeal, died of stomach cancer in 1985. He was fifty-four.

Michael Montgomery, a member of the Official IRA at the time of his arrest, became unsettled while in Long Kesh. Fellow survivor Kevin Hannaway tells of going to visit the hut where Montgomery was living. "I went to his cage to see someone else," Hannaway told me in 1991. "He started telling me about the colored rabbits in the ceiling. If you looked up at the ceiling there were holes in it where the outlets had been for the chimneys on potbellied stoves. So he pointed up, 'There they are,' and I thought he was slagging me and I pretended to go along with it. Then I turned around to talk to someone else and Montgomery picked up a mop—I thought he was going to mop the floor—and he put some lettuce on the end of the handle and held it up to the ceiling. He was trying to feed the rabbits."

"When he came out, we had a terrible life," Montgomery's wife Doris told me. "I couldn't turn on the Hoover. If you were turning a page in the newspaper, it affected him. The electric kettle, opening or closing a door affected him. If you dropped a spoon on the floor he went mad. He never slept. He twisted, turned, shouted, bawled at night. I was scared of him. After he came out he used to put a gun to my head and threaten to shoot me." In 1977, Doris Montgomery left her husband, who she says was a chronic alcoholic.

Michael Montgomery was able to do some things quite well, however. He was a well-known and popular man in the Creggan and Bogside areas of Londonderry and in October 1973, he was elected to the Derry City Council and served a four-year term. He did not run for re-election.

Michael Montgomery died of a heart attack on December 1, 1984. He was forty-nine.

Gerard McKerr, perhaps the most physically fit of the hooded men, began getting lumps on his neck not long after being moved to Long Kesh. He was diagnosed and subsequently treated for Hodgkin's disease. He was released from the camp after three years, returning home to find his job gone, his car beyond repair, and his physical stamina at low ebb.

In 1977, a stranger called at his door. When McKerr opened it, the man pulled a gun and fired, wounding McKerr in the groin. The stranger was later arrested and found to be a member of a Protestant paramilitary group. McKerr recovered. A few weeks after his release from the hospital, he walked out his front door with his children, intending to drive them to school, and spotted a bomb underneath his car. A British army bomb disposal crew dismantled it.

McKerr figured that his address was known because newspaper accounts of the hooded men's receipt of compensation from the government had included addresses of the recipients. He decided it was time to move. Today you will look in vain for a number on his front door.

LIAM SHANNON, one of the two men who were subjected to the hooded treatment months after the original dozen, came down with chronic diarrhea afterward and was ultimately diagnosed as having Crohn's disease. He underwent psychiatric treatment for depression. As compensation he received £25,000 (roughly $50,000), the largest award of any of the hooded men.

When I met him on New Year's Eve in 1990, I noted that he stood erect, that his hair was pure white, and that he looked to be about fifty-five. He later told me he was forty-two and that he had not worked since his ordeal.

A SURVIVOR WHO asked me not to use his name told me that he was arrested in the Republic of Ireland on charges that were later dropped. During the course of the incident, he said, he was locked in a cell and suddenly came to believe that he was in the custody of the Northern Irish police. He told me that he barricaded the door and that a psychiatrist was able to get him out only by having the guards change into civilian clothes. He later spent time in a mental hospital.

·   ·   ·

IN THE WAKE of the European Court decision in January 1978, an enraged Kevin Hannaway participated in a press conference in Dublin at which he insisted that the court was wrong, that he and the thirteen other men had indeed been tortured. Hannaway recalls that his Belfast address was printed in one of the Irish papers. A short time thereafter, shots were fired at his house. Hannaway was wounded twice and his twenty-month-old son was shot three times. Both recovered. At Christmas that year, a bomb was placed under his car. He spotted it, however, and British army bomb experts disposed of it.

When I met him in late 1991, he told me that the torture had several long-lasting effects on him, chief among them a strengthening of his resolve as a supporter of the Republican movement. He believes that he survived better than most of the other fourteen men because he came from a strong Republican background: his grandparents and his parents had been involved in the fight against the British. Hannaway told me that he had done a lot of reading about the British army's methods in other nations it had occupied, and so while others were stunned by the brutality they were subjected to, he was not surprised at all, nor was he ever in doubt as to why he had been chosen. "At this stage of my life," he said, "I wouldn't be surprised at anything. If I was arrested tomorrow and was skinned like a chicken, it wouldn't surprise me. So my background helped.

"I don't see us as a special case," he told me. "Our suffering is nothing compared to what families have suffered here over the last twenty years. Today, the British government is wiser, it is foxier, it knows how to hide what it is doing from the rest of the world. But nothing has changed. Amnesty International has been in here on a yearly basis [investigating incidents of torture]. Twenty years on, it has become a day-to-day thing, as common as breakfast or dinner. As sure as I am sitting here today it will happen tomorrow.

"As far as I am concerned I have been blessed. I have been the friend, comrade, prison mate, cellmate of men who have died on hunger strike or were shot."

I asked Hannaway what punishment he thought would be appropriate for the men who had tortured him. "I would be happy and content," he said, "just to see Britain remove every one of its troops from Ireland. It is not punishment that I would be seeking."

· · ·

FRANK McGUIGAN, who could not spell his name or count to ten during one of the interrogations, was, like Hannaway, one of the few active Republicans among the men who were subjected to the five techniques. (In Jim Auld's extended family, no one has ever been in jail; in McGuigan's family, everyone—his mother included—has seen the inside of a jail cell, and he boasts of being arrested for the first time at the age of twelve.) McGuigan left Long Kesh long before the British intended, walking out the front gate disguised as a priest on February 7, 1972. He has lived in the Republic of Ireland since and his days as an activist are now ancient history.

McGuigan told me that he had suffered a flashback while participating in a stress test for some curious psychologists in Dublin a few months after his escape. In the course of the test, he suddenly heard a noise similar to what was played throughout his time on the wall in 1971. He responded by kicking a door out of its frame, manhandling an orderly in the hallway, and running out of the clinic. He ran for several blocks until he found a phone booth. He called a friend, said that he was in danger of being taken in again, but would not tell his friend where he was for fear that those who wanted to take him away had tapped the phone.

Today McGuigan prides himself on the fact that he was able to take the test again six months later without incident. Although he recognizes that the torture had severe effect on other men, he insists that he is a better man because he survived. "I'm glad it happened to me," he told me twenty years after his ordeal. "It strengthened my character, it let me know what I could and couldn't take, and it's done me no harm in the long run."

He has an extremely vivid memory of the first cup of water he was given after the torture was over. The water in it was very cool, and a drop of condensation ran down the side of the mug. Accompanying the mug was a piece of dried bread. Today, he likes to have a piece of dried bread and mug of milk before going to bed. He runs cool water in the mug until a bead of condensation appears.

· · ·

PATRICK MCNALLY, a twenty-four-year-old bricklayer at the time
of his arrest, had a high profile in the civil rights movement in
Armagh before he was subjected to the five techniques. He recalls
that strangers from his hometown came up to him in Long Kesh
and told him that they had joined the IRA after hearing stories
of what he had been through. In Long Kesh, McNally says he was
unable to concentrate. "I could read a book two or three times," he told
me in August 1991, "because I couldn't remember what I had already
read.

"When I came out of Long Kesh I was totally changed. I went stone
mad. I drank every day for a couple years nonstop. I was forever in
fights. I wasn't a very nice person. I had been thinking that I was going
to be killed, and then I was interned, and when I got out, I just thought
I had a new lease on life, that I shouldn't be here, and I just went mad.
I enjoyed myself. Didn't care about anybody. I was losing friends.
Even the pubs I would drink in—I would insult the people who
owned the bar, maybe smash glasses out of badness. I remember firing
glasses behind the bar. I wasn't afraid of anybody. If anybody wanted
to fight with me, I would have had a go at them. It would have taken
two or three guys to put me out. That was the kind of person I was for
a while.

" Then I settled down. I was playing a bit of football, and I started to
realize that when I was going for a drink afterwards there wouldn't be
anybody who wanted to go with me. So I said, 'There is something
wrong here.' At first I thought it was the drink, and then I realized it
was just me. I eased off on the drink and started playing more football
and then I took a notion that I would go to Australia, and that is when
I really started settling down."

McNally's application for admission to Australia was rejected. He
attributes that rejection to the fact that he had been interned.

He never talked about the hooding treatment. His wife, who had
pressed him for details when she first visited him in Long Kesh, finally
heard a version of the full story in 1991, when McNally was interviewed by a television crew from the Republic of Ireland.

When I met him in 1991, he told me he still had a recurring dream
in which he is arrested and faces a soldier with a gun. The soldier
shoots him in the head. "I always thought when it was going on that

that is the way I was going to be killed," he says. "I really was con-vinced about that, and that is what I dreamed about afterwards."

In 1990, McNally and his wife began organizing fund-raising events to aid Romanian children. Because he was self-employed as a bricklayer, his schedule was more flexible than others involved in the effort, and so when it came time to distribute the food, clothing, and medicines collected, McNally made the delivery. He has since been back twice with additional supplies.

By COINCIDENCE, McNally and Michael Donnelly, the two bricklayers in the group of fourteen, ended up in the same cell at the Crumlin Road Jail when they were first brought back from the secret interro-gation center. The two men were from different parts of Northern Ireland and didn't know each other. Donnelly had seen no other pris-oners and when he set eyes on McNally, he recalls a certain period of silence. "He could have been a loyalist or anybody," Donnelly told me. "Finally I said to him, 'My God, you're in bad shape. It looks like you had a bad time.' He said to me, 'I was just about to say the same about you.' "

Donnelly was interned for three and a half years. His son, an infant when he was arrested, was almost five when they were reunited.

"I had nightmares for years, on and off," Donnelly told me in 1991. "If a blanket covered my head, I would wake up in a panic. It wouldn't have affected me before." He dreamt over and over again that he was in a big empty space and that behind him was a huge threepenny bit, a hexagonal coin no longer in circulation. The coin rolled faster and faster, and he had to run at greater and greater speed in order not to be run over.

Years after his release, he saw a policeman being interviewed on television about a murder investigation, and Donnelly recognized him as one of the men who had interrogated him during the hooded treat-ment. Donnelly called an activist priest, who in turn called a Catholic politician. The politician allegedly made inquiries and reported back that the policeman had been on holiday at the time of the torture and that Donnelly should be careful not to make reckless allegations.

That interrogator preyed on Donnelly's mind for years. During the course of the torture, the policeman had asked him, "If I come to Derry on my holidays when all this is over, will you put me up?"

"I remember fantasizing about putting him up and getting him upstairs and then killing him," Donnelly told me. "But that just wouldn't occur to me now. I would like to come face-to-face with him and discuss it with him, but I don't want to do anything violent to him anymore."

PADDY JOE McCLEAN, the schoolteacher who was one of the two survivors who testified before the European Commission of Human Rights, now has twelve children. There have been no attempts on his life since shots were fired at his house in June 1972, and he has recovered from the cancerous growth on his leg. He is still unable to stand excessive noise—he cites as an example a dance band. He says that he occasionally wakes up with "night chills" after dreaming of the torture, and that he has had slight memory blackouts ever since his ordeal. What amazes him particularly, however, is that even today, he can shut his eyes and see his own funeral, just as he saw it twenty-three years ago while hallucinating on the wall. The scene does not change: his children are the same age they were in 1971, which means that only eight of the twelve are in the picture.

When the European Court handed down its decision in 1978, McClean was serving as chairman of the Northern Ireland Civil Rights Association, and he has continued to maintain a high political profile, advocating nonviolence and civil rights. In 1972, he sued Defense Minister Lord Carrington for slander, citing Carrington's claim that the men subjected to the hooding treatment were "thugs and murderers." The suit never went to trial. McClean recalls that at some point his London-based solicitors came to feel that Carrington's remarks were too general—they were not directed at McClean personally—and that the political climate was such that pressing on would have been futile.

In 1991, I asked McClean what he would do if he were now asked to sit in judgment on his torturers. "I have thought about that for a long time," he said. "All I would want them to do would be to admit that they did it and to tell who told them to do it." The policemen and soldiers who carried out the torture, he said, should not be punished at all. He imagines that they were men with mortgages and families to support who were simply doing their job. He was not so forgiving of Lord Carrington. If Carrington ordered the torture, McClean said, then he should be held responsible for it, and if he did not give the orders, then he must be taken to account for not ferreting out those responsible and punishing them. In either event, McClean thinks the political opprobrium that would result from the truth would be punishment enough for Carrington and anyone else who might have been involved, since he imagines that "they have had to live with their consciences these last twenty years and I think that that is trouble enough for anybody."

BY THE TIME Jim Auld was hired to work on the DeLorean production line in 1979, many people who knew him might have said that he had recovered, that the torture he had endured eight years earlier no longer had much effect. In fact, Auld felt permanently scarred. He had become cynical of all political groups, from government officials to the Irish nationalists who hoped to replace them. He refused to vote (when I interviewed him, twenty years after his ordeal, he had yet to cast a ballot). The nightmares did not go away. He felt that no one could understand and that he could not explain what he had been through. He talked about it only with his friend and fellow survivor Joe Clarke. He cut all his social ties with anyone who might be perceived as an active Republican.

In the mid-1970s, he started doing volunteer work with the Samaritans, a charitable organization that helps the desperate and the suicidal. That work in turn led him to the West Belfast Auto Project, a program designed to help young car thieves, of which there were scores in Belfast's Catholic ghetto, to do something constructive with their skills. (Those teenagers were particularly careless. Their idea of a good time was to steal cars, drive them at army checkpoints, and refuse to stop. Being shot at was considered part of the fun.) Auld taught them how to rebuild and maintain engines, and the teenagers drove the cars they worked on in organized races.

While he was doing that in his spare time, Auld was rising through the ranks quickly at the DeLorean plant. When the company collapsed after its founder was arrested and charged with cocaine distribution, Auld was working as senior foreman in the test driving department. After the plant closed, Auld changed course. His volunteer work with teenage delinquents led to an offer of full-time work in that field, and in 1989, he was hired as manager of Challenge for Youth, a newly established agency that intended to provide support for teenagers in trouble, Catholic and Protestant.

Auld's clients included a significant number of torture victims. In Northern Ireland, Catholic and Protestant paramilitaries enforce order in their communities by shooting miscreants. This is commonly known as kneecapping, though offenders might be shot in any part of the leg, the arm, and, in extreme cases, the head. Most of those shot are young men, and some of those survivors were part of the client group that Auld had been working with as a volunteer with the Samaritans and the West Belfast Auto Project. Paramilitary groups, particularly the IRA, often follow the custom of giving a delinquent a warning that a kneecapper will soon call if the young man does not mend his ways. Once the Challenge for Youth office opened, young men who had been warned began to show up at Auld's office, referred by an ever-widening network of fellow delinquents, social workers, and associates of paramilitaries. After securing a promise of better behavior from the teenager, Auld began interceding with the IRA and the Ulster Volunteer Force, the leading Catholic and Protestant paramilitary groups, securing a period of probation for the threatened man. Thus far, Auld has succeeded in preventing physical harm in many cases, but in many others, the targeted young men have ultimately been shot. When I met Auld in his office at Challenge for Youth in January 1991, he had interceded on behalf of more than 120 people in the previous twelve months. Three years later, that number had almost doubled.

In 1991, twenty years after his arrest, he told me that he still suffers as a result of undergoing the five techniques. He said that his ability to write and spell vanished during his ordeal and that he can still read only for a short period of time before he loses concentration. He is easily startled, and the nightmares come back, particularly if he talks about the torture. As the twentieth anniversary of his ordeal approached, he gave two interviews, one to me and one to a reporter from a Belfast newspaper who was working on an anniversary story.

He came down with shingles and high blood pressure soon thereafter, and he spent the anniversary lying in bed in considerable pain.

When I last saw him in 1993, he told me that his torturers were enshrined in his memory, that he would never forget their faces. I asked him what would be an appropriate punishment for those men. "The real perpetrators," he said, "are the people that gave them the instructions to carry it out, the government of the day. They had full knowledge of it, I believe, and if they didn't have full knowledge, certainly their statements afterwards suggest that they were in full sympathy with it. And if that is the case, then they are quite capable of sanctioning another such attack, and I don't believe that anybody who is capable of doing that or ordering that to be done to another human being should be allowed to hold power."

And the actual perpetrators? I asked.

"The people who carried it out are animals," he said, "and that is an insult to animals. For somebody to do that to another human being is totally wrong and inexcusable. Over these past years in Northern Ireland I have seen many people whose minds were not working right, but none that did anything equivalent—it was so heartless, so cold, and so calculating over such a long period of time.

"They should be shot. They need to be killed, not for me, because I am over it, but because they are damaging other people. It is impossible for them to go on and live a normal life after what they did."

{14}

ISRAEL

"The Next Step Is to God"

O N APRIL 8, 1991, the three judges hearing the case of Col. Yehuda
Meir returned with a finding of guilty. The judges said that the
commands Meir had given were "shockingly out of the ordinary" and
that even if the orders had been transmitted by a superior officer, Meir
was obliged to disobey them because they were manifestly illegal.

The judges showed that they had felt some sympathy for Meir
when they reconvened for a sentencing hearing two weeks later. They
announced that they had decided against giving Meir a prison term
and would instead reduce his rank from colonel to private. They had
made this decision, they said, after considering the length of the prolonged trial, the suffering already inflicted on Meir and his family, and
the effect that the severe loss of rank would have on a man who held
such a high position in the IDF. The chief effect of the demotion was a
severe cut in Meir's pension. He stood to lose more than $100,000 over
the course of his life.

In commenting on the sentencing, Israeli journalists noted that
Meir's punishment was lighter than sentences given to soldiers of
lesser rank who had been convicted of offenses committed in the
intifada. The soldiers from the Givati Brigade who had been convicted of brutality in the wake of the murder of Hani al-Shami had
spent five and six months in prison. The soldiers who had buried the
four Palestinian youths in the village of Salem had received sentences
of four and five months, although those sentences were later cut in

half. Yossi Sarid, the member of the Knesset who had exposed the Beita and Hawara incidents in the newspaper *Ha'aretz,* pointed out that there was one system of justice for Arabs and another for Jews: Palestinian stone throwers who caused no damage were routinely receiving prison sentences of one and two years.

Both Meir and the prosecution had the opportunity to appeal the tribunal's sentence. Neither did.

I INTERVIEWED chief military prosecutor Menachem Finklestein and his assistant, Captain Yuval Horn, in February 1993, almost two years after the sentencing. Neither man felt at liberty to talk without getting permission from the IDF press office, and it took more than a dozen prodding phone calls to that office and six weeks of deliberation before permission was granted. An IDF press officer sat in on the session, running a tape recorder as we spoke and generally inhibiting conversation. Finklestein, who had initially seemed enthusiastic about talking about the prosecution, was very guarded. He declined to give me the names of the victims beaten in Hawara and Beita. He declined even to provide a list of injuries inflicted. He and Horn were anxious that I should understand that policemen in the United States and in other countries all over the world deal with rioters by using clubs, and they wanted to put the Israeli army's beatings in that context. The clubs had actually helped minimize fatalities, Finklestein said, since they were used as an alternative to rifles. There were some "regrettable excesses," the chief prosecutor said, but not many. Horn claimed that in every case in which there was an allegation of an illegitimate use of force, there was an investigation, and that no complaints were "trashed." That contradicted what I had earlier been told by military policeman Yoram Rabin, who had discovered the Hawara and Beita complaint in a notebook full of complaints that had not been investigated.

As for the Arabs, Finklestein said it was "a technical problem" to bring the witnesses: the scheduling of the court sessions was erratic and local curfews in the West Bank also made mobility there difficult. He said that some of the victims had moved to Jordan and that some of the others could not be located; he added, however, that he had never had any intention of bringing more than two to the court. Finklestein and Horn had submitted a list of medical records as evidence, and they were confident that those records, along with the testimony of the soldiers and the two Arabs, would make their case.

I asked Finklestein why he had prosecuted only Meir. He assured me that it had been a difficult decision, that he had considered also charging Captain Eldad Ben-Moshe. At the time of the indictment, he said, "there were allegations that only the low-ranking soldiers, the privates, the corporals, were paying the price, not the commanders or colonels or the superiors. . . . We wanted to show that if the commander was the bad guy, we would not hesitate to bring him to trial." The fact that Captain Ben-Moshe had been reluctant to obey the order, Finklestein said, and that there was such a gap in rank between Meir and the young captain, contributed to the decision to let Ben-Moshe off the hook.

Finklestein said that the second difficult decision he made on the case was not to appeal the judges' sentence. He told me that he had asked the judges for both jail time and a demotion and that he thought an appropriate sentence would be a reduction to the rank of lieutenant and "four or six or eight months imprisonment." But after reflecting upon the actual sentence, Finklestein decided that the judges had been wise, that they had sent a powerful message to all the troops by giving Meir such a severe demotion. Captain Horn compared the sentence to reducing a corporate president to the rank of mailroom worker.

As for the allegations concerning Major General Amram Mitzna and Brigadier General Ze'ev Livne—that both had known about the beatings at Beita and Hawara and had sanctioned them, before or after, directly or indirectly—the prosecutors said it made for interesting stories in the press, but made little difference in the case against Meir. Meir was guilty of causing serious bodily harm and giving a manifestly illegal order, they said, and that had nothing to do with whatever he heard or believed he heard from his superior officers and Defense Minister Rabin.

I HAD MET Yehuda Meir some weeks earlier. He had had no hesitation in granting an interview, and our meeting took place at his home in Oranit, a settlement full of modern houses and well-paved streets, suburban in appearance but not location. Oranit overlooks the village of Kfar Kassem, the site of the 1956 massacre of forty-seven Arabs, the incident that clarified the definition of illegal orders in Israeli law. Meir lives in a pleasantly furnished house with his wife, Orna, and their three children. As Orna spoke English better than her husband, she sat in on the interview as both translator and as commentator. I arrived prepared for a hostile atmosphere and found instead gracious company.

Meir was largely unrepentant. He saw himself as the victim of his superiors and believed his case would never have become a case at all if someone outside the country—in this case, the Red Cross—hadn't complained about it. (He did not know about the connection between military policeman Yoram Rabin and Lieutenant Omri Kochva, and at the time of the interview, I didn't either.) The army, he said, did not want to make a big issue out of what he had done, and he was certain that if the Association for Civil Rights in Israel had not filed a suit in the High Court, no big deal would have been made.

Meir had been dismissed from the army in the fall of 1989, six months before his trial began. At that point, his paycheck stopped, his army-issue car was taken away, and he was suddenly forced to find a new job. By that time he was notorious, and that notoriety did not help in his search for employment. He told me that his friends were not of much help in finding a job because most of them were in the army, not in the private sector. Eventually he took a job as a security guard, an extraordinary fall in prestige, rank, and salary from being the de facto ruler of the Nablus region for the Israel Defense Forces.

He considered emigrating. He went to Los Angeles on the invitation of a friend there, but he did not like it. "I think that to go in Los Angeles where the blacks are living is more dangerous than to go into Nablus," he told me. "Also when I was coming in on the airplane I thought that dollars would fall on my head, but nothing happened. No dollars, nothing. I went for one month and came back after three weeks."

He told me that he had gone to the military tribunal with some confidence. "I believed that I was clean from the beginning," he said. "I wanted to go to trial. I wanted all of the story to come out." He pointed out that he had been promoted from lieutenant colonel to colonel months after the incidents at Hawara and Beita, and he said that the senior command, who had approved the promotion, knew all about those particular incidents and his record in the Nablus region.

At the trial, Meir had said that it was harder to give an order to beat than to give an order to open fire, and I asked him to explain the remark. "It is something you do not learn in the army school," Meir said. "You don't know how to do it. I, myself, cannot see blood or see people suffer. It is very difficult for me. If you have to shoot somebody, it is far from you. You don't see him. And you are taught how to do it, to use the gun."

As for the incidents at Hawara and Beita, Meir said he thought he had chosen his soldiers wisely. "I had a lot of officers and soldiers," Meir said, "but Ben-Moshe was the best of them. I like him. He was my friend. Very good guy. . . . You must understand that I prefer to take Ben-Moshe to this mission, dirty mission, because I know that he will understand, that he will do only what is necessary." At that point, Orna Meir clarified her husband's statement, adding that Meir knew that Ben-Moshe would "not make it worse for the Arabs, would not torture them."

Some time after the end of his trial, Meir left his job as a security guard, thinking that he could do better if he formed his own company. There is a significant need for security on Israeli settlements, at Israeli schools, and at Israeli businesses—particularly those that operate in the occupied territories. In the security industry, Meir discovered that his notoriety was no handicap. He was viewed, he said, as a man "who knows how to beat Arabs."

His business grew quickly. When I met him, less than two years after his sentencing, he had 150 people on his payroll and twenty-five vehicles. He told me that running a business presented challenges he had not been prepared for and that he worked a very long day, but that in fact the quality of his life was much better now, that he was able to spend much more time with his family than he did when he was in the IDF.

When I arrived at Eldad Ben-Moshe's apartment in Tel Aviv on February 8, 1993, I met a man much more subdued, more thoughtful, and less physically imposing than Meir. Ben-Moshe is short, thin, and dark-skinned. His black hair was closely trimmed, and he was wearing black wire-rimmed glasses, sandals, blue jeans, and a red hooded sweatshirt. At that point he had been out of the army for five years. He had completed his studies in accounting, was soon to take the certification test, and was working for a large accounting firm in Tel Aviv. His chief mode of transportation was a motorcycle and his politics were liberal, but everything else about him seemed conservative.

He was doubtful that I—or anyone who hadn't served in the occupied territories in the first months of the intifada—could understand how he had come to order his men to break the arms and legs of complete strangers and abandon them on a winter evening in a muddy field in varying states of consciousness. "Intifada is a name that everybody gave it later," he told me. "[At the time], you didn't know what to call it, you didn't know how to treat it, you didn't know anything about it. The army didn't know what to do. On Sunday, they told you this. Monday, they told you don't do that, do this. The orders were very dynamic. It was something amazing.

"This order, when we are sitting here in this room, it seems something like a monster, but in this time, in this area, in this situation, it wasn't like that. Everybody did these things all the time. It wasn't something so bad. It wasn't something that dropped from the sky. It was something that you saw every day. All of the officers and [Defense Minister] Rabin were giving us orders, and I did not like these orders and I said it. It became a routine that they say something and I say I don't like it."

The idea of refusing to obey an order, however, never entered his mind. He knew about the massacre at Kfar Kassem, but he saw it as just a history lesson, not as something applicable to himself. When he received the order to break arms and legs, he decided he couldn't carry it out himself, but he never thought of not passing the order down the chain of command. He did offer his men the option of sitting out the action, and I asked if in so doing he wasn't running the risk of having everyone refuse the order.

"I can tell you now that I would be glad if all of them had said no," he said. "But to be honest, I knew that they would be glad to do it."

At Beita the first night, Ben-Moshe gave the orders and stayed near the bus. He expressed his misgivings the following day in meetings with both Meir and Brigadier General Ze'ev Livne, and on the second night, he stayed on the bus while the Arabs were led into the fields at

Hawara. At dawn on the third morning, Livne arrived and talked to the troops, and Ben-Moshe, feeling that Livne had cheated him by not dealing with the issues at hand, drove seventy kilometers to meet with his battalion commander, who phoned Major General Amram Mitzna and passed on Ben-Moshe's objections. Ben-Moshe told me that he felt he had done all that he could to convey his objections. "I went to Yehuda Meir, I went to Livne, I went to Mitzna," he said. "To me, as a young officer, the next step is to God."

When it became clear that there would be prosecutions resulting from the incident, Ben-Moshe said he felt confident. "I felt that honestly I did what I had to do, and if they put me in jail, okay, I will be in jail, but my conscience, if not clean, is something like clean."

Ben-Moshe told me that he felt bad not for what was done to the Palestinians, but for the act that he and his men had performed. He believed that the army's mistake had been to take on the job of the judiciary, levying punishment when it did not have the right to punish. When I asked him who was responsible for the two incidents, he indicated that he believed the entire chain of command was to blame, from Defense Minister Rabin down to the soldiers who did the beating, and that included himself. As for who was most responsible, he could not say.

The verdict in the case troubled Ben-Moshe. "I saw it in real life, and when I read the summary that the judge wrote, I see that all the facts are true and that the judge didn't understand anything." Ben-Moshe believed that Yehuda Meir took the fall for everyone else, and so when it came time for Meir to be sentenced, Ben-Moshe, who had been a witness for the prosecution, testified for the defense about Meir's strength of character. The young captain told the judges that unlike other commanders he had served in the field, Meir had never shirked responsibility when the going got rough—he had taken charge and had made the tough decisions.

After the verdict and sentencing, Ben-Moshe told me that he avoided the political Right in Israel, who he believed would have thought him a hero for his role in the beatings. He also declined offers by leftist politicians to appear at various forums and discuss the case. "I don't want politics in my life," he told me. "I expected that somebody from the army would call me to the officers' course to talk with young officers about this, about situations that an officer can meet even if he doesn't dream about them. Nobody has done this. I am not sure that I want to go, but nobody asks. This is the problem. Nobody learns from this situation, and the problem of the army is bigger than my problem. My problem is Hawara and Beita. The problem of the army is Hawara and Beita and more." He mentioned the similar incidents cited by Meir's attorney at the trial and said that the response from the Israeli public had been to put their hands over their ears. "This is my feeling about what everybody did."

At Meir's trial Ben-Moshe testified that during the beatings at Hawara, he had ordered the driver of the bus to rev the engine to drown out the screams. By the time of our interview, however, five years after the incident, he could not recall giving the order. He also had acquired the mistaken belief that the beatings had not resulted in any broken bones. (I had heard the same statement from Yehuda Meir. The belief was probably the by-product of the fact that the Arabs were not a significant presence at the trial.)

He seemed to see himself as someone who had carried out an inhumane order in as humane a fashion as he could, protesting all the while. I asked if he would call the beatings at Beita and Hawara torture.

"I don't call it torture," he said. "I prefer to call it punishment."

OMRI KOCHVA, who with fellow Lieutenant Ilan Shani directly supervised the beatings, spoke to me at his kibbutz on February 17, 1993. Kochva is physically impressive: he has a compact build, a rectangular face, short hair, and green eyes that do not look away even when he admits something he is ashamed of. He is a confident and competent man, just the sort you would want to have beside you on a battlefield. He provided the most shocking testimony at Meir's trial, shocking because he did not pull back, mince words, or soft-pedal; he straightforwardly described that the Nahal group had beaten the Arabs without mercy, paying no attention to their screams and cries. When I asked him what condition the Arabs were in when he left the fields in Beita and Hawara, he looked me right in the eye and said, "I thought they would never walk again."

He went on, "Hundreds of people ask me, 'How could you do it? We knew you before and we know you now and we know you are a reasonable person.' Or they say, 'I have known you from the day you were born, how could you do it?'" In answering that question, Kochva always describes in detail the atmosphere that led up to the beating in Beita: the chaos of the intifada, the filling of the jails, and the day's battle with the citizenry. In our interview, he went on to talk about the relationship between Yehuda Meir and the officers of the Nahal group. "He liked us very much. He knew us before it all began and it was more than an army relationship. We sat in his office and talked a lot before [the incidents]. I had a really good relationship with him. He likes me even today, I think."

So it was not some distant and perhaps disliked officer who gave the command, but someone whom Kochva liked and could relate to, an officer who knew what his men were going through because he was not bound to his desk. And Kochva indicated that they had done part of the job many times before, that they were accustomed to rounding up men whose names were on lists that came from the General Security Services (also known as Shin Bet and Shabback). He described his job as keeping peace in the villages by day and carrying out arrests for the GSS by night. "It is not our business to know why the Shabback wants this man," Kochva said. "Maybe they want this person to get information, but he is not a terrorist. Some of them are terrorists. But it isn't part of your job to ask questions. You do it, you don't ask too many questions, and anyway they don't give many answers."

Kochva also thought that the relative youth of the Nahal officers was a factor in their willingness to obey Meir's fateful order. Kochva had eventually, at the age of twenty-two, succeeded Ben-Moshe as commander of the Nahal group. "And still you are really a child," he said. "You have a very narrow world because you finish your high school, you go into the army, and in the army all the time you get orders, you give orders, you don't see much from the right, from the left. Now a few years later, I have grown up, I feel much more adult, but when you get eighty soldiers, young people, nineteen years old, a child like you but younger, and it is really dangerous, you can do things that a few years later you would do better. That is the main difference between Eldad, at twenty-two in command of a bus of forty people and a commander in the American army, twenty-six, twenty-seven, twenty-eight years old, much more adult. That was a very confused situation—confused orders, confused commander, confused soldiers, everyone was confused. And I appreciate Eldad because he told us we could become like the Americans in Vietnam, to become animals, and we didn't. We stayed as a group, as platoons, we trained, we practiced all the time, we talked about the things we did, we did not become animals."

Kochva also thought that the lack of training in the concept of legal and illegal orders had contributed to the willingness to break arms and legs. "The army expects the commanders to recognize orders with a red light behind them. You never learn, in officers' school, about legal or illegal orders, you never touch on this. You maybe touch, if you are lucky, the Kfar Kassem case. But everybody expects that because you are human, and you are an officer, and you are a good Jewish boy, when you get a very illegal order, you will refuse to do it. They expect us to do it and no one really talked about it before.

"When it happens, you don't have the time to stop and think reasonably. You never stop. The day after [Hawara] we went to another village, not to do the same thing. Life goes on. Nothing forced us to think immediately, even though we knew when it happened that there was something wrong with these two cases out of all the things that had been done before. I believe if it happened to our group, to our unit, it could happen to anyone. And that is the frightening thing. . . .

"Everybody has a part—me, Eldad, the other platoon commander, Eldad's deputy—very great persons. I like them, they are very good friends of mine, even now. Eldad has the biggest problem, of course. I feel very sorry for him, because everybody fingered him—Yehuda, Livne, we looked to Eldad to get orders. Eldad was a very intelligent man, and everybody looked to him from the higher ranks and the lower ranks. He was really in trouble because he had to get orders and give them. I just got orders. Eldad got orders and gave orders. He was the main person in this case. Yehuda only gave. Eldad tragically was the center of all this case, and I feel very sorry for him.

"Since the Holocaust, it really sounds bad when someone says, 'I got orders.' And I never use this excuse. All my family from my father's side are gone in the Holocaust, and also part of my mother's side. I said in court that I got the orders, but that was a fact—it doesn't excuse the things that we did."

I asked Kochva if he felt that he was in some way a victim in this situation. "I know, and every soldier knows, that we shouldn't have done it. I am a person who had the choice of what to do, and I chose the wrong way. So I am not a victim. Eldad is not a victim. It was a very hard decision, but he had the decision. And maybe we felt that we must do it, we must do it in this moment because Yehuda is waiting and Livne is sitting in the office and gave us the order—but we chose to do it. You have the right to say no, and we didn't."

Kochva told me that he would not have gone independently to the military police to file a report, that if he had not been a friend of military police investigator Yoram Rabin, the story of Beita and Hawara would probably never have surfaced. "I told the story," he said, "because I couldn't keep it in my heart," but he went on to say that he gave formal testimony only after prosecutor Finklestein promised him that none of the soldiers would be charged, that Meir alone would be prosecuted.

Because he was not charged or disciplined in any way, Kochva had no black marks in his military file, and by the end of his six years of service, he had risen to the rank of captain. He left the army in 1991, traveled to the Far East with his girlfriend for the better part of a year, and then returned to the kibbutz to enroll at a university. He was expecting to start his studies in the autumn after our interview.

"It doesn't break my heart and I don't cry for the Arabs," he told me, "but I feel that we did a very tragic thing that spoiled our army life and civilian life. Four or five years afterward I still talk about it and people are still interested. It took a place in my civilian life, so I feel very sorry for having done it. Sorry not for the Arabs, but for me, for Eldad, for the soldiers, that we didn't stop at the time. It will never pass from my life, and it is something that will always be inside me. I think every soldier who was involved, who hit or who was in the bus, will remember this forever. Some will tell you today that it was a good thing to do, but I think most of them understand that it was wrong."

I asked if he would call it torture. He defined torture as an act fueled by sadistic emotions or an act done to another person in order to get information or some desired result. This was different, he said. "It was a beating, a very strong beating, and a very inhuman thing, but it wasn't torture. I didn't expect one of the Arabs to tell me something if we did not hit him. We just hit him. I didn't expect that he would not throw stones the week after. We knew that they would hate us more than ever after this kind of thing. But it wasn't torture."

"And I have no sadistic emotions. And Eldad has none, and Ziv [Gefen—Ben-Moshe's deputy] has none, and Ilan [Shani] has none. In normal life, they are very normal. For it to be torture, you must expect something to happen as a result or you must get enjoyment from it. And we didn't expect something to happen and we did not enjoy it. So it isn't torture. It is a kind of punishment."

KOCHVA'S FRIEND, military police investigator Yoram Rabin, left the army after five years' service and had a year remaining in law school when I interviewed him in February 1993. He told me that his law school class had discussed the Meir case when he was a first-year student, but because he had not read the assigned material, his professor—unaware of Rabin's role in the case—would not let him take part in the discussion.

"In the beginning, I thought that what had happened was bad and I wanted to make a file on the case," Rabin told me. "But I didn't realize what a big mess would result. I didn't think at the time that it would explode. It was just another case. I knew it was something big, but I didn't know how big it was.

"In Israel it was far beyond the torture question. It was a question of how a society, an army, can rule another nation with the tools of law and with young soldiers, and if that mission is possible. To make the mission, you have to do things that do not go hand in hand with law. So it became an interesting question in a lot of other aspects."

Looking back on the case, he could see how the Nahal troops had come to participate so willingly. "The last war was in 1982, the Lebanon war, and these soldiers went to the army three years after that. And every second and every hour of their training, they train to act in a war. And there is no war. I train to make investigations and I make them. They train to make war, and there is no war. So when something happens, they think, 'This is war, this is the real thing.' And when something happens to a soldier like this, he can think about it, he can make his own conclusions, but he can never go to the military police because it is a war and the other soldier is his friend. If something happens, it happened. They can say it is good, it is bad, I can do it, I can't do it, but I never go and report that and be a hero in the press on the back of my friends. That is the strongest principle of the soldier.

"In this case, it was a very intelligent soldier, they knew about Kfar Kassem, they learned about it in school, but because they were so involved in the events, they saw no red light, no hearts, no nothing. And the argument was that it was a very illegal order, that you can see from one kilometer away that you are not supposed to do it. When you read it in the paper, when you see it in the TV, you say, 'That is obvious.' But if you talk to the soldier, you see it is not so obvious.

"But I think what is interesting here is not the torture by itself. What is interesting is how good people, good teenagers from good families from a good kibbutz, with the political ideas of the Left, do a thing like this. At the time they got the order, they did not say, 'It's bad and I have to do it.' They did not say, 'It's bad and I must do it or else someone will kill me.' They did not say, 'It's bad and I don't want to do it.' They did it, and just when they were twenty-five they said, 'Oh, what a mistake it was. You are not allowed to do what we did, and I don't know how I didn't catch it at the time that it happened.'

"I see Omri—he is very good, he cannot harm a fly—and he did it, and until today he can't understand why. And he says, 'It was a mistake and I hope that I will have the power not to do it again.' He doesn't say that because he was punished—he got away clean. That is what is interesting. That you can drive him to some situation where he will do it.

"I had great arguments with Omri. He told me, 'If you had come through the paratroopers, and I had gone into MPI, you would have done it and I would have investigated it.' Like it is all destiny, it is not how clever you are.

"I have an advantage on you because I lived it and I think about it a lot. And after all those years, this is what remains in my head—that you can take a good farmer—when he was fourteen, he was driving a tractor, a John Deere, on the kibbutz—and you can train him, tell him to do something, and he will do it. Everybody, even me. I didn't do it because I went to the MPI and they told me in the school, 'This is good. This is no good,' but I think maybe it can happen to me. And if it happened to me for the first time when I was a colonel, I would find myself in jail. And maybe that is what happened to Yehuda Meir. Maybe he is not a bad guy."

.   .   .

THE NAHAL OFFICERS' refusal to classify their acts in Beita and Hawara as torture can perhaps be better understood in light of the fact that in Israel there are more formal torture procedures executed on a systematic basis by the General Security Service. Those procedures, documented for many years by newspapers and human rights organizations, came to be openly admitted and embraced by the government.

The first major exposé appeared in the *Sunday Times* of London on June 19, 1977, alleging that the GSS and other Israeli security services used repeated cold showers, beatings, confinement in refrigerator cells, and electric shock, among other methods, and that the torture was "systematic" and "sanctioned at some level as deliberate policy." The government at the time denied the charges, but those denials rang hollow in the mid-1980s in the wake of two incidents, the Number 300 bus affair and the Nafsu case. In the former, two Palestinians who hijacked a bus were reported to have died in cross fire. Newspaper photographs, however, showed that the two were alive and well when they were taken into custody. It eventually became clear that the two had been executed by the GSS and that there had been a conspiracy to hide that fact. In the Nafsu case, an Israeli army officer named Izat Nafsu, sentenced to eighteen years for espionage, claimed that his confession had been extracted by torture. The GSS agents denied this under oath, but the Israeli High Court eventually decided that the agents had lied.

In the wake of those two incidents, the government appointed an investigating commission under the direction of former High Court Justice Moshe Landau, who had been the presiding judge in the 1961 trial of Nazi Sturmbannfuhrer Adolf Eichmann. Landau concluded that GSS agents had systematically committed perjury for sixteen years, lying about the fact that they used brutal physical and psychological methods to get confessions and information. He quoted from an internal GSS memo, written in 1982, that set out guidelines about what sort of lies should be told. In the public section of his report, Landau declined to spell out exactly what methods had been employed; the *Miami Herald* reported that the GSS admitted that its agents had "punched, slapped, and kicked suspects, spit and urinated on them, forced them under cold showers and then in front of air conditioners, hooded them and denied them food and sleep."

In Israel, Landau was considered a liberal. He had once declared a

Jewish criminal's confession tainted merely because a police officer had shouted at him. He was not so kind to the Palestinians who had been tortured. He recommended that no one in the GSS be prosecuted and that no cases be reopened. He went on to establish guidelines for the application of "moderate physical pressure" that could henceforth be used by GSS interrogators. Those guidelines were contained in a secret portion of Landau's report that has never been published, but it is clear that the judge was impressed by the British techniques used on the hooded men in Northern Ireland in 1971. In providing a legal background for his recommended interrogation methods, Landau cited the decision of the judges of the European Court of Human Rights in the case of *Ireland vs. the United Kingdom,* the decision that determined that the five techniques were inhuman and degrading but not torture. In the years after the Landau Commission filed its report, it became apparent that the GSS and the IDF had adopted and adapted the British methods wholesale. Although Landau claimed that the methods he was proposing in his secret guidelines were less severe than those used by the British, in actual practice the Israeli methods are at the very least equally brutal.

Various human rights organizations, including the International Committee of the Red Cross, Human Rights Watch, and the Israeli human rights group B'Tselem have found that the GSS interrogators hood detainees, deprive them of sleep, subject them to persistent and aggravating noise, tie and confine them in various positions that cause acute pain, lock them up in closetlike cells in which it is often impossible to sit or stand, and expose them to extreme heat or cold for hours at a time. Beatings and choking during interrogation are common, as is violent shaking of the prisoner so that his head jerks back and forth. (In July 1995, after 'Abd a-Samed Harizat died as a result of forceful shaking, Yitzhak Rabin, then prime minister, was quoted in *Ha'aretz* saying that eight thousand Palestinians had been subjected to that method of interrogation.) Prisoners are commonly denied access to a toilet for long periods of time, and when they are allowed to relieve themselves they are likely to discover that there is no soap, running water, or toilet paper. Until 1992, GSS agents commonly denied prisoners food and drink; today they provide both, but they are likely to do so in the brief moments when the prisoners are allowed to sit on a toilet; some former prisoners report that they had less than five minutes to relieve themselves and eat. In its 1994 report, *Torture and Ill-treatment: Israel's Interrogation of Palestinians from the Occupied Territories,* Human Rights Watch reported that Palestinian detainees can be subjected to all of these techniques for weeks, sometimes for months, getting a break in the routine only so that their interrogators can observe the Sabbath. In 1993, Human Rights Watch investigator Jim Ron and I interviewed Ahmed Husni al-Batsh, an aide to Faisal al-Husseini, director of the Arab Studies Society, who survived such treatment for seventy-five days, after which he was released without charge. Al-Batsh judged the kindness of his guards by what they did with his hood, which was removed when he was at the toilet. The nastier guards dropped the hood into the excrement and urine on the floor, then put it back on al-Batsh's head.

The Israeli human rights organization B'Tselem estimates that between 1987 and the end of 1994, approximately 20,000 Palestinians were tortured at the hands of the GSS. In its February 1998 report, *Routine Torture: Interrogation Methods of the General Security Service,* B'Tselem reported that at present, 1,000 to 1,500 Palestinians are being interrogated each year by the GSS and that 85 percent are subject to torture.

B'Tselem is limited in its access to torture survivors and depends largely upon the testimony of those who are released by the authorities. Delegates from the International Committee of the Red Cross, on the other hand, are allowed by the Israeli government to regularly interview Palestinians undergoing interrogation. The ICRC's policy is to make its reports available only to the responsible government, not to the public. In May 1992, however, the Red Cross took the unusual step of issuing a press release saying that it had found that Israel was using physical and psychological methods that constituted a violation of the Fourth Geneva Convention (which prohibits torture and inhuman and degrading treatment); that the agency had sent "numerous and detailed reports" to the government about the use of those methods; and that all those reports had had no effect.

On September 5, 1999, as this book went to press, the High Court in Israel ruled that the law forbade the methods so widely used by the Shin Bet. It remains to be seen, however, what will change as a result—the methods or the law. The court said that the Knesset, the Israeli parliament, might consider drafting special legislation authorizing physical pressure in exceptional cases. Gideon Ezra, a former deputy head of Shin Bet and now a member of the Knesset, said, "If it is forbidden to sit a detainee on a chair in a certain way, perhaps they will find a chair which is a little bit higher."

I WAS ABLE to locate and interview twelve of the twenty men who were attacked under the supervision of Kuchva, Shani, Ben-Moshe, and Meir. None of the men I spoke with noticed any soldiers who were reluctant participants. No one mentioned a noble captain who stayed on the bus. No one marveled at the transformation of a kibbutznik. Many asked why I was singling out the Meir incident when the torture being administered daily in the jails and detention centers was much worse. I took to anticipating the question, and began my later interviews with the explanation that I was aware of what else was going on, but that I felt this incident would make a stronger impression because it could not be disputed: no one could say that the victims were lying because the torturers themselves had confessed, under oath, in a courtroom.

Muhammad Beni Mufala, one of the two victims who had testified in court, welcomed me into his home in upper Beita on a cold day in February 1993. The house, like most in Beita and Hawara, seemed to have been made entirely of concrete. The room where visitors are received was lit by one bare lightbulb suspended from the ceiling and was furnished with two beds, a mattress, a stack of pillows, a table, and two chairs. The floors and walls were neat, clean, and entirely bare, and the wind blew through a sixty-square-inch hole in the window in the door. We sat as close as possible to an electric heater that seemed to warm an area about three feet square and two feet high. The room was very cold.

Mufala, a short man with a thin mustache and a stubble of beard, thirty-one years old, was the father of two children. He was employed in an auto body shop. His faith in Islam was very important to him, and at the end of our interview he briefly attempted to convert me.

Through a translator, he told me that on January 20, 1988, he ran into the Nahal troops on his way home from the mosque. Since he had not been out on the streets except to go to and from the mosque, he said, he was unaware that there was any fighting in the village and that the army had imposed a curfew. According to Mufala, the troops, swinging clubs, descended upon all of the worshipers. Mufala was caught and, when he could not produce his ID card (he had left it at home because he was only going the short distance to the mosque), he was beaten and then released. He told me that he arrived home, changed his wet and dirty clothes, and was sitting by the fire when soldiers came to the door to arrest him. They marched him off to the school yard where the bus was waiting. Mufala said he was beaten on his hands, arms, and legs during the course of the journey.

Once on the bus, Mufala and the other men whose names had been on the GSS list were ordered to sit on the floor. Mufala told me that when the soldiers boarded, they walked over the Beita men in order to get to their seats. (Several other Beita men said the same in their separate accounts of the incident.) When the bus stopped at the crossroads and the Palestinians were taken off into the orchard, Mufala thought the soldiers were going to tie them all to trees and let them go in the morning. It was not long, however, before Mufala realized the troops had different intentions. Two soldiers held his arms while others took deliberate aim at his legs. He tried to dodge the clubs, dancing about, at one point lifting both legs so that he was briefly held in the air by the two soldiers who were holding his arms. At that point, he said, he was hit in the head and dropped to the ground. He recalled trying to protect his legs only to be whacked on the arms and hands instead.

Of the dozen men I spoke with, Mufala displayed the most unusual reminder of the beatings. When I asked how the incident affected him today, he rolled up the cuff of his pants on one leg and displayed a lump about the size of half a walnut, a lump that he said had been much larger when he received it five years earlier. Then he put weight on his foot, and the walnut doubled in size. He proceeded to move back and forth, and the walnut alternately inflated and deflated as he walked. I later recalled that he had bared his leg to the judges at Meir's court-martial and realized that he had probably been displaying for them the same phenomenon, a display I could not see from my seat in the room. Mufala also suffered from headaches, which he attributed to the incident.

Mufala said that Ben-Moshe's men had asked him no questions and so he had no clue as to how he had been selected as a target. It was his first arrest, but it was not his last.

On April 6, 1988, a group of militant Jewish settlers from the Gush

Emunim (Bloc of the Faithful) movement decided to send some of their children on a provocative hiking trip. Two armed adults led fifteen teenagers into the fields around Beita, a trip designed to underscore the settlers' notion that, as the West Bank belongs to Israel, Jewish Israelis can go where they please. Palestinians often fear settlers more than the army, as settlers are regarded as well-armed fanatics without rules, sometimes winked at by the IDF. When villagers in Beita saw armed settlers heading toward them, they assumed the worst. Youths from the village began to throw stones. Roman Aldubi, one of the hikers' armed guards, then opened fire with his M-16, wounding one man and killing a second who was farming nearby. The marchers fled into the village, where news of the killing in the field had preceded them. Militant youths continued to throw stones, joined by the sister of the man whom Aldubi had killed. Aldubi opened fire again. The teenage settlers ran. Some were sheltered by Beita residents, others escaped from the village, and one remained behind: a fifteen-year-old girl named Tirza Porat, who lay on the ground with a bullet in her head.

The Gush Emunim teenagers said that the dead girl had been shot by a sniper firing from a rooftop, and in the wake of the incident, three cabinet ministers called for Beita to be leveled, one suggesting that it be replaced by a settlement named after the dead teenager. Yitzhak Shamir, Israel's prime minister, attended her burial service. Although forensic reports indicated that the dead girl had been killed not by Palestinians but by a shot fired by Aldubi, the village was severely punished. Within forty-eight hours of the incident, Major General Amram Mitzna ordered the demolition of fourteen houses in the village, including the home of a family that had sheltered one of the hikers. More than sixty people from Beita were arrested. Six were deported to Lebanon, and others later received prison sentences of varying terms. Muhammad Beni Mufala served twenty-two months in jail.

I INTERVIEWED FOUR other men from Beita who were among Meir's victims.

Tayseer Mousa Barham, twenty-nine at the time of the beating, said that he had also been beaten before he was ordered onto the bus, and that when it was all over, it was a month before he could stand up, two months before he could go back to work. He said he had no lingering effects. He had been arrested three times before the incident and thought that was why he was on the Shin Bet list.

Netham Hafeth Beni Shamseh, thirty-two, had a well-furnished home, the result of his success in the construction business, and he seemed a particularly unlikely candidate for a beating. He said that he was one of the last ones beaten, that many of the clubs had broken by the time the soldiers turned to him, and that he did not suffer as badly as the others because by that point the beatings had become so chaotic. He told of one soldier who kept hitting him with a rifle butt; the man was unable to get any leverage, Shamseh said, because his fellow soldiers kept getting in his way.

Shamseh said that he managed to roll onto his left side, and as a result his injuries were largely confined to his right hand and leg. When he regained consciousness, he found he was able to stand, but once he reached his home he was not able to repeat that performance for fifteen days. He had never been arrested before, he had not been arrested since, and he had no idea why he was on the list. He speculated that the list was made up of very religious Muslims, of which he was one, and PLO supporters, and he believed the purpose of the beating was to let the village know that you would be beaten whether you had done anything or not. He said the incident had had a strange effect on him: he had feared soldiers before, but not afterward.

Azam Hafeth Beni Chamous, thirty-one, could pass for a native of Germany: he has reddish blond hair, a handlebar mustache, and light blue eyes. He told me that he was beaten so well before the bus left the school yard that he had lost feeling in his legs. He recalled that while he was sitting on the bus he had the distinct fear that he had lost his shoes, but when he reached down to check, he discovered they were still on his feet. In the field he recalled screaming and shouting and being beaten everywhere except his head. Afterward he had enormous swelling but no broken bones.

Jihad Hamael was twenty years old when he was beaten. He said that when he arrived at the school yard, he was made to put his hands on the door of a jeep so that the soldiers could beat them with their clubs. When he was taken off the bus, his jacket was pulled over his head and he was pushed down into a small pool of water. He was hit mostly in his legs and hands, and he said the soldiers aimed particularly at his joints. When he regained consciousness, he could see cars passing on the road and he tried to cry out for help, but he could produce little sound. He recalled that some of the other men were nearly suffocating because they were lying face down in puddles. Some emerged thinking that their hearing had been damaged, only to discover that they had mud in their ears. Hamael was treated by an ambulance attendant. He described his body as "black and blue in Technicolor." It was a week before he could stand up, he said, and at that point he still had difficulty eating because he could hold nothing in his hands.

In reaction to the beating, Hamael decided to become a paramedic. He now drives an ambulance for the Red Crescent Society, a job that often has him coming to the rescue of wounded Palestinians.

"In Beita," Hamael told me, "they were practicing. In Hawara it was different—they had experience breaking bones."

In Hawara, I was able to locate seven of the twelve men beaten. The mukhtar's son, Muhammed Jihad Howary, was one of those unavailable for an interview. He was in prison at the time. Refideyeh Hospital records indicate that after the beating by Ben-Moshe's men, the mukhtar's son had multiple lacerations on both legs, a four-centimeter cut on his left leg, and a three-centimeter cut on his face.

The first victim I talked to was Jamal Jaber Audi, twenty-two at the time of the beating, who lives on the Nablus road. He told me that when he was taken to the hospital, his father was afraid that soldiers would follow and arrest the men and so he claimed that his son had been injured in a fall. Jamal told us that when he came home he was bruised all over his body, that his face was black and blue, that it was forty-five days before he could stand, and that for a month he had dreams in which he woke up screaming and attempting to defend himself from attackers. He believes that the twelve men who were beaten were chosen at random in order to intimidate the village. The beatings, he said, had the opposite effect. He told me that in a strange way his social standing in the village rose in the wake of

Captain Ben-Moshe's visit. "People began to view me as a good person," he said, "because I had been chosen to be beaten."

SAMIR HAMOUS ARRIVED for our interview with fellow victim Shehadeh Abdallah Shihad, and the two told their stories separately. Samir was seventeen at the time of the incident and the youngest of the victims I met. He had curly brown hair, a beard, a mustache, and brown eyes, and he told his story without expression or emotion. He said that when he regained consciousness after the beating he was in a car on the way to the hospital, unable to move because of the pain. His left leg was broken, his left arm swollen, other parts of his body well bruised. Like other men from Hawara and Beita, he fled the hospital after two days, having been warned by the mukhtar that there was a good chance that soldiers would come and arrest them. In the weeks that followed, Hamous and his friend Shihad took to sleeping in an abandoned building, a building with no electricity and no plumbing, because they were afraid the soldiers would come again.

Hamous told me that he had nightmares for "five or six months." Until the day of the beating, he had been commuting daily to a dishwashing job in Tel Aviv, but when I met him five years after the event he said he was too frightened to leave the West Bank. "It affects me mentally, economically, in everything I do," he said. "I became afraid of soldiers all the time. I don't go to the village or anywhere. I stay just at home." He told me that he supported himself by doing odd jobs with his brother and father.

Shehadeh Abdallah Shihad, a tall, clean-shaven man with an oval face, was not as depressed as his friend Samir and was physically the stronger of the two. He said that when the bus stopped on the Nablus road, he thought the soldiers were going to transfer some of the prisoners to a jeep because the bus was crowded. When he was marched into the field, he saw one of the men who had already been taken from the bus lying in the mud. "I thought he was dead," Shihad told me, "and that now it was my turn."

Shihad recalled his attack in some detail. He was kicked to the ground. A soldier shoved a cloth into his mouth. The officer supervising the soldiers put his muddy boot on Shihad's chest and, when the young Palestinian began to struggle, shifted the boot to Shihad's face.

Shihad said he was not hit on the arms, but that the soldiers became frustrated because he did not pass out. Shihad, who speaks Hebrew, recalled that one soldier remarked, "His legs must be made of iron."

Shihad had given a statement to Al Haq, the Palestinian human rights organization, seven days after the incident, and at that time he said that his legs were still bleeding. He showed me two ugly scars on his left leg and three on his right, oval in shape and about the size of a half dollar. He said that his feet hurt when he walked down stairs, that he could not run or do anything very strenuous with his legs, and that his nightmares sometimes caused him to wake up screaming. In one dream, he sees soldiers coming to beat him. In another, troops destroy his house and beat his mother.

I asked all of the Hawara and Beita victims I interviewed for permission to print their names. Shihad did not hesitate. "Nothing worse can happen to me," he said.

I INTERVIEWED Saber Salim Audi at the falafel stand he runs on the Nablus road, not far from the mukhtar's gas station. Salim was forty-one when I met him, with a weathered face lined with deep wrinkles. Like several of the other men, he had not been arrested before or since the incident. He was of the opinion that the men from Hawara were chosen at random. He found his departure from the bus terrifying because he thought he would be killed; if they were going to beat him, he thought, they could have done that in the village. He had no broken bones, but it was five months before he could use his hands again.

Saber's brother Ghaleb was also among the victims. Ghaleb, a former Bir Zeit University basketball player, had just returned from Jordan when I met him, and from where we sat on the porch of his brother's house we could see the fields, two hundred yards away, where the two men had been systematically beaten and abandoned. The cries of the two men that night were answered by their family. Ghaleb's left leg was broken, and he said that the injury put an end to his athletic activity. He left the West Bank a year after the incident and was teaching in an elementary school in Kuwait at the time of Meir's trial. Without being asked about dreams, he brought up the subject of nightmares, saying that he was surprised that he had them even when he was in Jordan, beyond the normal reach of Israeli troops.

KMAL DMADI, the son of a school headmaster, also lived within
about two hundred yards of the field where the men were beaten, but
his family heard no screams. His father had gone with him to the
mukhtar's gas station, was reassured by someone he believed was the
officer in charge that this was nothing more than a simple arrest, and
went home. While the headmaster was climbing back into bed, his
twenty-one-year-old son was being beaten in a muddy field two hundred yards away.

"They concentrated on my bones," Dmadi told me, "especially the
legs, the ankles, the joints, the shoulder, the back—especially in the
kidney. Also they beat my fingers. They destroyed my watch." Dmadi
said he was hit in the back of a head with the butt of a gun, but, as if
feeling a need to be fair, he hastily added that it was not a severe blow.

At Refideyeh Hospital he was given painkillers, but because he had
no broken bones there was little more that the doctors could do. "For
this type of injury there is no exact treatment," he said. "If you are hit
in the knee and blood has accumulated there, you cannot do anything
to treat that. Only time will cure it."

He also fled the hospital after two days. "I was paralyzed. I could
not walk, I could not eat. I was just lying in the bed. When I wanted to
go to the bathroom, some friends had to hold me." He estimated that it
was twenty-five days before he could stand and six weeks before he
could walk properly.

Three months after the incident, he was arrested a second time.
When I asked if he had been charged, he laughed and said yes, he had
been charged with throwing stones and putting obstacles in the street.
Palestinians regard those charges as automatic, having nothing to do
with reality. He was held for six months' administrative detention.

First, however, he was tortured. "The mind cannot imagine this.
The first day they blindfolded and handcuffed me, and I stayed two to
three days sitting on a chair made of concrete, day and night, outside,
under the rain, under the sunshine, under everything else. After this
they took me and beat me in the testicles, in the head, on the face, and
in the kidney. With their boots, their hands, and clubs made of hard
plastic.

"After this they take you to a small room, about one meter wide and two meters tall. I ate there, I went to the bathroom there, everything. For thirty-one days. And every day they took us and beat us."

Torture in the prison, Dmadi said, was more painful, but torture in the field was more terrifying. So many Palestinians have been tortured in the prisons and interrogation centers that most have an idea of what the routine will be, although they do not know how long the routine will last. While that knowledge does not make it less painful, for some it does diminish the terror. They know that while some men have died under torture, the number of deaths is minuscule compared to the total number of victims. Thus most prisoners know that they will probably survive what is done to them. Being taken from the bus and walked into the muddy field, Dmadi said, was more terrifying because it was unexpected, unpredictable, and what was going to happen was unknown.

I asked most of the men what they thought an appropriate punishment would be for their torturers. A good number said that under Islam, the perpetrators should be subjected to the same measures they used on their victims. Dmadi felt differently. "We are not like them," he said. "Maybe we will do nothing with them because we respect the human being."

NEMIR SALEH NEMIR talked to me in the auto parts store he runs on the outskirts of Nablus. He is a bulky man with a large head, friendly and kind to strangers, but with a worried expression on his face. Like Dmadi, he had also been through the torture routine in the prison: the confinement in a painful position while exposed to the weather, the beatings, and a second confinement in a miniature closet. He began to cough as he told his story, continued coughing at what seemed regular and precise intervals throughout the interview, and grew more and more withdrawn as the tale went on. By the end, every answer seemed an effort and was given in as few words as possible.

Nemir said that the Nahal troops had hit him primarily on the legs and lower back. No bones were broken, but he later had an operation on his kidney, which he believed was damaged in the beating. When I asked what an appropriate punishment would be for the men who did the beating, he said, "I would hang them."

NONE OF THE victims I spoke with had collected any compensation from the Israeli government for their injuries. Several had gone to Abed Assali, an Arab lawyer in Jerusalem, and had asked him to pursue their case, and so I visited Assali to see what might have happened. Assali has a long and honorable record in human rights cases and is mentioned in the groundbreaking exposé of torture in Israel published in the London *Sunday Times* in 1977. His practice was entirely in defending Palestinians in military court, and virtually no defendant ever wins there. He was not paid by the state, and sometimes the wages for his work did not cover the cost of the photocopies of court records. He was outspoken and unafraid, believing that Israel needed him—he was a lawyer who defended Palestinians in military court and thus part of the show of democracy at work.

Assali told me that nothing had been filed in the case of the victims of the Nahal beating, and it seemed certain to me that in all likelihood, nothing ever would be. He said he had advised the men who came to him that filing for damages on the basis of purely physical injuries was not worth the effort, that in most cases a lawyer's fees would amount to more than the paltry sums paid to such victims. Assali said that he thought the men were not sure that they wanted to press their claims, that they might fear going to court, that they might fear retaliation from the army if they did, though Assali believed fears of retaliation were groundless. He said he had advised the men to get a psychologist to document psychological damage. This would not be easy for the Nahal victims. There is no well-trodden path for them to follow, no ready bank of Palestinian and Israeli psychologists and psychiatrists who commonly make those sort of assessments, no lawyers who specialize solely in getting such compensation for their clients. The compensation-for-victims industry, so well developed in Northern Ireland, hardly exists at all in the Occupied Territories. A torturer has virtual immunity, as do his employers.

ON JUNE 23, 1992, Yitzhak Rabin, the author of the beatings policy, was elected prime minister of Israel. In 1994, he shared the Nobel Peace Prize with Palestinian leader Yasser Arafat and Israeli foreign minister Shimon Peres. Rabin was assassinated on November 4, 1995, by Yigal Amir, a right-wing Israeli university student.

{15}

CHICAGO

The Public Is Not Aroused

O N AUGUST 8, 1989, I watched Commander Burge and Detectives
O'Hara and Yucaitis walk out of Judge Duff's courtroom cleared
of all charges, secure in their jobs, and pleased with their lawyer,
William Kunkle, whose bills—having run into hundreds of thousands
of dollars—had been paid by city taxpayers. There was no great storm
of protest at the verdict. The city's two major daily newspapers—the
Tribune and the *Sun-Times,* had not paid much attention to the second
trial, failing to note the policemen's altered defense, the dependence
of that defense upon the word of a convicted perjurer, and the notion
that the radiator, broken during the first trial, was working during
the second. The papers reported the jury's decision, but said no more
about it.

Wilson's lawyers promised to appeal, though their resources by that
time had been severely stretched; they had spent years on the case
without compensation. Flint Taylor, Jeff Haas, and John Stainthorp
had reached a point during the interlude between the two civil trials
when they began to doubt whether they should carry on. Their emotional, psychological, and financial resources had been worn so thin,
and the prospect of another trial with Judge Duff had been so daunt-
ing, that when they raised the matter for a vote in the office at large,
there were strong and reasonable voices suggesting that they drop the
case. In an interview in September 1994, Taylor could no longer recall
the number of votes for and against, but did remember that the

margin was very thin. He said that although the second trial before
Judge Duff was even more frustrating than the first, morale in the
office and on the defense team actually improved; when the trial was
over, they felt they stood a good chance to prevail in the U.S. Court of
Appeals.

I should not give the impression that no one in the city was concerned with the torture allegations. Citizens Alert, a police watchdog
group that had some credibility with the Chicago Police Board, was
pestering board members and police superintendent LeRoy Martin
about the list of Area 2 victims that the PLO had compiled. Wilson's
lawyers and their supporters formed a group that called itself the
Task Force to Confront Police Violence, and they organized demonstrations and street protests, which they believe were pivotal and I
consider small and easily ignored. They did arouse the halfhearted
interest of various members of the city council, and as a result the
council eventually agreed to hold hearings. The first session, however,
was scheduled for Christmas Eve 1990, which seemed to be a parliamentary trick, an attempt to make certain that few would attend and
that news coverage would be minimal. Although the day's brief session ended with the promise that more would follow, none ever did.

In January 1991, Amnesty International issued a report asking for a
full-scale inquiry into the allegations that Area 2 detectives had systematically tortured criminal suspects between 1972 and 1984. While
the report contained no new evidence, it did lend the prestige of the
international human rights organization to the drive to get to the bottom of what occurred at Area 2. Wilson's lawyers and their task force
held a press conference and released the report. Asked to respond to
the issues Amnesty raised, Mayor Richard Daley said that the system
of investigating complaints was working just fine. Daley was running
for re-election at the time, and his defenders claimed the Amnesty
report was merely an attempt to tarnish the mayor in the eyes of the
voters.

In the meantime, however, David Fogel, the chief administrator of
the police department's Office of Professional Standards, had decided
that there was good reason to reopen the investigation that the agency
had botched so badly eight years earlier. Fogel had been appointed to
the position by Daley's predecessor, Harold Washington, the city's first

African American mayor, and on a few occasions during his tenure in office, Fogel showed himself to be something of a maverick. In one 1987 memo he had written that 30 percent of his investigators were "irremediably incompetent. . . . part of the inherited politically corrupt heritage" that the Washington administration was saddled with. "The troops love OPS," Fogel wrote. ". . . [It] actually operates to immunize police from internal discipline, increases their overtime, leads to an enormous 'paper storm' and has institutionalized lying. . . . I have come to the conclusion that OPS gives the appearance of formal justice, but actually helps to institutionalize subterfuge and injustice."

On March 27, 1990, with no publicity or fanfare, Fogel chose two of his best investigators and directed them to the Wilson case. He ordered Francine Sanders to analyze the particulars of the case and Michael Goldston to find out if there had indeed been a pattern of abuse by Area 2 detectives. Fogel retired a few weeks later, but his successor, Gayle Shines, an African American lawyer appointed by Mayor Daley, received the reports of the two investigators enthusiastically. She submitted the reports to police superintendent Martin in November 1990, two months before the Amnesty report was released, and in her cover letter she praised the work of her two investigators as "a masterful job."

Investigator Sanders had concluded that "the only reasonable explanation for Wilson's injuries" was that they "were sustained during Wilson's detention in an interview room on the second floor of Area Two Headquarters and that they occurred at the hands of the police and under the sanction of the officer in charge . . . Lieutenant Jon Burge." She did not shy away from difficult conclusions, finding that Burge had indeed administered electric shock and that Wilson had been burned. Sanders recommended that charges should be sustained against Burge, Yucaitis, and O'Hara.

In his separate report, investigator Goldston listed the names of fifty victims allegedly mistreated at Area 2 between 1973 and 1986, and grouped them by the techniques deployed by the perpetrators (electroshock, suffocation, hanging by handcuffs, etc.). He concluded that "abuse did occur and it was systematic. . . . The type of abuse described was not limited to the usual beating, but went into such esoteric areas as psychological techniques and planned torture. . . .

Particular command members were aware of the systematic abuse and perpetuated it either by actively participating in same or failing to take any action to bring it to an end."

Police superintendent Martin did not like what he had been given to read, perhaps in part because he had been Burge's supervisor at Area 2 for nine months in 1983 and hence seemed to be implicated, though not by name. He asked for clarifications and revisions, then sat on both reports for more than a year, doing nothing, as the date for his scheduled retirement approached. Finally, on November 8, 1991, the superintendent suspended Burge, Yucaitis, and O'Hara without pay, and formal charges were filed with the police board seeking their permanent dismissal.

The police board hearings were scheduled for February 10, 1992. On February 7, U.S. District Court Judge Milton Shadur ordered city attorneys to release both the Sanders and Goldston reports, which the city had fought hard to keep secret. The Chicago media gave the story prominent coverage, and as a result, almost twenty years after the first complaint of torture had been filed, the public got some impression of the scope of the situation. Mayor Daley found himself denouncing the work of his employees. "These are only allegations," he said. "These are not substantiated cases." Superintendent Martin said he was "furious" about the allegation that his department had condoned "poor conduct."

Surprisingly, the city's journalists did not seize on Goldston's list of victims as fertile territory for further investigation, but instead treated the report as a day's worth of news. The editorial pages were silent. The only commentary was provided by nationally syndicated *Tribune* columnist Mike Royko, who on February 27, 1992, sided with Burge and his comrades. Royko said that the Amnesty report had been "a publicity stunt that worked"; that the suspended policemen had "excellent records" (in fact, Burge had been cited in more than half of the incidents in the Goldston report in which the accused policemen could be identified); that the victims should not be believed because they were convicted criminals; and that if the case continued, half the inmates in Stateville penitentiary would come up with similar allegations against the three cops. Addressing the small group of protesters who had sought Burge's firing, Royko asked, "Have you had any first-hand experience with [the three police officers], and did they ever torture you? If not, get a life."

Mike Fahey, whose brother, Officer William Fahey, had been shot dead by Andrew Wilson, had long been incensed by what he saw as the continuing persecution of Burge, O'Hara, and Yucaitis, and he organized a benefit for the three, scheduled for February 25 at the auditorium of Teamsters Local 705. The event was announced at police roll calls throughout the city, attendance was encouraged, and tickets were sold at $20 each. Many policemen who didn't know the facts of the case were angered by the mere fact that it was still going on, that disciplinary hearings could be held against a policeman ten years after a complaint had first been filed. When I arrived at the Teamsters hall on the night of the event, it was packed with off-duty policemen. The Chicago Building Department's posted capacity for the hall was one thousand. Newspaper estimates put the crowd at four thousand; the entire Chicago police force numbers about twelve thousand. In the chaotic assembly, I spotted only two African Americans.

T shirts and badges were selling fast. Both proclaimed, "We support B.O.Y. Today Them. Tomorrow You? Burge, O'Hara, Yucaitis." Beer and pizza were served. Women passed through the crowd selling raffle tickets; the prizes included airline flights, hotel weekends, restaurant meals, and a .38-caliber snub-nosed revolver. When the ceremony began, a priest read the names of twenty-four Chicago police officers who had been killed in the line of duty since 1982 ("James Doyle, Richard O'Brien, William Fahey, Martin Darcy, Hamp McMikel, Larry J. Vincent . . .") while the Emerald Society Pipe and Drum Band played mournfully in the background. A series of speakers blamed Mayor Daley for the suspension of the three policemen, though Daley had never displayed any enthusiasm for the act. And when Burge, O'Hara, and Yucaitis were brought forth, the crowd roared in approval, clapping, yelling, and whistling with great enthusiasm. Burge thanked the organizing committee and the command personnel who had allowed their names to be used on the committee's masthead "even though it may have been politically unwise."

It was politically unwise because the city's lawyers had, in effect, changed sides. After denying that Wilson had been tortured during the two civil trials, they were now arguing just the opposite. To make that argument before the police board, the city recruited Dan Reidy, a former assistant U.S. attorney in private practice who was well known for having directed the prosecution of a series of corrupt judges and lawyers who had plagued Cook County courts for more than a decade. Wilson's attorneys watched from the sidelines as Reidy picked up where they had left off. The former prosecutor had a much easier task. He did not have to prove that Burge was guilty beyond a reasonable doubt; he was required only to show that "a preponderance of the evidence" indicated that Burge had abused Wilson. He did not have to contend with the man voted worst on the federal bench, nor was he bound by Judge Duff's narrow interpretation of the federal rules of evidence and so could call many victims to testify. The judge's chair in the police board case was occupied by hearing officer Michael Berland, a lawyer whose job was to conduct an orderly hearing and then pass on the transcript and evidence to the eight-member board. The board members would examine the transcript and evidence, consult with Berland on his impressions of the credibility of witnesses, and then decide the fate of Burge and his comrades.

The hearings lasted for five weeks. More than 3,800 pages of testimony and thousands of pages from previous court proceedings were turned over to the police board, and then the players sat back, waiting for an opinion. It was a long wait, but eleven months later, on February 10, 1993, the board issued a cautiously worded decision, as if they were afraid to shed too much light in so dark a corner. They mentioned the marks on Wilson's ears but offered no conclusions about how they got there. They said they were impressed by the testimony of Melvin Jones, the man allegedly shocked nine days before Wilson was arrested, but they never flatly stated that Burge had shocked anyone or that the commander had possessed any electrical devices. They concluded that Wilson was burned at Area 2 but they did not say who burned him. The board members never referred to the treatment as torture. Wilson instead received "physical abuse."

The board concluded that Burge "did . . . strike and/or kick and/or otherwise physically abuse or maltreat" Wilson, that as commanding officer he did not stop others from engaging in the abuse, and that he did not secure prompt medical attention when it was clearly called for. Detectives Yucaitis and O'Hara were judged guilty of failing to stop the abuse, failing to report it, and failing to secure medical attention in its wake. The board then said that it had voted to dismiss Commander Burge from the ranks of the police. The board members seemed to have decided that Detectives Yucaitis and O'Hara had already been punished enough, having gone fifteen months without pay—and so they were declared eligible for reinstatement.

Police Superintendent Matt Rodriguez, elevated to the post after LeRoy Martin's retirement, clearly had no difficulty accepting the idea that torture had occurred at Area 2. He attempted to impose his own punishment on O'Hara and Yucaitis, reducing their rank to patrolmen. In January 1994, however, a labor arbitrator ruled that the reduction in rank imposed by Rodriguez was a violation of the union contract, and Yucaitis and O'Hara were restored to the detective ranks and awarded back pay for the time they had served as patrolmen.

The three policemen appealed the board's ruling in Cook County Circuit Court. On February 10, 1994, Judge Thomas O'Brien issued a thirty-nine-page opinion on the matter. O'Brien was plainly uncomfortable with accepting the truthfulness of Andrew Wilson's testimony and clearly wanted to overturn the board, but he felt bound by the law, which, he said, required him to "defer to the Board on the weight of evidence and credibility of witnesses. In this case, the Court does so with the most difficult restraint."

O'Brien's ruling withstood appeals. Jon Burge and the Chicago Police Department were well and truly divorced.

IN THE MEANTIME, the PLO's appeal of the verdict in Andrew Wilson's civil trial had been heard by the judges of the U.S. Seventh Circuit Court of Appeals. On October 4, 1993, a three-judge panel headed by Chief Judge Richard Posner issued a decision expressing frank incredulity at what had gone on in Judge Duff's courtroom. Posner wrote that Duff had "stretched the concept of relevance beyond the breaking point," that he had allowed William Kunkle, the policemen's attorney, to load the jury with "a mass of inflammatory evidence having little or no relevance to the issues in this trial (as distinct from Wilson's murder trial) . . . and thus turn the trial of the defendants into a trial of the plaintiff." Among the examples Posner cited were Kunkle's use of Officer Fahey's service revolver in closing arguments, the display of Wilson's tattoo, and the introduction of Wilson's eyeglasses, found at the murder scene. "Even a murderer has a right to be free from torture," Posner wrote, "and the correlative right to present his claim of torture to a jury that has not been whipped into a frenzy of hatred."

Posner went on to say that Duff should not have dismissed the charges against Detective McKenna, O'Hara's partner, and should have allowed two of the victims the PLO had presented to testify. The appellate judge seemed particularly skeptical about the testimony of jailhouse informant William Coleman, who had appeared more credible than he should have because Judge Duff had closed various avenues of impeachment to Wilson's lawyers. Addressing Duff's exclusion of the testimony of British tabloid journalist Gregory Miskiw, Posner pointed out that it had been Miskiw's job to determine Coleman's reputation for trustworthiness and that in doing that job Miskiw had spent a fair amount of time with the convict and had interviewed members of Coleman's "community." As a result, Posner said, Miskiw had "an apparently well-substantiated opinion" that William Coleman was "a consummate liar," an opinion that was not hearsay but personal knowledge, and the reporter should have been allowed to convey that opinion to the jury.

In regard to the city's involvement—the question of whether the city had a policy of abusing people suspected of killing policemen—Posner and his two colleagues found that while the city may have been "careless, maybe even grossly so given the volume of complaints," Wilson's lawyers had not established a policy. Ineptitude on the part of a police chief, the court said, did not demonstrate approval. The three-judge panel dismissed the policy charges against the city and sent the rest of the case back to federal district court for a third trial.

AFTER SEEMING INVULNERABLE in the first two civil trials, Burge had now suffered a series of losses. The OPS investigation had concluded he was guilty. His old ally, police superintendent LeRoy Martin, had suspended him without pay. The police board took his job away, and the new police superintendent had made no objection and had offered no recognition of Burge's years of service. The Cook County Circuit Court had denied his appeal. And the United States

Court of Appeals had determined that he would have to stand trial in Wilson's civil suit one more time, this time with a new judge. There was some legal precedent that would allow that judge to simply adopt the findings of the police board regarding the policemen's guilt and hold a hearing simply to sort out the question of damages. If the judge did decide that a third trial was in order, he might allow the PLO to introduce into evidence the fact that Burge had lost his job because the police board believed that he had "physically abused" Andrew Wilson. It seemed likely that a parade of alleged victims would march to the stand, and their sheer numbers might outweigh their criminal histories in the minds of a jury. The repeated television broadcast of videotape of the beating of Rodney King by police in Los Angeles, a beating that had occurred after the two trials in Judge Duff's courtroom, might have raised the skepticism of the American public, and any jury selected for a third trial might have a lot less trouble believing that strange and brutal things could go on between policemen and African Americans accused of felonies. There was also the danger that a roach-clip defense might evoke laughter, not serious consideration. Jailhouse informant William Coleman might not cooperate, and even if he did, he might seem far less credible a second time around.

So there was some pressure on Burge, Yucaitis, and O'Hara's attorneys to arrange an out-of-court settlement, and they probably would have but for a brazen decision made by the city's attorneys. In March 1994, a month after the police board decision was upheld by Judge O'Brien in Cook County Circuit Court, the corporation counsel sent Burge and his colleagues a letter saying that they would not be indemnified, that the city would not pay for any damages awarded Wilson because they had "acted outside the scope of their employment," meaning they had acted for their own ends, not for the city's. This meant that Wilson's lawyers could only pursue the policemen's assets, and in Burge's case, there was allegedly not much to pursue. In the first civil trial Burge had said that he was less than solvent, that if you totaled all his assets and liabilities you would find he was $17,000 in the hole. The PLO had recorded more than six thousand hours of labor on the case, for which they had not received a penny. (In contrast, by May 1995, the city had paid almost $850,000 to William Kunkle, the policemen's attorney.)

If the city was able to establish a precedent of refusing to indemnify policemen in misconduct cases, they would essentially kill all subsequent lawsuits by victims, as no lawyers would take on such a case knowing that even if they won, they might not even recoup their costs, much less secure compensation for the victims.

The city's attorneys argued that the city had reached its decision "not in pursuit of any benefit, or to obtain an advantage in this litigation, but rather as a necessary consequence of its pursuit of the truth. . . . When police officers deviate from their investigation and cruelly torture a suspect and deny him necessary medical assistance, they are no longer serving the City's business. . . . Torture of arrestees cannot, as a matter of sound public policy and logic, be found to fall within the scope of Chicago police officers. . . . The city seeks to underscore its opposition to the abuse of police power by placing the financial costs of such abuses directly on the officers."

What made that argument particularly galling was its portrait of a client concerned with pursuing the truth and outraged by electric shock and police misconduct. The city had not pursued the truth; the truth had pursued the city. Had the city been interested in the truth, it would have acted upon receipt of the Sanders and Goldston reports; instead it sat on them for more than a year and then fought hard to prevent their release to the public. The city had disciplined none of the police officers accused in the other Area 2 cases of shock, suffocation, beating, and other abuse, even when those officers had been caught lying under oath. (By the time the corporation counsel was making its argument, the PLO's list of victims had grown to sixty-one men and one woman who claimed they were physically abused by Commander Burge or by detectives who were serving or had served under his command.) The corporation counsel's alleged outrage seemed to be directed at the sole case of electric shock that threatened the city's wallet.

In admitting that electric shock had been deployed in the Wilson and Jones cases and in using the word "torture" to describe it, the city attorneys were going beyond what had been said in the police board decision, the decision on which the city based its argument. (The police board had never used the word torture and had set down no conclusion regarding electric shock.) The corporation counsel seemed to be making these admissions not out of sincere outrage and horror but out of a desire to make Burge's actions seem as extreme as possible, and thus outside the scope of his employment, and thus outside the responsibility of the city and the realm of its treasury.

Oddly, the city's arguments had the effect of briefly uniting Wilson and Burge. Attorneys for both men argued that the city's position was preposterous.

U.S. District Court Judge Robert Gettleman had replaced Judge Duff as the case's arbiter, and he heard those arguments, the PLO's motion for summary judgment (Wilson's attorneys, citing ample legal precedent, asked the judge to adopt the findings of the police board rather than go through a third federal trial that would largely repeat the hearings held by the board), and the policemen's demands for a third trial. After sorting through all of those arguments and poring over reams of motions, Gettleman quietly did the remarkable. He dismissed the city's claim that it was not responsible and granted Wilson's motion for summary judgment. In mid-July 1996, he ordered the city to pay more than a million dollars in damages.

According to Gettleman's ruling, $900,016 was to be paid to Wilson's attorneys and $100,000 was to be paid to Wilson. That $100,000 would actually go to the widow and two children of Officer Fahey, whom Wilson had killed, as they had won a wrongful death suit years earlier that allowed them to garnish any money awarded Wilson in his civil rights suit.

The city appealed Gettleman's ruling. On July 21, 1997, the U.S. Court of Appeals ruled in Wilson's favor. Judge Posner, who had written the opinion expressing incredulity about what had gone on in Judge Duff's courtroom, concluded that the city's "beyond the scope of employment" argument "borders on the frivolous."

JUDGE GETTLEMAN's decision might have prompted a great deal of civic soul-searching. It did not. The People's Law Office abided by their client's wishes that they not seek publicity, and the month of July 1996 passed without a single newspaper, television, or radio station reporting that the most remarkable case of torture in the city's history had been settled in favor of the plaintiff. August went by without a single editorial, without a single politician demanding a full-scale investigation of the Area 2 allegations. By year's end, no one had yet reported that the corporation counsel of the city of Chicago had changed its mind and now embraced the idea that city policemen had tortured suspects with electric shock. Judge Posner's decision in July 1997 also achieved little notice. The *Chicago Sun-Times* gave it a single paragraph on page 24. The *Tribune* didn't mention it. Television and radio stations did not utter a word.

That coverage seemed to reflect the attitude of the community. People in Chicago cannot claim not to know that men were tortured in police custody. The police board's decision to dismiss Burge from the force had received prominent media coverage. The *Chicago Sun-Times,* for example, turned over its front page to a large color photograph of Burge and the headline "Cop Loses Job over Torture." At various times the story was mentioned in the national press (the *New York Times,* for example, mentioned it when the Fraternal Order of Police let it be known that it was going to feature Burge, Yucaitis, and O'Hara on its float in the St. Patrick's Day parade, a float that was to bear the legend "Miscarriages of Justice"). Public television stations around the country ran a documentary on the affair in 1994, and Burge's subsequent failure to win reinstatement by court order received additional coverage in the local media. While no one held full-scale hearings and neither of the main daily papers carried out an investigation, it cannot be said that the torture allegations were not publicized and known at some level by millions of people in the Chicago area and around the country.

The knowledge that torture had occurred, however, was not translated into any organized attempt to provide relief for the Area 2 victims, ten of whom sat on death row. Years passed with no public acknowledgment that many had been convicted by evil means, no notion that some of those convicted might be innocent, no wringing of hands about the impending execution of men whose guilt was questionable. None of the perpetrators were indicted or even effectively investigated.

The allegations did prompt some legislative action: a bill, signed by Governor Jim Edgar in 1992, not to aid victims but to shield perpetrators. The legislation established a five-year statute of limitations on administrative proceedings for police brutality. Commander Burge had been brought up on disciplinary charges nine years after he tortured Andrew Wilson, and the supporters of the bill felt that was unfair.

The legal community was not galvanized to action. The People's Law Office's list of sixty-two victims was not the result of sixty-two phone calls from defense attorneys, public defenders, and former prosecutors, each recalling an Area 2 case handled in the past. The PLO's list grew largely because one victim led to another and word traveled around various jailhouses that someone was trying to document torture at Area 2. No one made any formal attempt to locate victims in prisons or in the community (some of those allegedly tortured were never convicted and others were never charged).

Although the few federal judges who have heard Area 2 cases have sometimes sided with the victims, or at least have not shut the door on them, state and county judges have with few exceptions been happy to side with the perpetrators. The case of Stanley Howard, for example, was heard by Cook County Circuit Court Judge John Mannion, who saw no reason why he should be recused although he had previously been employed as a policeman at Area 2. In the case of Aaron Patterson, Judge John Morrissey refused to allow the defense to introduce photographs of etchings Patterson had made in a bench and on a door frame in the interrogation room. The etchings, made with a paper clip Patterson found on the floor, indicated that he had been tortured, denied a lawyer, and denied access to his father—a Chicago policeman. Judge Morrissey dismissed the etchings as "hearsay." Patterson was convicted of a double murder solely on the basis of his alleged confession, which he had refused to sign. No physical evidence linked him to the scene. Judge Thomas Maloney dismissed Darrell Cannon's claims that he had been shocked in the genitals by three of the seven officers whom OPS investigator Goldston would later name as "players"—policemen whose names came up regularly in the torture allegations. Cannon was convicted of murder and given a life sentence. Judge Maloney subsequently went to prison for taking bribes to fix murder cases, a practice that federal prosecutors say he engaged in both before and after he so cavalierly dismissed Cannon's claims of torture. U.S. Court of Appeals Judge Ilana Rovner later commented that Maloney may have operated his courtroom like a business: if he came down hard on a murder defendant who did not bribe him, he could both keep his conviction rate up and advertise the desirability of bribing the judge.

One of the exceptions among the state judiciary was Illinois Appellate Court Judge Dom Rizzi. In December 1989, before the Amnesty International report on Area 2, before OPS investigators Sanders and Goldston had begun their investigation, and long before Judge Gettleman ruled in the Wilson case, Rizzi addressed the issue of torture at Area 2 in *The People v. Gregory Banks*. Banks had testified that three Area 2 detectives put a gun in his mouth and threatened to blow his head off, beat him with a flashlight, kicked him about the ankle and stomach, and said, "We have something for niggers" just before putting a plastic bag over his head. He claimed he was suffocated twice before he agreed to give a statement confessing to involvement in a murder. During Banks's trial, his attorneys tried to introduce evidence that thirteen months before Banks was arrested, a man named Lee Holmes had accused the same detectives of precisely the same treatment: beating with a flashlight and suffocation with a plastic bag. The trial judge ruled that as the allegations were more than a year old, they were too remote to be admissible as evidence of the modus operandi of the detectives. Banks was convicted and sentenced to fifty years in jail.

Appellate Judge Rizzi issued his opinion six years later. He found it more likely that Area 2 detectives had tortured Banks than that they had not and he and the other two judges on the panel excoriated lower-court judges who seemed reluctant to act on claims of torture: "In this regard, trial judges must bear in mind that while we no longer see cases involving the use of the rack and the thumbscrew to obtain confessions, we are seeing cases, like the present case, involving punching, kicking, and placing a plastic bag over a suspect's head to obtain confessions. . . . When trial judges do not courageously and forthrightly exercise their responsibility to suppress confessions obtained by such means, they pervert our criminal justice system as much as the few misguided law enforcement officers who obtain confessions in utter disregard of the rights guaranteed to every citizen— including criminal suspects—by our constitution. Moreover, trial judges must be most circumspect when it appears that a right guaranteed to every citizen by our constitution may have been violated by police brutality or racial discrimination, for those affected are invariably the poorest, the weakest and the least educated, who are not sophisticated enough or do not have the resources to see and ensure that they are not denied the protections afforded by the rights and guarantees of our constitution." Banks was released from prison. The state declined to prosecute him again. In August 1993, the city paid him $92,500 to settle the civil suit he filed against the detectives. The detectives involved were not censured in any way.

The Illinois Supreme Court later referred to the *Banks* case in ruling on *The People v. Madison Hobley*. Hobley, a death-row inmate, alleged that he also had been abused by detectives at Area 2, one of whom had taken Banks's confession. At trial Hobley's attorneys had wanted to introduce evidence that the detectives who abused him had used the same methods on another man three years earlier. The Illinois Supreme Court looked to Rizzi's ruling in *Banks*. What they saw was not a pattern of abuse by Area 2 detectives, not a coincidence of both Hobley and Banks alleging suffocation in the same police station by detectives from the same unit, not the fact that one particular detective was involved in both cases. What the Supreme Court saw in the *Banks* ruling was a thirteen-month gap between torture incidents. The Supreme Court ruled that a thirteen-month gap made Banks's torture allegations relevant, while Hobley's allegations, separated by thirty-eight months, were "much more remote than in *Banks*" and could therefore be ignored.

Hobley remains on death row, awaiting execution for a crime he may not have committed.

THE AREA 2 CASES offered a chance for a Western democracy to show how torturers can be pursued and prosecuted. No coup was possible, as was the case in Chile or Argentina, where prosecution of torturers might have meant the end of the newly installed democratic regime. The police force would not have been decimated, since the number of alleged torturers was relatively small: although scores of detectives have worked at Area 2 in the last twenty years, the allegations of torture were made against a core group of about fifteen men, with other detectives appearing in single performances. That core group could have been easily identified: OPS investigator Goldston named a small group of "players"; the anonymous letter writer from Area 2 named a group of "Burge's Asskickers"; and two sets of defense attorneys have collated data that matches perpetrators with specific cases. Helpful officers might have been found by interviewing Area 2 detectives who disliked the Burge gang and their treatment of suspects—a list of detectives who held Burge in low esteem had been provided by the anonymous letter writer, who was certain that some would talk because they were disgusted about what had happened. Had any prosecutor shown interest, it seems entirely possible that the anonymous writer would have come forward, and he or she knew a lot (one of the letters, for example, claimed that Burge had gotten rid of one electrical device by throwing it over the side of his boat). For a federal prosecutor, the statute of limitations problems presented by the age of the cases could have been solved by prosecuting for perjury or deprivation of civil rights. For the Chicago City Council there was no statute of limitations, nor was there one for the local media. At the very least, some preventive steps might have been taken. According to a 1993 study by the Police Executive Research Forum, one-third of the nation's large police departments were videotaping interrogations and/or the taking of confessions. Nothing of the sort was then in the works for Chicago.

The citizens of Chicago were unmoved. The clergy showed no leadership; with the exception of a few mostly low-ranking ministers, religious officials were silent. In the absence of any clamor, politicians showed no interest. Reporters, hearing no complaint, conducted no investigations, and editorial writers launched no crusades. State and federal prosecutors, feeling no pressure from the press or the public, hearing no moral commentary from the religious quarter, prosecuted no one. Judges, seeing no officer indicted and hearing no officer speak against his comrades, could therefore comfortably dismiss claims of torture, and with few exceptions, they did.

I found I did not have to journey far to learn that torture is something we abhor only when it is done to someone we like, preferably someone we like who lives in another country.

AFTER HIS REMOVAL from the force, Jon Burge left Chicago and moved to Florida, where he now resides. Since he was never convicted of any crime related to the torture allegations, his pension was not disturbed by his firing.

During his final years as a Chicago policeman, he and I sat in various courtrooms day after day, month after month, year after year, listening to witnesses call him a fine policeman or a torturer. During breaks in those sessions we had occasional brief conversations, and he consented to an interview in September 1989, a time when he had been cleared of all charges by the second Wilson jury, a time when he seemed secure in his job as commander of Area 3 detectives, a time when few would have predicted the precipitous fall from grace he was about to endure.

His office at Area 3 was decorated with photographs of police softball and bowling teams, various sports trophies, an autographed picture of then Superintendent Martin (who would later suspend him), and a photo of the St. Jude's League parade (the league helps the families of police officers killed in action). Of his many commendations, the one that he had framed and hung on the wall was for his role in the investigation of the murders of Officers Fahey and O'Brien.

At that point the PLO's appeal was under way and the commander was limited in what he could say about the Wilson trials and the accusations against him. "The only statement I can make is that the jury has spoken," he said. "I testified at both trials. I did nothing wrong." He went on to say that the allegations that he had been abusing prisoners since 1968 were "gross misrepresentations."

In the course of our meeting, I brought up a couple of stories I had heard about him: the tale of how he had saved the life of a black woman who was pointing a gun at her head and the story, told to me by a former Area 2 detective, about how Burge had spotted a robbery of a Fotomat before it actually took place. He was surprised that I knew of the incidents and seemed uncomfortable telling a story in which he was a hero. He had a good sense of humor and didn't seem to take himself too seriously; I enjoyed his company. When we ran into each other in various courtrooms in the years that followed, he never displayed any resentment of the fact that I had concluded he was not innocent of the torture of Andrew Wilson and that I had said as much in print.

{16}

Bystanders

ALTHOUGH the men who tortured Jim Auld and the other hooded men were known to the authorities, none were ever punished. The politicians and army officers who gave the orders for the torture and protected those who carried it out did not suffer a moment in jail or even a moment's threat of indictment.

The men from the Nahal Brigade who broke bones on the orders of Colonel Meir were also never called to account. Meir did suffer emotionally during his long trial, and the penalty ultimately imposed on him diminished his pension significantly, but he did not spend a single day in jail. His notoriety subsequently proved to be an asset, and he is now more comfortable than he was before the men from Hawara and Beita were so viciously clubbed.

In Chicago, Commander Burge lost his job and Detectives O'Hara and Yucaitis served fifteen-month suspensions, but none of them were charged with any crime. Their colleagues at Area 2 who, according to Office of Professional Standards investigator Goldston, had participated in systematic abuse, were never called before any judge, jury, or hearing officer to answer for their crimes.

It takes no genius to see a pattern here, and that pattern is repeated throughout the world: torturers are rarely punished, and when they are, the punishment rarely corresponds to the severity of the crime.

. . .

WHEN A DICTATORSHIP is overthrown by a democratic regime, torture squads typically elude punishment because the new government is not entirely secure. After the junta fell in Argentina, for example, the new government lived in constant fear of a coup; the leaders of the ruling junta were prosecuted, but to avoid riling the armed forces further, there was no great purge of torturers, no indictments of whole companies of men. In other countries in which civilian governments have taken over from a regime that practiced torture, the new leaders, seeing the need for order and continuity, have decided it was not practical to replace every judge, prosecutor, and policeman who held office during the dark ages; as a result, the bureaucracy that supported or tolerated torture remains in place, a bureaucracy understandably not interested in investigating the sins of the past. In other nations where torture has been systematic, reform governments have become convinced that what their country needs is reconciliation and healing, that prosecution of torturers would once again polarize society, that the best course is to avoid indictments for human rights violations. Other liberating governments have declined to prosecute either because they quickly find the torturer's tools quite useful or because the liberators have a history of torture themselves.

Democracies and authoritarian regimes sometimes offer the same rationales for failing to prosecute torturers. The morale of the security forces, for example, is as sacred in a democracy as it is in an undemocratic regime. Putting soldiers or policemen on the witness stand is politically dangerous. They might, after all, name high-ranking officers or public officials who sanctioned the treatment.

Furthermore, it is often difficult to mount an effective prosecution. Torture usually occurs in a closed room without independent witnesses. Sometimes the victims have been blindfolded or they are dead, so although their injuries indicate they were tortured and it is not hard to determine what unit was responsible for their custody, it may be impossible to determine which man in particular attached the electrodes, performed the rape, the near drowning, or the severe beating. Without predetention medical examinations, it is often difficult to prove that a victim's injuries were sustained in custody.

A prosecutor's task is made more difficult by the fact that torturers are often decorated soldiers or policemen who have served their country in time of need, men who often represent popular belief: they were tough on crime, or they were saving the country from subversion or immorality. The victims, on the other hand, may hold political or religious beliefs not in favor in the larger society, or they may come from some lesser class that is viewed as a threat to the society at large: gooks, niggers, Paddies, Arabs, Jews, criminals, agitators, heretics, labor organizers, stone throwers, flag wavers, singers of nationalist songs, terrorists, friends of terrorists, and so on. A judge or jury choosing between an erect and courageous torturer and an unpopular victim often has an easier time identifying with the torturer.

In various nations in which notorious regimes have fallen, there has been a public acknowledgment that people were tortured. In democracies of long standing in which torture has taken place, however, denial takes hold and official acknowledgment is extremely slow in coming, if it appears at all. The response of those societies is fairly predictable and can be charted in thematic, if not chronological, stages.

Consider, for example, the British reaction to the revelations that they were torturing the Northern Irish in 1971. The first stage of response was absolute and complete denial, accompanied by attacks on those who exposed the treatment. Northern Irish Prime Minister Brian Faulkner announced that there had been "no brutality of any kind." The London *Sunday Times* was denounced for printing "the fantasies of terrorists."

The second stage was to minimize the abuse. The government referred to it not as torture but as "interrogation in depth." Home Secretary Reginald Maulding proclaimed that there was "no permanent lasting injury whatever, physical or mental, to any of the men." The majority report of the Parker Commission proclaimed that any mental disorientation should disappear within hours, and, if it didn't, it might be the men's own fault, the product of anxiety caused by "guilty knowledge" and "fear of reprisals" from comrades for having allegedly given information. In the Compton Report, Sir Edmund Compton and his colleagues concluded that part of the torture had been done for the men's own good: the hooding kept the prisoners from identifying each other, thus preserving each man's security. The beating of Joe Clarke's hands had not occurred; his hands had been massaged by guards in order to restore circulation. The guards who forced men to perform strenuous exercises were merely trying to keep the prisoners warm.

A third stage is to disparage the victims. Lord Carrington judged them to be "thugs and murderers," while Reginald Maulding proclaimed, "It was necessary to take measures to fight terrorists, the murderous enemy. We must recognize them for what they are. They are criminals who wish to impose their own will by violence and terror." Yet after extensive torture and ostensibly extensive confessions about their acts of "violence and terror," none of the hooded men were charged with any crime.

A fourth stage is to justify the treatment on the grounds that it was effective or appropriate under the circumstances. Lord Balniel, junior minister of defense, said that there was no evidence of torture, ill-treatment, or brainwashing, and that the methods employed had produced "invaluable" information about a brutal, callous, and barbaric enemy. Compton proclaimed that the five techniques had been used on the men because it was "operationally necessary to obtain [information] as rapidly as possible in the interest of saving lives." On November 21, 1971, the *Sunday Times* poked holes in the apologists' claims, pointing out that if the interrogation methods used on the hooded men "were approved for use in any British police station, where the need for information is sometimes just as urgent as in Ulster, there would be universal outrage." The *Sunday Times* editorial staff dismissed the claim that cruel treatment was justified if it saved lives. How can you be sure, the paper asked, that the prisoner has the information you seek, that the lack of that information will indeed mean someone will die, and that cruel methods extract reliable information? The claim that lives were saved became even more suspect as time passed. The IRA was invigorated by new recruits inspired by the cruel treatment accorded the Catholic community, and in the calendar year following the introduction of internment, the number of shootings rose by 605 percent, the number of armed robberies increased 441 percent, and the number of deaths rose 268 percent.

A fifth component of a torturing society's defense is to charge that those who take up the cause of those tortured are aiding the enemies of the state. So when the Republic of Ireland persisted in its suit against the United Kingdom on behalf of the victims, the *Guardian* argued that the republic's government was "torturing Northern Ireland" by "force feeding the Provisionals [the Provisional IRA] with propaganda."

A sixth defense is that the torture is no longer occurring, and anyone who raises the issue is therefore "raking up the past." Northern Ireland Secretary Merlyn Rees leveled that charge at the Irish government when it persisted in its pursuit of the victims' cause five years after their ordeal. Fifteen years later, there was widespread support throughout the United Kingdom for the War Crimes Bill, which became law in May 1991 and which allowed for the prosecution of former Nazi officials for crimes committed fifty years earlier. (Lord Carrington and former Prime Minister Edwin Heath opposed the bill.) It is always easier to see torture in another country than in one's own.

A seventh component of a torturing bureaucracy is to put the blame on a few bad apples. In defending themselves before the European Court, the British proclaimed that it was not an administrative practice, but rather a few men exceeding their orders. If this had been the case, however, there would seem to be no reason why the torturers could not have been publicly named and prosecuted.

An eighth stage in a society's rationalization of its policy of torture is the common torturer's defense, presented to me by most of the former torturers I interviewed, that someone else does or has done much worse things. When the subject of the hooded men arose, it was common for the British government spokesmen and many editorial writers to respond by denouncing the IRA for its callous campaign of random murder, as if that justified the torture of randomly chosen men who, on the whole, were not members of the IRA. In the wake of the European Commission decision labeling the five techniques torture, the *Times* of London hastened to point out that Britain should not be "lumped together with regimes past or present in Greece, Brazil, Iran, Argentina." The *Times* argued that the techniques employed by those regimes put the victim in terror of the continuation of pain, and that that terror forced the victim to submit to the interrogator. The British techniques, the *Times* said, were not as evil because they were not designed to induce terror, but rather to induce a state of mental disorientation so that the victim's will to resist was lost.

A final rationalization of a torturing nation is that the victims will get over it. In a 1982 interview, General Harry Tuzo, the Oxford-educated commander of the army in Northern Ireland at the time Jim Auld and the others were tortured, claimed that the victims, who in

Tuzo's words had suffered not torture but "acute discomfort and humiliation," had been "very well compensated and looked after." "I personally would have thought," Tuzo said, "that they had got over it by now." Similarly, General Jacques Massu, the French commander who throughout his life staunchly defended the widespread use of torture by his troops during the Algerian war, dismissed the pains suffered by Henri Alleg, the European-born Jew who wrote a book about his experience as a victim of Massu's policy (*The Question,* George Braziller, 1958). Massu saw Alleg in 1970, thirteen years after he was tortured, and based on that viewing discerned that the torture survivor was in "reassuringly vigorous condition."

It is perhaps understandable that public officials accused of a crime as heinous as torture would react defensively and follow a predictable route of denial. What is perhaps more difficult to understand is the rampant indifference that grips most societies in the face of revelations of torture.

The indifference demonstrated by bystanders in the face of other people's suffering has been widely studied, particularly since the murder of twenty-eight-year-old Kitty Genovese on March 13, 1964, in Queens, New York. The murder was witnessed by thirty-eight of the victim's neighbors. During the thirty minutes that it took the killer to complete his act, not one of those thirty-eight people called the police or came to the young woman's aid.

In considering that incident, psychologists John Darley and Bibb Latane wondered if Genovese might have fared better had there been fewer onlookers. The two psychologists then designed a series of experiments to test the hypothesis that the greater the number of people who witness an emergency, the less likely it is that anyone will do anything about it.

In one experiment, New York University students were led, one by one, to small rooms. Each was told that he or she was part of a group of students, all sitting alone in similar rooms, all connected by microphones and headsets. During the course of a discussion about the pressures that students faced, the subjects heard one student—actually a confederate of the experimenters—confess that he was prone to seizures when tense. A few minutes later, subjects heard that same student break down and plead for help. The subjects had been led to believe that no instructor would be monitoring their conversation, so no one hearing the seizure was clearly in charge.

In an article on the experiment published in the *Journal of Personality and Social Psychology,* Darley and Latane reproduced a portion of the victim's speech, the ending of which went as follows: "I-er-if somebody could help me out it would-it would-er-er s-s-sure be-sure be good . . . because-er-there-er-er-a cause I-er-I-uh-I've got a-a one of the-er-sei—er-er-things coming on and-and-and I could really-er-use some help so if somebody would-er-give me a little h-help-uh-er-er-er-er-er could somebody-er-er-help-er-uh-uh-uh [choking sounds]. . . . I'm gonna die-er-er-I'm . . . gonna die-er-help-er-er-seizure-er [chokes, then quiet]."

The experiment was designed so that the subjects believed they could not communicate directly with each other—all believed that their microphones were turned off when it was not their turn to speak. Some subjects believed that they were part of a two-person group, and that therefore they alone had heard the young man's seizure. Other subjects believed that one other student had also heard the victim's pleas (a three-person group), and still others thought that four other people were listening when the breakdown occurred (a six-person group). The dependent variable was the time elapsed from the start of the victim's fit until the subject sought help. If six minutes passed after the end of the fit and the subject had not left his or her room, the experimenter entered the room and terminated the session.

Darley and Latane's theory about bystanders proved to be correct. All of the subjects who thought that they alone had heard the victim's seizure tried to get help, most leaving their room before the victim had even finished his speech. Eighty percent of those in the three-person groups sought help, albeit it a little more slowly than those in the two-person groups. But only 62 percent of those in the six-person groups left their room, and they moved at a considerably slower pace: 50 percent of the single bystanders bolted from the room within forty-five seconds of the start of the seizure, by which time none of the people in the six-person groups had yet reached the door. Males and females responded to the emergency with almost exactly the same frequency and speed.

Surprisingly, Darley and Latane did not find that the subjects who stayed in their seats were apathetic or unconcerned; in fact, those who did not respond to the emergency seemed more upset than those who did, often asking the experimenter who entered their rooms if the victim was all right. The two psychologists concluded that nonintervening subjects had not responded because they were mired in a state of indecision and internal conflict: "On the one hand, subjects worried about the guilt and shame they would feel if they did not help the person in distress. On the other hand, they were concerned not to make fools of themselves by overreacting, not to ruin the ongoing experiment by leaving their intercom, and not to destroy the anonymous nature of the situation which the experimenter had earlier stressed as important. . . . Caught between the two negative alternatives of letting the victim continue to suffer or the costs of rushing in to help, the nonresponding bystanders vacillated between them rather than choosing not to respond. This distinction may be academic to the victim, since he got no help in either case, but it is an extremely important one for arriving at an understanding of the causes of bystanders' failures to help."

Darley and Latane concluded by saying that individuals are not "noninterveners" because of some flaw in their personality, but rather because responsibility is diffused. As in the murder of Kitty Genovese, isolated individuals, knowing that others were also aware of the emergency but not knowing how those others were responding, did not attempt to intervene because they did not feel personally responsible.

Darley and Latane wondered if the results would be different if those individuals were not isolated, if they could talk to other bystanders. A layperson might imagine that when strangers are able to talk to each other about an emergency, they will be more likely to arrive at a decisive course of action—the old notion that two or three or six heads are better than one. Darley and Latane, however, suspected that the opposite might be true.

To test their beliefs, they established a situation in which varying numbers of male Columbia University students filled out forms in a room that slowly filled with smoke. The students were witnessing a potential emergency that threatened themselves as well as others. It was not a subtle process: many of the subjects noticed the smoke within five seconds of its introduction, and after four minutes, subjects were coughing, rubbing their eyes, and attempting to open the window. At six minutes, when the experiment was terminated if no one had bothered to seek help, vision was obscured by the amount of smoke in the room.

In their sample of students, three out of four of those tested alone reported the smoke, but only one out of eight students who were tested in groups of three saw fit to report the emergency.

In their accounts of the experiment, which appeared in the *Journal of Personality and Social Psychology* and *Psychology Today,* Darley and Latane wrote that when the subjects who reported the smoke were debriefed after the experiment, they often mentioned that they had considered the possibility that the building was on fire. By contrast, those who sat through the six minutes without moving came up with an astonishing variety of alternative explanations for the smoke, none of which mentioned the word "fire." Two students from different groups actually suggested that the smoke was a truth gas deployed to induce them to answer the questionnaire accurately. (Darley and Latane reported that the two who offered this explanation did not seem in the least disturbed by it.) In essence, the inactive bystanders were concocting reasons why they should be absolved for their inaction.

The two psychologists concluded that individuals are less likely to engage in socially responsible action if they think other bystanders are present. "If each member of a group of bystanders is aware that other people are also present, he will be less likely to notice the emergency, less likely to decide that it is an emergency, and less likely to act even if he thinks there is an emergency."

Darley and Latane's experiments and others inspired by the Genovese murder have led psychologists to conclude that people tend to look to others to define events. Someone who sees something that may be an emergency looks to see if other witnesses are also alarmed. If everyone seems calm or indifferent, the observer often concludes that no emergency is taking place. The group defines the event, and most people follow the spoken and unspoken norms of the group and are unwilling to risk the embarrassment of overreacting in public. Furthermore, even if people recognize that they are witnessing an event in which help is called for, they remain unsure who is responsible for providing that help: in a group of strangers there is no captain.

Responsibility is therefore diffused, and so is the guilt felt by those who do nothing.

Social psychologists also explain the passivity of human beings in the face of emergencies by citing the human tendency to believe that there is some order to the universe—that the guilty are punished, the innocent are rewarded, and justice prevails. Various studies indicate that most of us are given to this "just world thinking," and that we will rearrange our perception of people and events so that it seems as though everyone gets what they deserve. Upon seeing an innocent person punished, for example, most people will adjust their interpretation of what they have witnessed: the person being punished "must have done something," must somehow be inferior or dangerous or evil, or must be suffering because some higher cause is being served.

This phenomenon was illustrated in an experiment conducted by psychologists Melvin Lerner and Carolyn Simmons in which seventy-two female undergraduates watched a peer receive severe and painful electric shocks when she gave wrong answers to questions put to her. (The "victim" was in league with the experimenters and was not actually shocked.) Some observers were told that they could stop the shocks after the experiment's first ten-minute session, and that for the second session they could place the victim in a position to earn a fair sum of money for her participation. Other participants were told that they had no control over the experiment, and after witnessing the first session of painful shocks, they believed their colleague was going to suffer more of the same. The students who thought that they controlled the fate of the victim described her in much more positive terms than those who thought they had no influence. Lerner and Simmons concluded that those who believed the suffering was unstoppable devalued the victim so that they could justify what they had witnessed.

Psychologists are also quick to point out that helping often conflicts with norms or rules of appropriate behavior. A man escorting a woman to a dark place in a park could seem like a cause for alarm, but it is considered perverse and impolite to follow a couple into the bushes. Speaking out for a man unjustly imprisoned sounds noble in the abstract, but when that man is from one of the torturable classes, those who speak for him can expect few pats on the back.

The Chicago cases seem to speak to all of these points. It wasn't a case of five people hearing a seizure and doing nothing or acting slowly; it was a case of millions of people knowing of an emergency and doing nothing. People looked about, saw no great crusade forming, saw protests only from the usual agitators, and assumed there was no cause for alarm. Responsibility was diffused. Citizens offended by torture could easily retreat into the notion that they lived in a just world, that the experts would sort things out, that the press, prosecutors, the judiciary, the legislature, or the police department's Office of Professional Standards would take care of the matter. Furthermore, the victims were easily devalued. Some were on death row, many were gang members with extensive police records, and those who were neither were tainted by their association with those who were—"if they were tortured, they must have been guilty because look who else was tortured."

Seeing this play out in my hometown made me wonder: If the Area 2 victims could not rely on public outrage, on the press, on state or federal prosecutors, on politicians, or on the judiciary, what hope is there? Who does help?

ONE SMALL STUDY of people who helped Jews during the Holocaust, described by Perry London in "The Rescuers: Motivational Hypotheses about Christians Who Saved Jews from the Nazis" (a chapter in the 1970 book *Altruism and Helping Behavior,* edited by J. Macaulay and L. Berkowitz), found evidence to indicate that altruistic behavior was related to three personality traits: a spirit of adventurousness, an intense identification with a parent who set a high standard of moral conduct, and a sense of being socially marginal. In London's small sample, the spirit of adventurousness was perhaps best exemplified by a man whose prewar hobby was to race motorcycles on courses that required driving over narrow boards that spanned deep ditches. Once the war began, that man and his friends got a kick out of putting sugar in the gas tanks of German army vehicles, a practice that disabled the engines. The identification with a parent with high moral standards was prominent in the case of a Seventh-Day Adventist minister from the Netherlands whose father had gone to jail for his beliefs; the minister described himself as mildly anti-Semitic, but during the war he organized a large-scale operation for rescuing Jews, believing simply that it was a Christian's duty. That minister, who belonged to a religious group with an extremely small number of followers in Holland, was also cited as an example of what the researchers called "social marginality": a social separateness, a feeling of being an outsider, that seemed to allow the rescuers to have less fear about losing their attachment to the majority group. One highly effective German rescuer, also part of London's sample, had been a stutterer as a child and in an interview confessed that he had always felt friendless. The residents of the French village of Le Chambon, who saved thousands of Jews during the war, also had a certain social marginality: they were Huguenots in overwhelmingly Catholic France.

Amherst professor Dr. Ervin Staub, perhaps the world's foremost authority on bystanders, has staged his own experiments designed to identify the qualities of those who help during emergencies. In one of those experiments, described in "Helping a Distressed Person: Social, Personality, and Stimulus Determinants" (a chapter in the book *Advances in Experimental Social Psychology,* edited by L. Berkowitz), male undergraduates filling out a questionnaire became aware of moaning coming from the next room. Some of the students believed they were working on a timed task, while others had been given no directions concerning time. If the student went into the room to discover the source of the noise, he found another male undergraduate complaining that his stomach was "killing him" and that he had run out of pills. If the subject did not investigate the noise, the allegedly ill confederate eventually entered the testing room, mentioned his ailment and his lack of pills, and asked if he could sit on a couch nearby.

Some of those who helped the ailing student were so enthusiastic that, in an attempt to get medicine at a nearby pharmacy, they ran down twelve flights of stairs rather than wait for an elevator, and one student was so fast that the experimenters didn't catch up with him until he actually got to the drugstore. Those helpers, however, were a small minority. In the sample of 122 students, 73 percent did little or nothing.

While other psychologists have had a hard time gathering results that show any correlation between personality and helping behavior, Staub found a strong correlation in this particular experiment. Subjects who valued cleanliness highly were generally less helpful. Staub interpreted this to indicate that college students "who endorse cleanliness may be highly conventional, and conventional values seem to be different from concern for others." Students who ranked ambition highly as a value were less willing to interrupt their work on the assigned task for longer periods of time (Staub believed that the more ambitious may have experienced more conflict in determining a course of action). The subjects whose personality profiles showed a significant prosocial orientation were more likely to help, but only when the circumstances permitted it: the prosocial students who believed they were working on a timed task were less responsive than those who were unconcerned about the passage of time. Subjects who valued courage highly were more apt to initiate action in response to the moans, those who were taken with adventure and novel experiences seemed more likely to initiate help, and those who valued helpfulness tended to be more responsive when they were asked to collect a prescription.

In his book *The Roots of Evil: The Origins of Genocide and Other Group Violence,* Staub argues that helping is infectious, that helpful bystanders, if they are not devalued by the perpetrators and inactive bystanders, break the uniformity of views, chip away at widespread antagonism toward a particular group, affirm the humanity of the victims, call attention to values disregarded by perpetrators and passive bystanders, and make it clear that persecution can have consequences for the persecutor. Staub points out that the citizens of Le Chambon seemed to have a profound effect on the Vichy police charged with rounding up the Jews: anonymous callers, believed to be policemen, warned the local pastor of impending raids.

Staub argues that helpful bystanders can also inspire victims. Staub points out that during World War II, Belgians resisted the Third Reich's anti-Semitic orders, and Belgian Jews did more on their own behalf than Jews in other Nazi-dominated countries because they did not feel abandoned, helpless, and alone.

It also seems, however, that helping is an infection that is not easily spread. Those who rescued Jews during the Holocaust were often personally approached by someone in dire need, and the same can be said of those who helped the student in pain in Dr. Staub's experiment. Most men and women who are tortured are like the Chicago victims—locked up, unable to knock on anyone's door. Dr. Staub's work indicates that if it is easy to escape without helping, most people will escape: in one Staub experiment in which a confederate feigned a heart attack on a public street, far fewer people helped when the victim was across the street than when he was in their path. Staub noted that some of his subjects observed the victim in agony and then immediately turned their heads and looked away, never turning back.

Furthermore, in places where torture takes place, it is often well known to thousands and sometimes millions of people. That means that responsibility is diffused. Many bystanders simply don't know what to do, how to help, even if they are inclined to—certainly a situation faced by many good Germans during the years of the Holocaust—and they remain immobilized, like the students in the Darley and Latane experiment who heard a colleague plead for help with his seizure. It is not so difficult for many bystanders to adapt their beliefs, to buy into the idea that what is being done is not an abomination, but a service to humanity—that, for example, innocent lives are being saved because men and women are being tortured. Observe, for example, the case of Israel, where there is no large-scale protest over the widely reported torture of more than twenty thousand Palestinians, many of them mere stone throwers.

While helping is infectious, so is torture. The Soviet Union, China, and North Korea provided the inspiration for the British use of the five techniques. The British methods inspired the Israelis. Israeli methods have in turn inspired the Palestinians, who now have their own torturable class in the West Bank and Gaza.

For the victims of the Area 2 detectives, for the Palestinians tortured by Israelis, for the Northern Irish tortured by the British security forces, for most torture victims, there can be little hope of help from their fellow citizens or outsiders. A few will be rescued by the clamor of human rights activists and the chain of events that that clamor initiates, but for most, any rescuing done will be done by the victims themselves, using their own internal resources, shoring up themselves and their fellow victims as best as they can during the process, and perhaps—if they or their families are very resourceful—getting some psychological help if they are released. Only a tiny fraction of working torturers will ever be punished, and those who are can expect their punishment to be slight compared to their crime.

It seems a very small leap to argue that torture is the perfect crime. There are exceptions, yes, but in the vast majority of cases, only the victim pays.

Bibliographical Note

I am indebted to many journalists, historians, and human rights activists, living and dead, who have written about torture.

Belfast

The chapters on the hooded men were informed by the work of human rights activists Father Denis Faul and Father Raymond Murray, who in July 1974 published a 129-page book, *The Hooded Men*. That book included formal statements taken from the victims not long after their ordeal. In 1976, Faul and Murray also published *The RUC: The Black and Blue Book*, which contains statements from Jim Auld and Joe Clarke taken in 1974 and 1975. RUC is the acronym for the Royal Ulster Constabulary, the Northern Ireland police force.

Equally valuable was John McGuffin's book *The Guineapigs* (Penguin, 1974), which includes later interviews with some of the hooded men. McGuffin's history of internment in Ireland was also useful (*Internment,* Tralee, Ireland: Anvil Books, 1973).

There were five major reports written on the torture. Amnesty International published *Report of an Enquiry into Allegations of Ill-Treatment in Northern Ireland* on March 13, 1972. Amnesty's investigating commission was headed by Thomas Hammarberg, then chairman of the Swedish section of Amnesty International. Among other things, the report included a legal analysis of the government's acts that concluded that both national and international law had been violated. Citing J. E. S. Fawcett's *The Application of the European Convention of Human Rights*

(Oxford University Press, 1969), Amnesty pointed out that the United Kingdom had ratified the European Convention for the Protection of Human Rights and Fundamental Freedoms in 1951, that the convention provided that no one should be subjected to torture or to inhuman or degrading treatment or punishment, and that when the convention was still in draft form, the British government had proposed to extend it to cover "imprisonment with such an excess of light, darkness, noise, or silence as to cause mental suffering."

The Compton and Parker reports, which I discuss in chapter 5, were published by Her Majesty's Stationery Office. The Compton Report is formally known as *Report of the enquiry into allegations against the security forces of physical brutality in Northern Ireland arising out of events on the 9th August, 1971* (November 1971). Lord Parker's document is entitled *Report of the Committee of Privy Counsellors appointed to consider authorised procedures for the interrogation of persons suspected of terrorism* (March 1972).

The European Commission of Human Rights report, adopted on January 25, 1976, can be located by its case number and legal title: *Application No. 5310/71, Ireland against The United Kingdom of Great Britain and Northern Ireland, Report of the Commission*. The European Court of Human Rights's ruling of January 18, 1978, is entitled *Case of Ireland against the United Kingdom Judgment*. Both documents were published by the Council of Europe in Strasbourg. Judge Sir Gerald Fitzmaurice's claim that the five techniques did not qualify even as inhuman treatment can be found in his dissent, which follows the Court's ruling. In that dissent, Fitzmaurice argues that to call the methods inhuman is to "debase the currency of normal speech."

Lord Carrington's accusation that the hooded men were thugs and murderers was made on the BBC and Independent Television on November 16, 1971. *The Guardian* and *The Times* (all mention of *The Times* and *The Sunday Times* refer to papers published in London, not the daily published in New York), made mention of the charge on November 18, 1971, when, in the course of reporting on the previous day's Parliamentary debate on the Compton report, they recorded Shadow Home Secretary James Callaghan's denunciation of Carrington for leveling that accusation against people who had been "neither tried nor convicted" (see "Brutality Charges 'Demolished' " in *The Times* and "Calumnies Against Police and Troops Disposed Of, Says Home Secretary" in *The Guardian*). The *Sunday Times* Insight Team's book, *Northern Ireland: A Report on the Conflict* (Vintage Books, 1972) also mentions Carrington's characterization of the hooded men (the book itself is worthwhile for its account of the buildup of the conflict and the introduction of internment). On February 28, 1972, *The Guardian* reported the filing of Paddy Joe McClean's libel suit against Carrington ("Internee Sues Carrington for Libel"). I was unable to check Mr. McClean's recollections of the reasons for the demise of his suit, which bore the action number reference Queen's Bench Decision 1972 M. No 863. In a letter written to me on May 28, 1993, Keith Topley, the Senior Master of the Queen's Bench Division, said that records were retained for ten years and that no trace of the action could be found. The London firm that represented McClean has dissolved.

In December 1993, I sent a letter to Carrington, asking him who knew the nature of the interrogation methods before they were deployed, who authorized their use, how the victims were chosen, whether he stood by the "thugs and murderers" characterization, whether the perpetrators should have been punished or censured, and who made the decision to keep British government officials from testifying in the case of *Ireland against the United Kingdom*. In a letter dated January 20, 1994, Katie Roberton, secretary to Lord Carrington, indicated that he felt "unable to comment on this incident."

I sent a similar letter and list of questions to former Prime Minister Edward Heath and received a similar response. "It was most kind of you to contact Sir Edward regarding the book you are currently writing," wrote Nick Edgar, Heath's private secretary, on December 14, 1993. "However, Sir Edward very much regrets that he is unable to contribute on this occasion. As you can imagine, Sir Edward receives many requests of this nature and simply cannot respond positively to them all." I had also been unsuccessful in getting comment from Carrington and Heath in 1991, when I was working on an article about the hooded men that appeared in *Granta* ("The Internment," issue number 39, "The Body").

On October 18, 1971, *The Times* reported Northern Irish Prime Minister Brian Faulkner's claim that there had "been no brutality of any kind" in an article bearing the headline "Inquiry on 'Brain Washing.'" Almost five years later, the *Irish Times* recorded Faulkner's statement that he did not know the details of the interrogation methods before they were introduced ("Faulkner, Taylor 'Did Not Know' of Specific Methods," September 3, 1976). The same story included the claim of John Taylor, Faulkner's minister of home affairs, that the only politicians who knew the details of the methods were Carrington and Heath.

Reginald Maulding's statement that "There was no permanent lasting

260

injury whatever, physical or mental, to any of the men concerned" was made in the Parliamentary debate on the Compton report, as was Lord Balniel's claim that "there was no brutality, no torture, no brainwashing, no physical injury, and no mental injury." Those statements can be found in *The Times* of November 18, 1971 ("Interrogation of Ulster Internees Yielded Valuable Information"). A more complete excerpt of the Parliamentary debate can be found in Faul and Murray's book *The Hooded Men*. In a phone conversation with me on September 19, 1991, Lord Balniel, later known as the Earl of Crawford and Balcarres, declined to be interviewed.

In chapters 13 and 16, I refer to General Harry Tuzo's claim that the torture amounted to "acute discomfort and humiliation," that it had been inflicted "to save life and safeguard the well-being of perhaps a million people," that the recipients of the treatment were well looked after in the wake of their experience, and that they would have "got over it by now." Those statements were captured on camera by Brian McKenna for his documentary *The Hooded Men,* broadcast by the Canadian Broadcasting Corporation on March 23, 1982. I am grateful to Amnesty International for lending me a copy of the program. General Tuzo declined to be interviewed in a phone conversation on July 31, 1991.

I am also grateful to the survivors of the hooded treatment who signed release forms allowing me to look at medical and psychological reports dealing with their recovery from the torture. A few of those forms were signed by next of kin, since some of the victims were dead by the time I came looking for them. With those consent forms I was able to gain access to the psychiatric and medical reports cited in this book. Much of that information came from documents provided by a Northern Irish solicitor who requested that he not be identified. Those consent forms also allowed me to interview Dr. Robert Daly, the psychiatrist who testified for the Irish government before the European Commission on Human Rights. Results of Daly's first interviews with the hooded men were reported in an article by Martin Huckerby in the *Irish Times* on July 9, 1973 ("Mental Harm from Ulster Hooding, Expert Says"). On May 13, 1976, the *Irish Times* reported on Daly's follow-up study, five years after the torture, a story based on a presentation Daly gave at a meeting of the American Psychiatric Association. Daly also discussed the case of the hooded men in a November 1980 article in the *Danish Medical Bulletin* ("Compensation and Rehabilitation of Victims of Torture," volume 27, number 5). In his testimony before the European Commission, Daly cited "Communist Interrogation and Indoctrination of 'Enemies of the

States,' " written by Lawrence Hinkle Jr. and Harold G. Wolff and published in the American Medical Association's *Archives of Neurology and Psychiatry* (volume 76 [1956], pages 115–74).

The Guardian's report that Sean McKenna and Jim Auld had begun to display severe psychiatric disorders while in Long Kesh was written by Simon Hoggart and appeared on May 6, 1972 ("Hooding Effect on Mind").

In chapter 9 I refer to the British government's obfuscation of the work of the European Commission on Human Rights. This is detailed in several places in the commission's report, in the European Court of Human Rights judgment (see Judge Patrick O'Donoghue's dissent), and in various press reports (see, for example, Anne McHardy's article "Britain Was Guilty of Torture," *The Guardian,* August 27, 1976; Alan Smith's report "Britain Found Guilty of Torture," *The Guardian,* September 3, 1976; and Derek Brown's article "Why Ireland Dragged Britain into the Dock," *The Guardian,* September 3, 1976).

In the course of my discussion of the British policy of obstruction, I mention that years earlier the Greek government had allowed commission delegates to visit three torture sites. The junta refused, however, to allow the commission to inspect several others. See *The Greek Case,* Council of Europe, European Commission of Human Rights, Report of the Commission (Application Nos. 3321/67, 3322/67, 3323/67, 3344/67), volume 1, pages 7–8.

On September 4, 1976, the day the European Commission's finding of torture was reported in the press, the *Irish Times* ran an article stating that the five techniques were still being taught to British military personnel ("British Servicemen Still Being Trained in In-Depth Interrogation"). That story quoted Minister of State for Defense William Rodgers defending the policy, saying that it was designed to prepare servicemen who might be "captured by an unscrupulous enemy."

That day's *Irish Times* also included a summary of the reaction of the British press to the European Commission's finding ("British Papers Keen to Forget Torture Affair"). A year and a half later, when the European Court ruled that the five techniques were not torture, the *Irish Times* ran a similar summary of British press response ("British Press Gloats in the Wake of Strasbourg Finding," January 20, 1978).

The positions of the British and Irish legal teams in their submissions to the European Court, which I discuss in chapter 13, were reported in *The Guardian* by Anne McHardy on February 7, 8, 9, and 10, 1977 (see "Britain in Court," "Britain's Answer to Torture," "Britain Drops

Torture Defence," "British Pledge on Northern Ireland Torture," "No More Torture, Britain Promises," "Irish Press on Despite UK Torture Pledge").

In the book's final chapter, I report on the various justifications torturing nations use in justifying their practices. Northern Irish Prime Minister Brian Faulkner's claim that there had "been no brutality of any kind" appeared in *The Times,* October 18, 1971 ("Inquiry on 'Brain Washing' "). The *Sunday Times* mentions that it was denounced for printing the fantasies of terrorists in its editorial "A Lowering of Civilized Standards," November 21, 1971, page 14. Reginald Maulding's statement that "There was no permanent lasting injury whatever, physical or mental, to any of the men concerned" appeared in *The Times* of November 18, 1971 ("Interrogation of Ulster Internees Yielded Valuable Information"). The Parker Commission's assertion that any mental disorientation would disappear within hours, unless it was the men's own fault, caused by "guilty knowledge" and "fear of reprisals," can be found on page 4 of the aforementioned *Report of the Committee of Privy Counsellors appointed to consider authorised procedures for the interrogation of persons suspected of terrorism.* The Compton report concluded that the hooding was done for the prisoner's own good (see page 13); that Joe Clarke's hands had not been beaten but rather massaged by guards to restore normal feeling (page 18); that strenuous exercises were imposed simply to keep the prisoners warm (page 36); and that the men were believed to possess "information of a kind which it was operationally necessary to obtain as rapidly as possible in the interest of saving lives" (page 13). Reginald Maulding's claim that "vigorous measures" were needed to "fight terrorists, the murderous enemy" can be found in coverage of the Parliamentary debate on the Compton report (*The Times,* November 18, 1971, "Interrogation of Ulster Internees Yielded Valuable Information"). The *Sunday Times*'s argument that Britain would react in horror if the same methods were used in local police stations is in the editorial "A Lowering of Civilised Standards" (*The Sunday Times,* November 21, 1971). The statistics on the rise in shootings, armed robberies, and deaths in Northern Ireland after the introduction of internment are based on my own calculations from statistics provided by the Royal Ulster Constabulary and the British army.

Merlyn Rees's denunciation of the Irish government for "raking over the events of five years ago" was reported by David McKittrick in the *Irish Times* on September 3, 1976 ("Rees Attacks 'Raking Over Events of Five Years Ago' "). The *Guardian*'s claim that Ireland was torturing

Northern Ireland in its persistence in pressing the case on the European Court can be found on the paper's editorial page on September 3, 1976.

The passage of the War Crimes Bill was reported in the *Chicago Tribune* on May 2, 1991 ("Britain OKs War Crime Bill, Ignores House of Lords"). Edwin Heath's opposition to the legislation was noted in *The Times* of March 20, 1990 ("Police Team to Pursue War Crimes Inquiry"). Heath said that show trials would result from the bill, that those who read coverage of those trials in "the gutter press" would want retribution and revenge, and that the bill appealed to "the lowest instincts." Lord Carrington, noting that he had been part of a force that had liberated a concentration camp, opposed the bill in the debate in the House of Lords ("Lords Majority of 133 against War Crimes Bill," *The Times,* June 5, 1990).

Britain's use of the "few bad apples" defense is analyzed on page 274 of *The New Scientist* of August 5, 1976 ("Taking the Hood off British Torture," by William Ristow and Tim Shallice), which notes that the British legal team was making the claim that the five techniques "were not a matter of 'administrative practice' approved by government officials. Rather they simply involved individuals exceeding their orders."

In the book's final chapter I also assert that when the subject of the hooded men arose, it was common for British government spokesmen and editorial writers to respond by denouncing the IRA, as if that justified the torture. For an example of this, see the *Daily Express* editorial on September 3, 1976, in which the writer points out that "The IRA thinks nothing of torture. It maims, hurts, and kills without worrying at all about what the European Commission of Human Rights may think about it." Also see *The Times* article of May 14, 1976, "Report on Alleged Torture of Ulster Detainees Claims It Caused Range of Mental and Physical Disorders," in which the government's Northern Ireland Office responds to Dr. Daly's presentation to the American Psychiatric Association: "It would be interesting to see the same amount of dedicated research and publicity given to the 'drastic psychiatric after effects' on the many hundreds of people widowed and orphaned in Northern Ireland as a result of the activities of bombers and gunmen. All of the men referred to in the report have claimed compensation and twelve have already been paid."

The Times's claim that British torture was more humane than the torture deployed in Greece, Brazil, Iran, and Argentina was made on September 3, 1976 ("A Shameful Chapter That Should Now Be Closed").

Other useful material for those doing research on the hooded men:

Jack Holland's article, "Strasbourg: The Men behind the Torture," published in *Hibernia,* October 8, 1976; "The Torturers' Who's Who," published in *The Leveller,* December 1976; "How Ulster Internees Are Made to Talk," by John Whale, *London Sunday Times,* October 17, 1971; "Internees—New Cruelty Allegations," by John Whale and Lewis Chester, *London Sunday Times,* October 24, 1971; "The Debacle of Ulster Internment," by Tom Hadden, *New Society,* February 6, 1975; "'The Hooded Men': Victims of Psychological Research?," by Steven B. Kennedy, a chapter in the book *Psychology and Torture,* edited by Peter Suedfeld, Hemisphere Publishing Corporation, 1990.

Israel

My descriptions of the villages of Beita and Hawara in chapter 2 are based on personal observation. My description of Colonel Yehuda Meir is based on the same. The account of his career was compiled from my interview with him on January 25, 1993, from his testimony at his court-martial, from Anat Tal-Shir's October 11, 1989, article in *Yediot Ahronot* ("He Was the Sheriff"), and from Alex Fishman's April 28, 1989, article in *Hadashot* ("Who Is Afraid of Colonel Yehuda Meir?"). The description of Meir as a man who did not command from a chair came from those articles as well as from Captain Eldad Ben-Moshe and Lieutenant Omri Kochva.

The biographical material on Ben-Moshe, Kochva, and Yoram Rabin came from interviews with them. My account of the events preceeding the breaking of arms and legs in Beita comes from interviews with Kochva, Ben-Moshe, and Meir, and from their testimony at Meir's court-martial. I benefited from the generosity of members of Yesh Gvul, who provided me with translated excerpts of testimony given at Meir's trial. (Yesh Gvul is an organization of Israeli soldiers who refused to serve in the Occupied Territories. *Yesh gvul* means both "There is a limit" and "There is a border.") Other excerpts were taken from news reports of the trial. Ben-Moshe's testimony is quoted at some length, for example, in the April 13, 1990, edition of *Hadashot* ("That I Would Refuse an Order?," by Alex Fishman). Kochva's testimony was also quoted, albeit more briefly, in many newspapers. See, for example, the *Jerusalem Post* of March 30, 1990 ("'Not Guilty' Plea at 'Break Bones' Trial," by Joshua Brilliant), and the *Jerusalem Post International* dated April 7, 1990 ("Colonel Meir Goes on Trial; Charged with Brutality," also written by Mr. Brilliant).

In chapter 2 I describe the eight men from Beita as nonviolent ("Some had participated in demonstrations . . ."). That assessment came from the testimony given by "Lieutenant Colonel S." on the first day of Meir's trial

(March 29, 1990). In military trials in Israel it is common for certain officers to be identified by an initial, rather than by their full name, for reasons of security. Lieutenant Colonel S. was the intelligence officer Meir
dispatched to get the list from the Shin Bet, and his testimony was
reported in the *Jerusalem Post* on March 30, 1990, and the *Jerusalem Post
International* on April 7, 1990 (articles cited above). The dismissal of Mike
Herzog, son of the president of Israel, from further duties that night
comes from the testimony of the same intelligence officer. I found that
particular passage in an excerpt of testimony provided to me by Yesh
Gvul. Reference to the dismissal of Herzog can also be found in news
accounts in the Hebrew dailies; see, for example, Eitan Rabin's trial cov-
erage in *Ha'aretz* on April 4, 1990 ("Witness in the Trial of Yehuda Meir:
Soldiers Even Entered the Hospital and Started Hitting") and Yehuda
Meltzer's column in *Hadashot* on April 5, 1990 ("The Meir Trial—the Big
Bang").

Yitzhak Rabin's directive to suppress the intifada using "force, might,
beatings" can be found in the *Jerusalem Post,* January 20, 1988 ("Defence
Establishment Still at a Loss on How to Put Down the Unrest," by Joshua
Brilliant). The same article contains the defense department spokesman's
explanation of the logic of the policy that I quote in chapter 2, the belief
that a stone thrower sent to prison might be incarcerated for eighteen
days, "but if troops break his hand, he won't be able to throw stones for a
month and a half."

Captain Ben-Moshe and Lieutenant Kochva testified about receiving
Meir's command to break arms and legs, as did other soldiers who participated in the beatings. At his trial on November 8, 1990, Meir admitted
that he gave the order to beat, but he denied telling the soldiers to tie up
the men, to gag them, or to beat them with clubs (see "Colonel Pleads
Guilty to Relaying Illegal Order; Meir Admits Ordering Blows," by
Bradley Burston, *Jerusalem Post,* November 9, 1990). My description of
Ben-Moshe's acts in Beita comes from his testimony at trial, from my
interview with him, from the testimony of Kochva and Shmuel Shefi,
and from press coverage of the trial (see, for example, the aforementioned
Alex Fishman piece in the April 13, 1990, edition of *Hadashot,* "That I
Would Refuse an Order?"). My depiction of the chaos that accompanied
the execution of Ben-Moshe's order came from descriptions by Kochva
(in his testimony and in his February 17, 1993, interview with me) and
from the men from Beita who were beaten, whom I interviewed in January and February 1993. Shmuel Shefi's story of dragging one of the victims off the road can be found in his court testimony, dated April 5, 1990.

Captain Ben-Moshe's account of meeting with his men after the Beita beating, of his visit to Meir's office the following day, and of his meeting with Brigadier General Livne come from his court testimony and his interview with me.

In court, both Ben-Moshe and Captain Ziv Gefen provided details about Major Danny Gabriel and the plan to involve the mukhtar in the round-up of the Hawara victims. (An account of Gefen's testimony by journalist Batya Feldman can be found in *Hadashot* on June 4, 1990.) My description of the mukhtar Jihad Hamdan Howary and his meeting with Major Gabriel comes from my interview with the mukhtar on February 12, 1993. The gathering of the Hawara residents, the loading of them on the bus, their subsequent mauling, and the inferiority of the soldier's clubs was described to me by Kochva and the Hawara victims, and it was also detailed by Yossi Sarid in his article "The Night of the Broken Clubs" (*Ha'aretz,* May 4, 1989). At Meir's trial, Ben-Moshe testified that he had ordered the bus driver to accelerate the engine (see Fishman's *Hadashot* piece "That I Would Refuse an Order?"). When I interviewed Ben-Moshe in February 1993, he could not recall giving that order, only that "somebody mentioned it at the trial."

Kochva told me that Ben-Moshe had ordered that the mukhtar's son be spared, and my report that the son was nonetheless badly beaten was based on medical records from Refideyeh Hospital. On February 15, 1993, a staff member at the hospital, saying he feared being arrested for what he was about to do, opened the medical records of nine men from Hawara and Beita for me and my translator. The nine men had been treated at the hospital after being beaten by Ben-Moshe's troops, and it was those records that indicated that the mukhtar's son had been listed in fair condition, that he had multiple lacerations in both legs, and that he had a cut on his face three centimeters in length.

When testifying in Meir's court-martial, Brigadier General Livne admitted that he had met with Ben-Moshe and that he had subsequently visited the Nahal troops (see Alex Fishman's article "What Surprises Life Has in Store for Brigadier General Ze'ev Livne," *Hadashot,* May 4, 1990). Ben-Moshe's recollection of that visit was related to me in my interview with him, and his recollection matches his testimony at the court-martial.

In chapter 6, my account of how military police investigations were carried out—or not carried out, as was often the case—is based on my interview with military police investigator Yoram Rabin, on an article by Dan Sagir in *Ha'aretz* ("Criminal Investigation Division Probes," February 2, 1989), and on chapter 2 of *The Israeli Army and the Intifada,* a book published by Middle East Watch in August 1990 (Middle East Watch is now known as Human Rights Watch/Middle East). Lieutenant Yuval Horn, whom I interviewed with Colonel Finklestein, admitted that newspapers are not used as sources of possible prosecutions (see *The Israeli Army and the Intifada,* page 95). I interviewed Kochva and Rabin together, and they both explained how Kochva had come to talk about the incidents at Hawara and Beita. Both men claimed that chief military prosecutor Colonel Menachem Finklestein had promised that if prosecution resulted, it would be directed solely at Meir.

Brigadier General Amnon Strashnow's decision to charge Meir only with exceeding authority was reported in Alex Fishman's article "Who Is Afraid of Colonel Yehuda Meir?" (*Hadashot,* April 28, 1989). Chief of staff Dan Shomron's delivery of that decision ("Good Morning, Severe Reprimand") was reported in the *Jerusalem Post* (" 'Beatings Were Not Aberrant Behavior,' " by Joshua Brilliant, June 24, 1990). My account of the arrangement that Strashnow, Shomron, and chief of army personnel Yimri Olmert worked out so that Meir could be loaned to the GSS for two years, and thus keep his pension, came from multiple sources: from my interviews with Meir and Joshua Schoffman of the Association for Civil Rights in Israel (ACRI), from Yossi Sarid's article in *Ha'aretz* "Why He Came to Me," June 28, 1990, and from a document composed by Olmert outlining the terms of Meir's termination from army service. Meir's subsequent meeting with Sarid was described by Meir on the witness stand and in his interview with me, and Sarid described the same session in his "Why He Came to Me" article.

The description of ACRI's role in the case came from my interview with Schoffman and from the petition Schoffman submitted to the High Court. The IDF's position can be found in their submission to the High Court. Strashnow's statement, "Along with respecting the rights of Palestinians one must also consider the rights of an officer who has served in the Israeli army for twenty years," was reported in *Ha'aretz* on October 22, 1989 ("Puzzling Forgiveness," by Gideon Alon).

Yoram Rabin told me of his concern that he had put his friend Kochva in jeopardy once his investigation reached the High Court, and the military police investigator also told me of his conversation with Colonel Finklestein about the matter. *The Israeli Army and the Intifada* reported that the High Court's decision in the case was the first time in Israel's history that the High Court had overruled a prosecutorial decision by the judge advocate general (see page 184).

In chapter 10 I relate the story of the slaughter at Kfar Kassem. (The

village's name, when translated into English, is sometimes spelled Kafr
Kasim, Kafr Qasim, Kfar Kassem, Kefer Qesem). Shmuel Malinki and
ten other officers of the border patrol were tried before the District Military Tribunal in Jerusalem (case number M.T. 3/57; known on appeal as
Ofer *v.* Chief Military Prosecutor [1960] 44 P.E. 362). Although forty-
seven people were killed in the massacre, the officers were charged only
with the murder of forty-three, as it was not clear who exactly had shot
four of the residents of the village. The tribunal began on January 15,
1957. Testimony ended on January 5, 1958, and the judges delivered their
verdict on October 13, 1958. Malinki's remark, "May Allah have mercy
on their souls," was testified to by several officers, including First Inspector Arye Menashes, who disobeyed Malinki's orders (see "I Could Not
Kill Women, Children," *Jerusalem Post,* July 25, 1957), Deputy Arie
Alexandroni, and Company Commander Haim Levy ("Authorship of
'May Allah Have Mercy' Quote Debated," *Jerusalem Post,* January 27,
1959). Malinki's superior officer, Aluf-Mishne Issachar Shadmi, who was
charged with murder and exceeding authority and was tried separately
("Shadmi Charged with Murder," *Jerusalem Post,* November 2, 1958),
later admitted to uttering the same blessing (see "Shadmi Claims He Was
Quoted out of Context," *Jerusalem Post,* February 6, 1959) but claimed he
said it when he was asked how a soldier could differentiate between
fedayeen (Palestinian guerrillas) and Israeli Arabs moving around army
posts at night.

Malinki's statement that a few deaths would impress the villagers was
testified to by Segen Gavriel Dehan ("Kasim Accused Details How Vil-
lagers Were Killed," by Macabee Kaskin, *Jerusalem Post,* April 2, 1957)
and by Inspector Yehuda Frankental ("Officer Claims Malinki's Orders
Were 'Murderous,' " by Macabee Kaskin, *Jerusalem Post,* May 2, 1957).
The "mow them down" command was testified to by two villagers
who were shot and survived by pretending to be dead (see "Kafr Kasim
Court Strikes Out Testimony on Mukhtar's Blame," by Macabee Kaskin,
Jerusalem Post, May 24, 1957, and "Wounded Farmer Describes Kafr
Kasim Killing," *Jerusalem Post,* May 28, 1957). The slaughter of the
truckload of women was testified to by several witnesses, including Mah-
mud Mohammed Farif, another wounded survivor, who heard the
women beg for mercy ("Prosecution in Kasim Trial Winding Up Next
Week," by Macabee Kaskin, *Jerusalem Post,* approximately June 7, 1957—
the copy in the *Post*'s archive bears no date).

Lance Corporal Shalom Ofer admitted killing the fifteen bicyclists,
the villagers who rode on three trucks, and five other people who were

riding in a wagon (see Macabee Kaskin's article of April 2, 1957, "Kasim Accused Details How Villagers Were Killed").

Of the eleven officers tried in 1957, Malinki and seven others were found guilty ("Eight Guilty; Three Freed," by Macabee Kaskin, *Jerusalem Post,* October 13, 1958). Malinki was sentenced to seventeen years, but this was later reduced to seven years by the president of Israel, and on November 13, 1959, the *Jerusalem Post* reported that with time off for good behavior, Malinki would be released in August 1961, less than three years after he had been found guilty. Ofer and Dehan, the two officers who were accused of having done the bulk of the killing, were originally sentenced to fifteen years, but in the end they also served less than three years ("Kafr Kasim N.C.O. to Be Freed Today," *Jerusalem Post,* November 10, 1959, and "Sentences Cut for Malinki and Dehan," *Jerusalem Post,* November 13, 1959).

Excerpts from Judge Benjamin Halevi's "black flag" opinion in the Kfar Kasim case appeared in Moshe Negbi's "Legal Analysis" column in *Hadashot* on November 10, 1989, and in Joshua Brilliant's story in the *Jerusalem Post,* "Two Military Legal Experts Warn of Criminal Liability in Beatings," January 26, 1988. The judge advocate general's summary in the Meir case, which I obtained from ACRI, stated that "a black flag" hung over Colonel Meir's order.

My explanation of the context of the Beita and Hawara beatings comes from several sources. Joshua Brilliant's story " 'No Beating for Beating's Sake'—Rabin" (*Jerusalem Post,* January 27, 1988) was the basis for my report that two members of the Israeli parliament had seen two hundred Arabs in Gaza whose limbs had been broken by the IDF. (The two politicians were Yossi Sarid and Dedi Zucker.) The beating incident filmed by CBS was shown on CBS, and my source for the fact that the beating was filmed continuously for forty-five minutes is the Physicians for Human Rights report, *The Casualties of Conflict: Medical Care and Human Rights in the West Bank and Gaza Strip* (published March 30, 1988). That same report is my source for the statement that the beating policy had unleased an "uncontrolled epidemic of violence by police and soldiers. . . . The word 'beating' does not properly convey the literal pounding and mauling . . . we saw."

The beating death of Hani al-Shami and the subsequent court-martial of the four soldiers from the Givati Brigade were widely covered by the Israeli press, and I was also able to work with transcripts of trial testimony, already translated into English, thanks to the generosity of Igal Ezraty of Yesh Gvul. The testimony of military police investigator

Sergeant Major Wein Re'a was my source for the defendants' admissions that they had beaten two children, a teenage boy, and Mr. al-Shami; that they had beaten the teenager and his father with rifle butts and a broomstick; that one soldier had jumped off a bed onto al-Shami; that the soldiers admitted there was no resistance once the beating started. The investigator also testified that a sign on the camp bulletin board said, "The battalion will observe and detain and beat rioters, day and night," and he testified that the soldiers had told him they were ordered to "break bones so that they cannot walk on their feet. The meaning is not to break bones deliberately, but to beat them hard so that they aren't able to walk. If a bone breaks in the process, so it breaks." First Sergeant Yitzhak Adler testified that he continued beating even after father and son were motionless, and it was Adler who said, "Every now and then he got a blow to the leg, so that no thought goes up to his head."

The sentences of the four Givati soldiers were reported in the *New York Times* on June 16, 1989 ("Four Israel Soldiers Are Sentenced in Beating Death of a Palestinian," by Alan Cowell). The first soldier to be pardoned was released on September 7, 1989 ("Givati Soldier's Jail Sentence Reduced," *Jerusalem Post,* September 8, 1989). *Ha'aretz*'s report that army morale was suffering due to the widespread sentiment that the soldiers had taken the fall for the senior command appeared on September 29, 1989, the same day that *Ma'ariv* reported that Defense Minister Rabin wanted the remaining soldiers to be pardoned. The pardons were issued that day, three and a half months after the men were sentenced, so the soldiers could spend Rosh Hashanah with their families ("Givati Men Freed, but Barred from Returning to Brigade," by Kenneth Kaplan, *Jerusalem Post,* October 2, 1989).

Colonel Finklestein's view that Meir's trial would refute the notion, common after the Givati case, that only the lowly would be punished, was conveyed to me in my interview with him. Judge Advocate General Strashnow's summary of the military police investigation characterizes Meir as "the father of all sin."

In chapter 10, my summary of Meir's view of the case—that he was being singled out when thousands of arms and legs were being broken at the time, that beating prisoners was standard operating procedure, and that Defense Minister Rabin was the father of all sin—came from points he made with me during our interview and from what he said on the witness stand. In that chapter, the quotes I attribute to Kochva, Avirash, Shefi, Ben-Moshe, and Meir come directly from their testimony. My sources for Livne's testimony were two articles in *Hadashot* on May 4,

1990—Alex Fishman's "What Surprises Life Has in Store for Brigadier General Zev Livne" and Yehuda Meltzer's "Next Week Mitzna." My sources for Mitzna's testimony were "Mitzna: The Command of Colonel Meir—A Black Flag Flies over It," by Hadas Manor (*Ha'aretz,* May 11, 1990); "Mitzna: The Company Commander Should Have Refused Meir's Order," by Batya Feldman (*Hadashot,* May 5, 1990); the similarly titled "Mitzna: The Company Commander Should Have Refused Meir's Command" (*Hadashot,* May 11, 1990); and "Mitzna: I Did Not Say 'to Break Bones,' " by Eitan Mor (*Yediot Ahronot,* May 15, 1990). Yehuda Meltzer's column suggesting that either Livne or Mitzna was lying or that one of the two had a severe hearing or speaking disability appeared in *Hadashot* on May 18, 1990 ("One of Them Is Lying"). Uri Milstein, writing in *Ha Ir,* a Tel Aviv weekly, suggested that Mitzne and Livne were senile, or liars, or unable to control their troops ("The Trial of the Colonels," May 18, 1990). Yossi Sarid accused Mitzna of locking the black flag in the central command's closet in *Ha'aretz* on May 17, 1990 ("Why I Am Suing Rabin"), the same article in which he stated that Yitzhak Rabin should have also been a defendant. Sarid's citation of four other incidents in which Palestinians were beaten in similar or worse fashion, incidents for which there had been no courts-martial, were contained in an open letter that he and fellow parliamentarian Dede Zucker wrote after Mitzna's first day of testimony. The letter, addressed to then prime minister Yitzhak Shamir and army chief of staff Dan Shomron, was excerpted in Yehuda Meltzer's column "One of Them Is Lying."

Defense Minister Rabin's denial that he told anyone to break bones was reported by the *International Herald Tribune* on June 23, 1990.

The background I provide on Meir's army career in chapter 10 comes from Anat Tal-Shir's "He Was the Sheriff," and from Alex Fishman's "Who Is Afraid of Colonel Yehuda Meir?" Rabin's assurance that those who carried out his orders to beat would not be prosecuted was confirmed by Rabin in an interview on Israeli radio on June 22, 1990, according to a Reuters story published in the *International Herald Tribune* on June 23, 1990 ("Rabin Ordered Beating, Colonel Says"). Itim, the Israeli wire service, quoted Rabin making a similar statement (see *Ha'aretz,* June 7, 1990).

The statements of Lieutenant Colonel Zvi Barkai and Chief Superintendent Mose Viltzig that I quote here come directly from their testimony at Meir's trial. My statement that the prosecution found it difficult to get the Beita and Hawara victims to testify is based on my interview with Joshua Schoffman of ACRI. ACRI had tried to get some of the

Palestinians to come to the court-martial without success. From my interviews with the victims, I learned that some of them were not in the country at the time of the trial.

My account of the testimony of Samir Hamous was based on an article by Etti Hasid that appeared in *Ha'aretz*'s weekly magazine on April 6, 1990, and on trial coverage in *Ha'aretz* ("Witness in the Trial of Yehuda Meir: Soldiers Even Entered the Hospital and Started Beating," by Eitan Rabin, April 2, 1990); *Hadashot* ("We Discussed the Technique and Went into Details," by Batya Feldman, April 6, 1990); and *Al Hamishmar* ("Colonel Meir Said to Us: Take Him and Break One of His Arms or Legs," April 2, 1990). I was present in court for the testimony of Muhammad Beni Mufala and had his testimony translated. My presentation of prosecutor Finklestein's concerns is based on my interview with him.

In chapter 14: My report of the verdict and sentencing in the Meir case was based on four articles by Bradley Burston in the *Jerusalem Post:* "Colonel Meir Found Guilty of Ordering Beatings" (April 9, 1991); "Colonel Meir Demoted in 'Limb-Breaking' Trial" (April 24, 1991); "More Officer Trials Possible on Intifada" (April 25, 1991); and "IDF Lawyers to Let Meir's Sentence Stand Unchallenged" (May 9, 1991). Yossi Sarid's comment that there was one system of justice for Jews and another for Arabs was quoted in Asher Wallfish's addition to Burston's *Jerusalem Post* story "More Officer Trials Possible on Intifada" (April 25, 1991).

In my discussion of the torture commonly practiced in Israel today, I refer to the London *Sunday Times* Insight Team's report "Israel and Torture." That article appeared on June 19, 1977. The paper reported that allegations of systematic torture had been persistent for almost a decade and the reporters concluded that torture of Palestinians was standard operating procedure and sanctioned as deliberate policy. The Landau Commission report outlines the basic facts of the Number 300 bus affair and the Izzat Nafsu case. For a brief description of those cases and the role they played in establishing the Landau Commission, see *The Interrogation of Palestinians during the Intifada: Ill-Treatment, "Moderate Physical Pressure," or Torture?,* a book published by the Israeli human rights group B'Tselem in March 1991. The *Miami Herald*'s article reporting on the methods of torture that the GSS admitted deploying was written by Juan Tamayo and appeared on December 6, 1987 ("Torture Scandal Rocks Israel's Secret Service"). The same article identifies Landau as a liberal who threw out the confession of an Israeli Jew because a police officer had orally abused him. The suspect, Yisrael Artsi, was an income tax investigator suspected of taking a bribe, and his case is discussed in slightly greater detail in "Moderate Physical Pressure: Interrogation Methods in Israel," a symposium conducted on December 7, 1990, in the wake of the Landau Commission report (the symposium report was published by The Public Committee Against Torture in Israel, whose office is in Jerusalem).

I cite the work of Human Rights Watch, B'Tselem, and the International Committee of the Red Cross as finding that Israel routinely tortures Arab detainees. Human Rights Watch/Middle East published a 316-page book, *Torture and Ill-Treatment: Israel's Interrogation of Palestinians from the Occupied Territories,* in June 1994, detailing the Israeli methods. Appendix C (starting on page 287) contains an account of two interviews that Human Rights Watch investigator James Ron conducted with Ahmed Husni al-Batsh, whose seventy-five days of torture I mention briefly. I participated in one of those interviews. B'Tselem's report *Routine Torture: Interrogation Methods of the General Security Service* was published in February 1998. The International Committee of the Red Cross's condemnation of Israeli methods appeared in its press release number 1717, May 21, 1992. Prime Minister Yitzhak Rabin's admission that eight thousand Palestinians had been subjected to forceful shaking was made on the radio program *Yoman Hashavua* on July 29, 1995, and the remark was quoted the following day in *Ha'aretz* ("Rabin Attacked Landor Report: 'It's Impossible to Interrogate a Terrorist on a Cup of Coffee,' " by Yerah Tal). My report on the High Court's ruling on torture as this book went to press is based on "Israel's Supreme Court Bans Torture during Interrogation," by Alan Philps, a story that appeared in the *Chicago Sun-Times* on September 6, 1999.

My account of the Jewish settlers' provocative hiking trip through Beita was taken from the following sources: "The Army Stands by Its Findings" (*Jerusalem Post,* April 11, 1988); "Town without Pity," by Mary Curtius, *Boston Globe,* August 20, 1989; and *Punishing a Nation: Human Rights Violations during the Palestinian Uprising, December 1987–1988,* published by Al Haq, the Palestinian human rights organization, December 1988 (see pages 172–3 and page 187).

Those interested in the subject of torture in Israel should also see: "In Israel, Coercing Prisoners Is Becoming Law of the Land," by Serge Schmemann, *New York Times,* May 8, 1997; *Routine Torture: Interrogation Methods of the General Security Service,* published by B'Tselem in February 1998; *The Interrogation of Palestinians during the Intifada: Follow-up to the March 1991 B'Tselem Report,* published by B'Tselem, March 1992; *Denial and Acknowledgement: The Impact of Information about Human Rights Violations,* by Stanley Cohen, published by The Center for Human Rights, Faculty of Law, Hebrew University of Jerusalem, 1995; *Israel Law Review,* volume 23, numbers 2–3, spring–summer 1989, an issue devoted to torture and the Landau Commission's report; the annual reports of the Public Committee against Torture in Israel; and *Tikkun* (volume 6, numbers 5 and 6), where the articles "The Wrong Arm of the Law: Torture Disclosed and Deflected in Israeli Politics" and "Talking about Torture in Israel" appeared, the former attributed to B'Tselem, the latter to Stanley Cohen.

Chicago

I have been reporting on the allegations of torture at Area 2 since 1989, and anyone wishing to learn more about those cases may wish to consult my articles in the *Chicago Reader.* To date, those articles are "House of Screams" (January 26, 1990); "Town without Pity" (January 12, 1996); "The Shocking Truth" (January 10, 1997); "Shot in the Dark" (November 6, 1998); and "Poison in the System" (June 25, 1999). All of the stories are posted on the *Reader*'s Web site at www.chicagoreader.com. My source for some of the information used in this book was testimony I heard during the course of covering Andrew Wilson's civil suit trials, and to guide anyone searching for that material I have cited the dates of the testimony below.

Mrs. Fahey told me of her husband's tendency to point out "dirty" cars when I sat next to her in the courtroom of Judge Duff in the first days of Andrew Wilson's civil suit. The details of the killing of Officers Fahey and O'Brien can be found in Area 2 Violent Crime's supplementary report, written by Detectives Thomas McKenna, Patrick O'Hara, and Fred Hill. The accounts of various witnesses, including Dwayne Hardin, Andre Coulter, Tyrone Sims, Solomon Morgan, and Donald White are included in that report. The police department's description of the getaway car is contained in the Chicago Police Department's *Daily Bulletin,* volume 23, number 42, February 11, 1982.

The excessive force used by police during the manhunt for the Wilson brothers is described in the *Chicago Sun-Times,* "3 Brutality Charges Filed in Manhunt" (February 13, 1982) and in six stories by Chinta Strausberg in the *Chicago Defender:* "Brzeczek Pressed to Act on Cop Brutality" (February 22, 1982); "End 'War Zone'—Jesse Jackson" (February 11, 1982); "Citizens Tell of Verbal, Physical Abuse" (February 22, 1982); "Jesse Jackson Rips Cop 'Manhunt Tactics' " (February 15, 1982);

"Police Tactics 'Shock' Community" (February 16, 1982); and "Sleeping Family Startled by Police Search" (February 11, 1982). Doris Miller described being abused in the Area 2 headquarters in her testimony at a hearing on a motion to suppress Wilson's confession before he was tried for the murders of Fahey and O'Brien in 1982.

Wilson's civil suit is known as *Andrew Wilson v. City of Chicago, Richard Brzeczek, Jon Burge, Patrick O'Hara, Thomas McKenna, and John Yucaitis,* No. 86 C 2360 in U.S. District Court, Northern District of Illinois, Eastern Division.

The arrest of Andrew Wilson was described by Commander Burge when he testified in Judge Duff's courtroom starting on March 13, 1989, and Officer Chester Batey, testifying on March 22 and 23, 1989, provided the details of the arrest of Jackie Wilson. The Illinois Supreme Court concluded that Andrew Wilson had "suffered his injuries while in police custody" in its ruling in *People v. Andrew Wilson,* 106 Ill. Dec. 771, 506 N.E. 2d 571 (Ill. 1987).

Wilson's charges against the officers at Area 2 are detailed in the "Second Amended Complaint" filed in his civil suit. Burge described his family background to me in an interview on September 18, 1989. His military history is outlined briefly in his testimony in Judge Duff's courtroom. His actions in saving the life of Erma Moody, the woman threatening suicide, are outlined in a memo dated February 4, 1972, from the Third District commander recommending Burge for a Department Commendation Award. Two newspapers also carried accounts of the incident (see "Cop Grabs Gun, Saves Mom's Life," by William Clements, *Chicago Daily News,* January 27, 1972, and "Heroic Policemen Thwart Suicide," by Jim Casey, *Chicago Sun-Times,* January 28, 1972). The story behind Burge's 1980 commendation for apprehending the armed robbers of the Fotomat can be found in Personnel Order No. 80-139 (the department commendation signed by Superintendent Richard Brzeczek, dated May 31, 1980). Burge provided additional details when I asked him about it during our interview.

The presentencing report written by social worker Jill Miller was my source for the biographical data on Andrew Wilson. The report was dated June 15, 1988.

The camera store allegedly robbed by the Wilson brothers was World Camera at 11511 S. Michigan in Chicago. The police department's supplementary report on the robbery was written by Detective Thomas McKenna, who would later be charged in Wilson's civil suit, and was dated December 13, 1981 (the investigation was assigned Records Division number C 457 495). The robbery of Levada Downs, which Andrew Wilson carried out while disguised as a postman, occurred on February 4, 1982. The supplementary report, written again by Detective McKenna, can be located under the Records Division number D 038 977.

The *Chicago Lawyer* article rating federal judges was published in the March 1989 issue ("Our Federal Judges—The Best, the Worst"). My background on Wilson's lawyers and on William Kunkle, who defended the policemen, is based primarily on interviews with them. Kunkle's response to seeing Wilson break down ("I love to see him cry") is recorded on page 172 of Andrew Wilson's deposition, taken December 15, 1988, at Pontiac Correctional Center. Wilson's testimony in Duff's courtroom began on February 22, 1989.

My source for the specifics of Wilson's confession is the statement itself. The refusal of the lockup keeper to accept Wilson was testified to during Wilson's civil suit by Officer Mario Ferro, one of the two wagon-men who took Wilson to Mercy Hospital. Ferro gave a deposition from his home in Florida on January 6, 1989, and the deposition was read in court on March 6, 1989. Mercy Hospital records, included in appendix J of the People's Law Office's January 18, 1989, submission, support the testimony of Patricia Crossen and Dr. Geoffrey Korn, both of whom took the witness stand on March 7, 1989.

Detective O'Hara's testimony began on March 16, 1989, McKenna's began on March 21, and Yucaitis took the stand on March 22. All three said Wilson had been taken to Interview Room Number Two. On the basis of the recollections of various officers that the radiator in that room did not work, the police argued Wilson could not have burned himself. In the second trial in the civil suit, the police argued Wilson was in Interview Room Number One and burned himself on a working radiator. An analysis of that changing story can be found in OPS investigator Francine Sanders's "Special Project Investigative Summary Report," dated October 26, 1990 (see pages 33, 37, 39, and 61), and her "Supplemental Summary Report," dated September 23, 1991 (see pages 25 and 26). Dr. Raymond Warpeha, the burn expert, testified on March 27. Dr. Robert Kirschner's deposition is dated February 9, 1982. He testified in Duff's courtroom on March 9, 1989.

On February 15, 1989, Julia Davis testified about the police ransacking her house. Roy Wade Brown told of being suffocated by the police on February 28. The letter from Dr. John Raba to Superintendent Brzeczek, dated February 17, 1982, is appendix L of the People's Law Office's January 18, 1989, submission. On February 25, 1982, Brzeczek forwarded

Raba's letter to then State's Attorney Richard Daley and asked for guidance. Brzeczek's letter to Daley can be found in appendix J (the file of OPS investigator Keith Griffiths). Brzeczek's testimony began on February 15, 1988. OPS investigator Griffiths testified on March 6, 1989.

Closing arguments in the first civil trial began on March 29, 1989. My account of the jury's debate is based on interviews with them after they returned with their verdict.

The police officer who wrote the anonymous letters to the People's Law Office informing them of the existence of other victims asked that his or her letters be kept confidential, but the letters ultimately became part of the court file in Wilson's civil suit. The transcript of Melvin Jones's motion-to-suppress hearing can be found in his case file in Cook County Circuit Court, Number 82 C 1605. The PLO's motion for recusal of Judge Duff is dated April 7, 1989, and it includes transcripts of the "scum of the earth" debate.

The list of men who claimed they were tortured at Area 2, including Anthony Holmes, George Powell, Lawrence Poree, Gregory Banks, Darrell Cannon, and Willie Porch, was submitted by the People's Law Office in Wilson's civil suit, but it was subsequently amended as additional victims surfaced. The PLO has now submitted the list in several cases. See, for example, the "affidavit of G. Flint Taylor" in the case file of *Marcus Wiggins v. Jon Burge, et al,* Number 93 C 0199 in the United States District Court for the Northern District of Illinois, Eastern Division.

The background material on William Coleman came from material submitted to the court by the People's Law Office in Wilson's civil suit. The filing contained an Interpol document listing Coleman's description, aliases, convictions, and the warning, "Liable to commit theft and fraud. . . . It would be advisable to keep a watch on him if in your country." Gregory Miskiw's story about Coleman, "Amazing Royal Smear of Billy Liar" appeared in the *Sunday Mirror,* March 2, 1988. He testified in court, with the jury excused, and I interviewed him briefly after that testimony.

My taped interview with Allen Gall occurred on September 13, 1989.

The Amnesty International report *Allegations of Police Torture in Chicago, Illinois* is dated December 1990. Amnesty's index number for the report is AMR/51/42/90. David Fogel's October 19, 1987, memo, "Proposed Revamping of Office of Professional Standards," in which he states that OPS "institutionalizes lying," can be found attached as exhibit A in the People's Law Office document "Plaintiff's Reply to Defendant City's

Memorandum in Response to Plaintiff's Motion for Summary Judgment," filed June 23, 1995, in the courtroom of Judge Robert Gettleman, who presided over Wilson's civil suit after the U.S. Court of Appeals granted Wilson another trial.

The assessment of Sanders and Goldston as two of Fogel's best investigators is based on my interviews with David Fogel on October 13 and 17, 1994. Their reports, collectively known as "Chicago Police Department Office of Professional Standards Special Project," were released on February 7, 1992, by Judge Milton Shadur during the course of hearing *Fallon v. Dillon,* case number 90 C 6722. Mike Royko's column dismissing the case against Burge appeared in the *Chicago Tribune* on February 27, 1992 ("Facts Don't Add Up to Police Brutality"). Royko's remarks were analyzed by Michael Miner in the pages of the *Chicago Reader* on March 6, 1992 (see "Royko's Tortured Reasoning," page 4).

Though the three officers charged before the Police Board each had their own case number (Burge's case number was 91-1856; O'Hara's was 91-1857; and Yucaitis's was 92-1858), the board's "Findings and Decision" is contained in a single document bearing all three numbers. The board also filed a "Supplemental Opinion on Legal Issues" with the police superintendent on March 8, 1993. Judge Thomas O'Brien's ruling is also a single document, though it contains two case numbers: 93 CH 2215 (for O'Hara and Yucaitis) and 93 CH 2265 (for Burge). It can be found in the files of the Chancery Division, Cook County Circuit Court. The U.S. Seventh Circuit Court of Appeals ruling awarding Wilson a third trial in his civil suit was issued on October 4, 1993; it bears the numbers 89-3747 and 90-2216.

The restoration of O'Hara and Yucaitis to detective rank, ordered by an arbitrator, was reported in the *Chicago Sun-Times* ("2 Detectives in Brutality Case Regain Their Rank," by Charles Nicodemus) and in the *Chicago Tribune* ("Demoted Detectives Win Reinstatement") on January 28, 1994. The arbitrator, Alex Elson, made the decision after a grievance was filed on the officers' behalf by the Fraternal Order of Police.

My report that by May 1995 the city had paid Kunkle almost $850,000 is based on the city's response to my Freedom of Information Act request. That response, dated April 24, 1995, said that as of that date, $848,156.94 had been paid to Kunkle's law firm for the defense of Burge and his colleagues.

The letter from the city corporation counsel's office stating that the city would henceforth deny indemnification to the officers because they had acted outside the scope of their employment was dated March 28,

1994, and was addressed to William Kunkle. The city's argument that it had reached that decision "as a necessary consequence of its pursuit of truth" can be found in "City of Chicago's Memorandum in Response to Plaintiff Andrew Wilson's Motion for Summary Judgment," dated May 15, 1995, filed in U.S. District Judge Gettleman's courtroom, case number 86 C 2360. Judge Gettleman's ruling and the judgment orders for damages and attorneys' fees can be found in that case file.

The Seventh Circuit of the U.S. Court of Appeals, which had previously ordered that Wilson should receive a third trial, decided on July 21, 1997, that the city's scope of employment argument "borders on the frivolous." The decision, written by Judge Richard Posner, carries the number 96-3083. The *Chicago Sun-Times* devoted one paragraph to the decision on page 24 ("City's Brutality Appeal Denied"). The *Chicago Tribune* failed to mention it at all.

In discussing the publicity given to the Burge controversy, I mention the large color photograph of Burge that took over the front page of the *Chicago Sun-Times* the day after the Police Board decision was announced. That photo ran on February 11, 1993, and was accompanied by three articles on page 5. The *Chicago Tribune* also placed the story prominently—at the top of page 1 (see "Police Board Fires Burge, Reinstates 2 Detectives," by Sharman Stein, February 11, 1993). The *New York Times* story on the Fraternal Order of Police's desire to put Burge, Yucaitis, and O'Hara on its float in one of the city's two St. Patrick's Day parades can be found in the paper on March 10, 1993 ("Citing a Race Angle in Float, Parade Bars a Police Entry"). The float was banned by the organizers of the south side parade. The south side parade is privately organized, is staged in a largely white neighborhood, and is not considered to be the city's official St. Patrick's Day parade. The documentary shown on public television stations about the torture at Area 2 was "The End of the Nightstick," made by Peter Kuttner, Cyndi Moran, and Eric Scholl. It was shown on PBS's *P.O.V.* program.

The passage of legislation to shield perpetrators of torture in Illinois was reported by Michael Miner in the *Chicago Reader* ("Cop Stoppers' Textbook," August 14, 1992) and by Hugh Dellios and Rob Karwath in the September 4, 1992, edition of the *Chicago Tribune* ("Law Curbs Prosecution of Brutality").

In my discussion of Cook County Circuit Court judges I mention the following cases, all from the criminal court: Stanley Howard (case number 84 C 13134); Aaron Patterson (86 C 6091); Darrell Cannon (83 C 11830). In Howard's case, police department personnel records, subpoenaed by his attorney, reveal that Judge John Mannion served as a policeman at Area 2, and two affidavits sworn to by Mannion, available in Howard's case file, present arguments against his being recused. In neither affidavit does he mention that he served as a policeman at Area 2. Howard's case was allowed to remain on Mannion's docket.

In Aaron Patterson's case, Judge John Morrissey dismissed the defendent's etchings as "hearsay" on September 15, 1989, and anyone wishing to see the full text of his remarks can consult the transcript for that date. In discussing Darrell Cannon's case I refer to Judge Thomas Maloney's conviction on charges of taking bribes to fix murder cases. For background, see "Judge Maloney Found Guilty in Corruption Case," by Matt O'Connor (*Chicago Tribune,* April 17, 1993).

Judge Rizzi's decision in *People v. Gregory Banks* was issued on December 28, 1989, and carries the case number 1-85-2746. Its law library citation is 140 Ill.Dec. 115, 549 N.E.2d 766 (Ill. App. 1 Dist. 1989). Judges P. J. Freeman and J. White concurred. In Cook Country Criminal Court, Banks's case number was 83 C 1247801. Banks's civil suit in U.S. District Court, Northern District of Illinois (case number 91 C 6470) was settled on August 18, 1993.

The Illinois Supreme Court ruling in *People v. Madison Hobley* was handed down on March 31, 1994, and carries the Supreme Court case number 71184 (a copy of the decision can be found at 1994 WL 106576 [Ill.]). In Cook Country Criminal Court, Hobley's case number is 87C 2356.

It should also be noted that Judge Brian Duff resigned from the federal bench in 1996. Duff's letter of resignation indicated that he wished to retire on disability, but the *Tribune* reported that the resignation came "in the face of a judicial disciplinary complaint filed by the U.S. Department of Justice" (see "Controversial Judge Steps Down from U.S. Bench," by Maurice Possley and Matt O'Connor, *Chicago Tribune,* October 11, 1996). Possley and O'Connor reported that Duff had "earned a reputation for a hot temper and erratic rulings." Among the examples the reporters cited was Duff's then recent threat to lawyers in a narcotics case. "If I find someone talking to the press," the judge said, "I'm going to bore them a new orifice."

Chapter 4—History and Method

In recounting the history of torture, I am much indebted to two fine books: Edward Peters's *Torture* (Basil Blackwell, 1985) and John Langbein's *Torture and the Law of Proof* (University of Chicago Press, 1976). Aristotle's embrace of torture in extracting evidence was cited by Peters (see pages 13–14). St. Augustine recognized torture as unjust, but nonetheless thought it necessary (*Encyclopaedia Britannica,* 1926, volume 27). Peters describes the Roman system of torture (see pages 18–36) and in his second chapter he delineates how, once instituted, the punishments intended only for the lowest of classes came to be applied across a broader spectrum of society. The *Encyclopaedia Britannica* (1929, volume 22, page 311), details the methods used in Rome as postconviction punishment. The history of the Catholic Church's stance can be found on the same page.

The belief that God would offer signs to determine guilt or innocence, those signs being the survival of an ordeal, is discussed in Peters's chapter 2, which also describes the revolution in legal theory of the twelfth century and the methods of torture deployed thereafter. Langbein's passage on the German criminal code of 1532, which forbade suggestive questioning so that the accused would confess to specific details of the crime, can be found in "Torture and Plea-Bargaining" (*University of Chicago Law Review,* volume 46, number 1, fall 1978, page 7). The idea that prisons in the Middle Ages were places of detention, not punishment, can be found in Langbein's *Torture and the Law of Proof* (page 28). His explanation of the German criminal code of 1532 appears on the preceding page. Langbein mentions the Elizabethan England hanging rate—eight hundred a year—on page 82, and the account of what was done to traitors, felons, heretics, and lesser offenders appears on page 77.

The end of torture as an acceptable form of legal investigation is described in Langbein's chapter 2 and Peters's chapter 3. I found Victor Hugo's claim ("Torture has ceased to exist") in Rita Maran's book *Torture: The Role of Ideology in the French-Algerian War* (Praeger Publishers, 1989, page 4). The description of the Cheka's method involving the deployment of a rat can be found in Peters's *Torture* (see page 129), and four pages later the author describes how the widespread use of torture by the French in Algeria in the late 1950s laid waste to the notion that torture was "an aberration of psychotic or degenerate governments, lacking popular support." Sartre's characterization of torture as "a plague infecting our whole era" can be found in his introduction to Henri Alleg's account of his torture by French paratroopers (*The Question,* George Braziller, 1958, page 26).

The torture of blasphemers, heretics, Quakers, thieves, forgers, and burglars in colonial America is described in chapter 11 of Alice Morse Earle's *Curious Punishments of Bygone Days* (originally published in 1896; reissued, Detroit: Singing Tree Press, 1968). The Works Progress Administration interviews of former slaves whipped for learning to read, for spilling coffee, or for praying for freedom are contained in *Bullwhip Days: The Slaves Remember,* edited by James Mellon (Weidenfeld & Nicolson, 1988). Flogging in Delaware is described in detail in Robert Graham Caldwell's *Red Hannah: Delaware's Whipping Post* (University of Pennsylvania Press, 1947); the decline in the use of the post after 1941 is explained on page 70.

The National Commission on Law Observance and Enforcement, commonly known as the Wickersham Commission, submitted its *Report on Lawlessness in Law Enforcement* to President Herbert Hoover in 1931 (the Government Printing Office published the report). Chapter 2 contains a description of torture methods used by police in fifteen cities in the United States. Mention of the electric chair used in Helena, Arkansas, can be found in the appendix, page 239. *Our Lawless Police,* by Wickersham Commission field investigator Ernest Hopkins, is a less clinical account of what the commission uncovered (originally published by Viking Press in 1931; reissued, Da Capo Press, 1972).

The story of the torture at the Tucker State Prison Farm can be found in *Humanistic Perspectives in Medical Ethics,* edited by Maurice Visscher (Prometheus Books, 1972). Chapter 11, "Prison Doctors," by Tom Murton, describes what he and others uncovered in the Arkansas prison system. The abuses of the Massachusetts juvenile correctional system in the late 1960s are detailed in *Last One over the Wall,* by Jerome Miller (Ohio State University Press, 1998).

Police in New Orleans resorted to torture in November 1980 in the wake of the shooting of a policeman. *See Singletary et al. v. Parsons et al.,* #81-496 (E.D. La.) and *U.S. v. McKenzie,* 768 F.2d 602 (5th Cir. 1985). The torture of suspects by New York police using stun guns was detailed in the *New York Times* (see "Student Tells Jury 2 Officers Burned Him with Stun Gun," April 19, 1986; "Lawyers Clash on Evidence in Officers' Stun-Gun Trial," May 1, 1988; "Two Queens Officers Convicted in Stun-Gun Trial," May 3, 1986; "Stun Gun Trial Ends with Four Being Convicted," February 25, 1988, all stories by Joseph Fried, and "Queens Police Are Accused of Torture" [February 2, 1988] by Stacey Okun).

The practices of the K-9 unit of the Los Angeles Police Department are explained in two 1992 reports: Amnesty International's *Torture, Ill-Treatment, and Excessive Force by Police in Los Angeles, California* (see chapter 5), and *Analysis and Recommendations: Los Angeles Police Department K-9 Program,* prepared for the Los Angeles Police Commission by the American Civil Liberties Union Foundation of Southern California and five other civil and human rights groups. My report that Chicago police dogs had bitten only thirty-two people in a three-year period (as compared to more than nine hundred in Los Angeles) is based on the Chicago police department's response to my Freedom of Information Act request; the figures were supplied by John P. Sullivan, commander of the Public Transportation Section, in a memo written February 8, 1995.

Menachem Begin's description of the effects of sleep deprivation in *White Nights: The Story of a Prisoner in Russia* (Harper & Row, 1977) can be found on pages 107 and 108. The humiliating practices of the Northern Ireland police in the late 1970s were described in *Report of an Amnesty International Mission to Northern Ireland* (Amnesty International, June 1978). The practices of the Nazis, making prisoners live in their own excrement, are described in Terence Des Pres, *The Survivor: An Anatomy of Life in the Death Camps* (Oxford University Press, 1976, chapter 3). Alexander Donat's recollection of the impending doom of anyone who did not wash in the camps can be found on page 173 of his memoir *The Holocaust Kingdom* (Holt, Rinehart, and Winston, 1965).

The Israeli journalist Yossi Melman's account of his participation in the mock execution of a Palestinian farm worker was published in the *Chicago Tribune* on May 23, 1994 ("Facing up to Israel as an Oppressor"). James LeMoyne's story of Honduran interrogator Florencio Caballero and the "psychological methods" he was taught by instructors from the United States can be found in the *New York Times Magazine,* June 5, 1988 ("Testifying to Torture," page 44). The Uruguayan methods of psychological torture detailed in this book come from Lawrence Weschler's *A Miracle, a Universe: Settling Accounts with Torturers* (Pantheon, 1990).

The United Nations' attempts to define torture can be found in two documents, the 1975 Declaration against Torture and the Convention against Torture and Other Cruel, Inhuman, and Degrading Treatment or Punishment (passed December 10, 1984). An examination of the 1975 definition and the difficulty in applying it can be found in Amnesty International's report *Torture in the Eighties* (Amnesty International, 1984, pages 13 to 17). Particular attention is paid in that passage to the European Court of Human Rights 1978 ruling in the case of Northern Ireland's hooded men. A discussion of the UN's 1984 Convention against Torture and what it requires can be found in the journal *Torture* ("Practices against Governmental Sanctioned Torture," by Bent Sorensen, volume 5, number 2, [1995]).

In *Strategic Models for the Abolition of Torture,* a paper prepared for the University of Chicago Human Rights Program conference "Investigating and Combating Torture" (March 4–7, 1999), Eric Prokosch, theme research coordinator of Amnesty International, stated, "Amnesty International receives reports of torture or ill-treatment in over 100 countries each year, and torture and ill-treatment can be said to be widespread or recurrent in over 60 countries."

Chapter 8—Perpetrators

Psychologists Mika Haritos-Fatouros and Janice Gibson have written several articles about the Greek torturers from the ETA. Together they published "The Education of a Torturer" (*Psychology Today,* November 1986). Haritos-Fatouros has written "Antecedent Conditions Leading to the Behavior of a Torturer: Fallacy or Reality," an unpublished manuscript that she kindly provided to me, and "The Official Torturer: A Learning Model for Obedience to an Authority of Violence" (*Journal of Applied Social Psychology,* volume 18 [1988], pages 1107–20; reprinted with two additional tables in *The Politics of Pain,* Leiden, the Netherlands: publication #45, edited by Ronald Crelinsten and Alex Schmid, The Center for Study of Social Conflicts). Gibson published "Training People to Inflict Pain: State Terror and Social Learning" (*Journal of Humanistic Psychology,* volume 31, number 2, spring 1991, pages 72–87) and "Factors Contributing to the Creation of a Torturer" (a chapter in the book *Psychology and Torture,* edited by Peter Suedfeld; Washington, D.C.: Hemisphere,1990).

Haritos-Fatouros also does an extraordinary interview of Greek torturer Michaelis Petrou in the Danish film *Your Neighbor's Son* (1982), an interview in which Petrou admits he would have performed any sort of torture he was asked to perform, including the torture of children before the eyes of their father. I quote from that interview later in chapter 8 when I state that Petrou said he never thought he could do anything but obey. That specific remark appears in the transcript of the Haritos-Fatouros interview, but it is not part of the film. Later in the chapter I also discuss how Mika Haritos-Fatouros came to do her research on torturers by first winning the confidence of one member of the unit. That account came from my interview with her at the University of Thessaloniki. The information that one of the ESA men married one of the prisoners can be found in table 1 of Haritos-Fatouros's article in the *Journal of Applied Psychology.*

My description of the My Lai massacre is based on *Crimes of Obedience,* by Herbert Kelman and V. Lee Hamilton (Yale University Press, 1989); *Four Hours in My Lai,* by Michael Bilton and Kevin Sim (Viking, 1992);

and Seymour Hersh's two books *My Lai 4: A Report on the Massacre and Its Aftermath* (Random House, 1970) and *Cover-Up: The Army's Secret Investigation of the Massacre at My Lai 4* (Vintage, 1972). Various figures have been published as the body count for the day. On the first page of their book, Bilton and Sim quote the Peers Commission Report: "The precise number of Vietnamese cannot be determined but was at least 175 and may exceed 400."

Molly Harrower's article "Rorschach Records of the Nazi War Criminals: An Experimental Study after Thirty Years" appeared in the *Journal of Personality Assessment* (volume 40 [1976]). Ervin Staub describes the professional backgrounds of members of the Einsatzgruppen in *The Roots of Evil* (Cambridge University Press, 1989, page 136).

Bruce Moore-King's fictional memoir, *White Man, Black War* (Harare, Zimbabwe: Baobab Books, 1988) includes scenes of torture that he witnessed, but he uses a novelist's approach, and thus his own role in the stories told in the book is not clear.

My description of the Stanley Milgram experiments on obedience comes from his book *Obedience to Authority* (Harper & Row, 1974). His account of Elinor Rosenblum's participation can be found on pages 79–84. Ervin Staub cautions against viewing obedience as the sole motive for acts of human destructiveness in *The Roots of Evil* (page 29). Staub's book also describes the continuum of destruction that takes place in genocidal nations.

Robert Jay Lifton's description of the doctors at Auschwitz who felt sorry not for their victims but for themselves can be found in "Medicalized Killing in Auschwitz" (*Psychiatry,* volume 45 [November 1982], page 295). The metalworker from Bremerhaven serving in the Nazi's Reserve Police Battalion 101 who "humanely" kills only children explains his reasoning in Christopher Browning's book *Ordinary Men* (HarperCollins, 1992, page 73).

Jean-Pierre Vittori's *Confessions d'un professional de la torture* (Paris: Editions Ramsay, 1980), a book based on the recollections of a French torturer in Algeria, is unfortunately out of print and was never translated into English. The torturer's assertion that the Algerians found native interrogators more frightening than the French can be found on pages 55 and 109. General Jacques Massu's admission that torture had been used by the French in Algeria was quoted by Alistair Horne in his book *A Savage War of Peace: Algeria 1954–1962* (Penguin, 1985, page 196). Horne discusses the effectiveness of the torture starting on page 204. He quotes Edward Behr (author of *The Algerian Problem,* London, 1961) who states that the Battle of Algiers could not have been won without the use of torture; Horne then goes on to make the argument that the war would have ended sooner had torture not been deployed. Horne's discussion of the Wuillaume report is not to be missed (page 197). Wuillaume, a senior civil servant, proposed that torture should be institutionalized because it had become so prevalent, that doing so would restore police morale, and that torture by electricity and by the "water pipe method" (filling the victim with water) was more painful psychologically than physically and did not constitute excessive cruelty. Wuillaume and his reasoning are also analyzed in Rita Maran's aforementioned book, *Torture: The Role of Ideology in the French-Algerian War.*

Henri Alleg's book, *La Question* (George Braziller, 1958), details his torture at the hands of the French. In his introduction to the book, Jean-Paul Sartre makes the point that the torture occurred not because lives were in danger but only to find the name of the man who had hid Alleg (page 27).

Don Dzagulones, the former Americal Division interrogator, talked to me in his apartment outside Detroit on August 9, 1995. He also testified at hearings conducted by Vietnam Veterans against the War in 1971. The proceedings of those hearings were later inserted into the Congressional Record of April 6, 1971 (see pages 9,947 to 10,055; Dzagulones is introduced on page 9,988 and his remarks begin on page 9,996). An edited collection of the testimony at the hearings was published by Beacon Press in 1972 (*The Winter Soldier Investigation: An Inquiry into American War Crimes,* by Vietnam Veterans against the War), and a brief version of Dzagulones's statement can be found on page 115.

The text of the U.S. military's pocket card, "The Enemy in Your Hands," issued to all members of the American armed forces in Vietnam starting in late 1967, can be found in Lieutenant General William R. Peers's book *The My Lai Inquiry* (W. W. Norton, 1979), starting on page 264. Peers notes that the holders of the cards often neglected to read them. "In any case," Peers wrote, "after a couple of monsoon rains, they became mangled and useless."

Chapter 12—Victims

Dr. Liber Mandressi's account of being tortured in Uruguay by people who had no desire for information can be found on page 125 of Lawrence Weschler's book *A Miracle, a Universe: Settling Accounts with Torturers* (Pantheon, 1990). Dr. Ole Vedel Rasmussen's report on his survey of two hundred torture victims can be found in the *Danish Medical Bulletin*

("Medical Aspects of Torture," volume 37, supplement number 1 [January 1990]). *The Guardian Weekly* carried the report of the man, who, under torture by the African National Congress, confessed to murdering himself (the interrogator was confused by code names) (see "ANC Officials Denounced for Prison Camp Terror," by David Beresford, October 25, 1992). Beresford's article also tells of a man who confessed to his ANC torturers that he had killed people who were subsequently found to be alive.

Mauricio Rosencof's account of the fantasies he used to cope with his confinement in Uruguay were related in Weschler's *A Miracle, a Universe* (page 146). Dr. Hugo Sacchi related his preparations for being tortured in *Estudias* ("No hay que ser un heroe, solamente un ser humano," volume 84 [October–December 1982]). Major Stewart Wolf and Lieutenant Colonel Herbert Ripley's study of victims of torture by the Japanese can be found in the *American Journal of Psychiatry*, "Reactions among Allied Prisoners of War Subjected to Three Years of Imprisonment and Torture by the Japanese" (volume 104, pages 180–93).

My paragraphs on coping mechanisms deployed by torture victims are based on the following: "Group Formation and Its Significance in the Nazi Concentration Camps," by Shamai Davidson (*Israel Journal of Psychiatry and Related Sciences*, volume 22, numbers 1–2 [1985], pages 41–50); "Psychotherapy for Victims of Torture," by F. Somnier and Inge Genefke (*British Journal of Psychiatry*, volume 149 [1986], pages 323–29; the previously cited article "Communist Interrogation and Indoctrination of 'Enemies of the States,' " by Lawrence Hinkle Jr. and Harold G. Wolff; and Vittori's aforementioned *Confessions d'un professional de la torture*.

Iain Guest's report on his interview with Chilean torturer Andres Valenzuela ("Portrait of a Torturer") can be found in *The Guardian*, December 7, 1989. The accusations of torture leveled against the government of Robert Mugabe are documented in *Zimbabwe: A Break with the Past?*, an Africa Watch report published in October 1989, and mention of Mugabe's tirade against "Amnesty Lies International" can be found on page 19 of that report.

In my discussion of the long-term effects of torture on those who survive it, I discuss various theories about what sort of torture victim fares better in the long run. Bruno Bettelheim suggested that politically active people had an easier time coping with their experiences in concentration camps (see his "Individual and Mass Behavior in Extreme Situations," *Journal of Abnormal Social Psychology*, volume 38 [1943], pages 417–52). An article by J. Kieler in the *Danish Medical Bulletin* ("Immediate Reactions to Capture and Deportation," volume 27 [1980], pages 215–20) also argues that the politically active coped better. Tony Horwitz, writing in the *Wall Street Journal* on October 12, 1992 ("London Foundation Offers Care to Victims of World's Dictators"), quotes social worker Hilda Blank of the London Medical Foundation for the Care of Victims of Torture as saying that committed dissidents could find a way to explain the pain they suffered. Horwitz then goes on to report that "people swept up in random police raids or mass arrests often are paralyzed by what seems a senseless turn of fate." Based on a sample of 211 Holocaust survivors, Dr. William Helmreich, author of *Against All Odds: Holocaust Survivors and the Successful Lives They Made in America* (Simon & Schuster, 1992), came to believe that the people in his sample had certain strength-of-character traits—adaptability, initiative, and tenacity—that accounted for their survival and their later success in the United States.

Wolf and Ripley's assessment of the two dominant personality types in their sample can be found on page 186 of the aforementioned "Reactions Among Allied Prisoners of War Subjected to Three Years of Imprisonment and Torture by the Japanese." The study of 253 Vietnam veterans who were prisoners of war, conducted by Robert Ursano, James Boydstun, and Richard Wheatley, can be found in the *American Journal of Psychiatry* ("Psychiatric Illness in U.S. Air Force Viet Nam Prisoners of War: A Five-Year Follow-Up," March 1981). The study of sixty-two former World War II prisoners of war ("Posttraumatic Stress Disorder as a Consequence of the POW Experience") that appeared in the *Journal of Mental and Nervous Disease* (volume 177, number 3 [1989]), was conducted by Nancy Speed, Brian Engdahl, Joseph Schwartz, and Raina Eberly. The study of Holocaust survivors conducted by Zev Harel, Boaz Kahana, and Eva Kahana was cited in the *New York Times* on October 6, 1992 ("Holocaust Survivors Had Skills to Prosper," by Daniel Goleman), and the same article quotes author and cartoonist Art Spiegelman saying that his parents, both Holocaust survivors, woke up howling every night.

"Psychotherapy for Victims of Torture," by Dr. Finn Somnier and Dr. Inge Genefke appeared in the *British Journal of Psychiatry* (volume 149 [1986], pages 323–29). Dr. Rasmussen's survey of two hundred victims appeared in the aforementioned "Medical Aspects of Torture." My account of the blindness experienced by Cambodian women in California was taken from "A Changed Vision of God," by Alec Wilkinson (*The New Yorker,* January 24, 1994) and "They Cried Until They Could Not See" by Patrick Cooke (*New York Times Magazine,* June 23, 1991).

A text of Richard Juma Oketch's statement before Congress on May 8, 1996, was provided to me by The Center for Victims of Torture in Minneapolis. Oketch testified before the House Committee on International Relations' Subcommittee on International Operations and Human Rights.

I refer to two studies of Americans held as prisoners of war by the Japanese and Koreans. One, published in 1975, was conducted by Gilbert Beebe ("Follow-up Studies of World War II and Korean War Prisoners," *American Journal of Epidemiology,* volume 101, number 5, page 400). The other, published five years earlier, was conducted by M. Dean Nefzger ("Follow-up Studies of World War II and Korean War Prisoners," *American Journal of Epidemiology,* volume 91, number 2, page 123). Beebe makes reference to the results of several studies of concentration camp survivors, including Leo Eitinger's *Concentration Camp Survivors in Norway and Israel* (Allen and Unvin, 1964) and an article by P. Thygesen, K. Hermann, and R. Willanger ("Concentration Camp Survivors in Denmark: Persecution, Disease, Disability, Compensation," *Danish Medical Bulletin,* volume 17 [1970], pages 65–108).

The study of children whose parents had been tortured in Chile, which was conducted by Jorgen Cohn and six of his colleagues at the International Rehabilitation and Research Centre for Torture Victims in Copenhagen, can be found in *The Lancet* (August 24, 1985, pages 437–38). The results of three studies of the children of torture victims from Chile, Argentina, and Mexico were reported in "Psychological Consequences of Torture: A Need to Formulate New Strategies for Research," by Barbara Melamed, Jodi Melamed, and Jacqueline Bouhoutsos (a chapter in the book *Psychology and Torture,* edited by Peter Suedfeld, mentioned earlier).

Chapter 16—Bystanders

I report that in Chicago, the Area 2 colleagues of Commander Burge and Detectives O'Hara and Yucaitis who participated in the systematic abuse were never called before any judge, jury, or hearing officer to answer for their crimes. Area 2 detectives did testify in various cases in which a victim alleged he had been tortured, but in those cases it was the victim who was charged with a crime, not the detectives.

The problems of democratic regimes that succeed dictatorships and the unwillingness of those new governments to prosecute torturers is discussed in a collection of papers from a conference held in November 1989, *State Crimes: Punishment or Pardon* (Queenstown, Md.: Aspen Institute, 1989).

The sources for my analysis of the British reactions to the revelations that they were torturing the Northern Irish can be found in the section of this bibliography on the case of the hooded men.

I found General Massu's comment that Henri Alleg was reassuringly vigorous thirteen years after being tortured in Rita Maran's previously mentioned book *Torture: The Role of Ideology in the French-Algerian War* (page 172).

The bystander experiment conducted with New York University students who heard a colleague call for help was reported in the *Journal of Personality and Social Psychology* ("Bystander Intervention in Emergencies: Diffusion of Responsibility," by John Darley and Bibb Latane, volume 8, number 4 [1968], page 377). Latane and Darley's smoke-filled-room experiment, conducted with Columbia University students as subjects, was presented in "Group Inhibition of Bystander Intervention in Emergencies" (*Journal of Personality and Social Psychology,* volume 10, number 3 [1968], pages 215–21) and in "When Will People Help in a Crisis?" (*Psychology Today,* December 1968, page 54).

A brief discussion of the commonly held belief that we live in a "just world" can be found on page 79 of Ervin Staub's *The Roots of Evil* (mentioned earlier). An experiment that demonstrates the belief is "Observer's Reaction to the 'Innocent Victim': Compassion or Rejection," by Melvin Lerner and Carolyn Simmons (*Journal of Personality and Social Psychology,* volume 4 [1966], pages 203–10).

Perry London's theories of altruistic behavior can be found in "The Rescuers: Motivational Hypotheses about Christians Who Saved Jews from the Nazis" (a chapter in *Altruism and Helping Behavior,* edited by J. Macaulay and L. Berkowitz, Academic Press, 1970). There have since been other studies of rescuers who saved the lives of Jews, and they are far broader than London's small sample, but they seem to me to be consistent with his findings. For a discussion of London's work and four other studies, see Ervin Staub's *The Roots of Evil* (page 166).

Accounts of two of Staub's experiments mentioned in this chapter—the experiment in which a student seeks help by saying his stomach is "killing him" and the experiment in which someone feigns a heart attack on a public street—are described in Staub's article "Helping a Distressed Person: Social, Personality, and Stimulus Determinants" (a chapter in the book *Advances in Experimental Social Psychology,* edited by L. Berkowitz, Academic Press, 1974). Staub's argument that helping is infectious can be found in *The Roots of Evil* (page 165), and he cites Philip Hallie's book about the village of Le Chambon (*Lest Innocent Blood Be Shed,* Harper & Row, 1979). Staub's discussion of Belgian actions to prevent Jews from being persecuted and the response of the Jewish community to such support appears in *The Roots of Evil* (page 165).

Acknowledgments

I have been helped by a great number of people. The John D. and Catherine T. MacArthur Foundation and the J. Roderick MacArthur Foundation both provided grants to fund my initial research. I'd like to thank those at both foundations who believed that something worthy would result from my proposal and those who supervised my work, particularly Ruth Adams, Kennette Benedict, Kate Early, and Lance Lindblom. The Ragdale Foundation provided me with a quiet and supportive place to work at various points along the way, and Mike Wilkerson, Sonja Carlborg, and Sylvia Brown made life easy during those visits.

Even with that foundation support, the book would never have seen the light of day without the tolerance, encouragement, and wisdom of my colleagues at the *Chicago Reader*. The publisher and editors of the *Reader* allowed me to follow the story of torture at Area 2 for almost a decade when no one else in town was paying it much attention, and they did so at considerable expense, since my articles took a long time to produce, required extensive legal review, and once led me into federal court to obtain documents, a very expensive path. I cannot thank them enough, particularly Bob Roth, Jane Levine, Mike Lenehan, Alison True, and Michael Miner. I am grateful also to have had David Andich, the *Reader*'s attorney, in my corner. He has been a great fighter on my behalf.

Ann Close, my editor at Knopf, has been understanding and wonderful to work with. This book was her idea, and I would probably not have taken it on had it been proposed by someone else. Wendy Weil, my agent, deserves canonization, nothing less.

Nomination for sainthood is also due to Marjorie Benton, who advised me all the way through this project. Without her intercession at the start, I'd never have reached the end. Marianne Philbin helped me obtain funding back when she was director of the Chicago Peace Museum, and I am grateful to her and to the museum.

In 1989, fellow writer Mary Ann Williams, then with *The Chicago Lawyer,* alerted me to Andrew Wilson's civil suit before it went to trial, and as a result I was there from day one. She could have seen me as a competitor and kept the story to herself, at least for a time. Dr. Robert Kirschner and Dr. Antonio Martinez gave kindly of their time, and Dr. Irena Martinez gave kindly from her bank of painful memory. Jess Brodnax provided a personal clipping service, finding articles and books I would never have thought to look for, and Eugene Raikhel proved to be a fine researcher, dogged in his pursuit of the obscure. Bonnie Samuelson translated a whole volume for me at bargain rates. Tony Judge, champion of Chicago writers for twenty years, helped me locate two former torturers. Pat Clinton, Alex Kotlowitz, Paul Engleman, Ted Hearne, Paul Wertheimer, Grant Pick, Kathy Richland, Tom Terranova, Michael Blitstein, Peter Lukidis, Chris Stewart, Wanda Rohm, and Harriet Choice helped in ways they took for granted but which meant a great deal to me. Francine Sanders kindly answered many questions, almost always, it seemed, at the eleventh hour. Erik Hudson was a tireless source. So, too, was Flint Taylor.

I am grateful for the efforts of Amnesty International staff who helped me at various points: Halya Gowan and Gillian Hoffman in London, Pia Hallonsten in Sweden, Stig Michaelsen in Norway, and Marjory Byler, Judy Hatcher, Ruth Barrett, Toni Moore, and Maureen Kelly in Chicago.

In Northern Ireland, I thank the hooded men who consented to be interviewed, particularly Jim Auld and Paddy Joe McClean. I am also grateful to Monica Davison and Marian and Patrick Harte, who hosted me on my many trips.

In London, Richard Taylor and Peter Taylor nobly shared sources. Michael VerMeulen came to my aid, providing resources and a magazine assignment when I needed both. He deserved a much longer life. Helen Bamber, of the Medical Foundation for Victims of Torture, opened the foundation's clipping files to me, and that was most helpful.

In Israel, sheer luck brought me into contact with Jihad Abdal Raheem Mohareb, my resourceful guide to Hawara and Beita; Igal Ezraty of Yesh Gvul, who provided counsel as well as numerous news clippings and translated transcripts; and James Ron of Human Rights Watch, who allowed me to accompany him on several interviews, thus sparing me the cost of a translator, and who later provided guidance after reading a draft of the Israeli chapters in this book. My thanks to them, to the men from Hawara and Beita who told me their stories, and to Jessica Montell at B'Tselem, Stanley Cohen and Nachman Ben-Yehuda at Hebrew University, Anita Vitullo at the Palestinian Human Rights Information Center, Lisa Talesnick at the *Boston Globe,* Tom Hundley of the *Chicago Tribune,* and Dan Almagor of Yesh Gvul.

In Greece, Mika Haritos-Fatouros was extraordinarily kind. She has probably interviewed more torturers than anyone else in the world, and she kindly opened the door for me to meet two of them at a time when I was not sure I would ever meet anyone who had held the job. Dr. Maria Piniou-Kalli, a victim of the junta, was a gracious host and provided an office in which I could meet the ETA men. Marianna Zervopoulou was an able translator, refusing my attempt to pay her.

In Norway, Dr. Kirsti Oskarsson helped beyond measure. In Konigsberg, Aage Ingebrethsen, managing editor of *Laagendalspoften,* provided a complete and total stranger with a room in which to conduct an interview.

In Denmark, I am indebted to the International Rehabilitation Council for Torture Victims, particularly to Peter Vesti, Svend Bitsch Christensen, Johanne Cummings, Kirsti Sparrevohn, and the helpful staff of the documentation center.

In Zimbabwe, I thank Bishop Patrick Mutume for his time and story and Sue Moore-King for her hospitality.

Finally, my deepest thanks to my wife, Colette, my son, Matthew, and my daughter, Sarah, who lived with this project in the house for far too long.

Index

Adler, Yitzhak, 270
African National Congress, 170
Africa Watch, 177
Against All Odds (Helmreich), 179
Aldubi, Roman, 217
Algeria, 32, 112, 113, 174, 247, 286
Al Haq, 221
Alleg, Henri, 113, 247
American Journal of Psychiatry, 118
Amir, Yigal, 224
Amnesty International, 38, 108, 177,
    187, 191, 226, 228, 257
*Application of the European Convention
    of Human Rights, The* (Fawcett),
    257–8
Archives of Neurology and Psychology,
    127, 174, 261
Argentina, 105, 111, 170–2, 175, 182,
    243
Arkansas, 32–3
Assali, Abed, 224
Association for Civil Rights in Israel,
    56–7, 202, 271
Audi, Ghaleb, 221
Audi, Jamal Jaber, 219–20

Audi, Saber Salim, 221
Auld, Jim, 3–10, 39, 40–1, 42, 123–5,
    174, 182, 184–5, 192, 196–8, 242
authority, obedience to, 96–102, 110
Avirash, Amiram, 144

Balniel, Lord, 43, 188, 245, 260
Banks, Gregory, 162, 238–9
Barham, Tayseer Mousa, 217–18
Barkai, Zvi, 154–5
Barrow, Rev. Willie, 24
Bastiaans, Dr. Jan, 133–4, 135–6
Batey, Chester, 25
Batsh, Ahmed Husni al-, 214, 273
Beccaria, Cesare, 31
Beebe, Gilbert, 181–2
Begin, Menachem, 34
Beiski, Justice Moshe, 58–9
Beita, West Bank, 11–16, 142, 215–19,
    242
    court-martial of Yehuda Meir, 59,
        139–57, 199–201, 205, 216, 242
    investigation of beatings at, 48–59

Ben-Moshe, Eldad, 12, 48, 201, 203–6,
    208, 209, 210
  arrests and beatings in Beita and
    Hawara and, 13–20, 53, 56,
    144–5, 152, 153–4, 157, 203,
    204–6, 208, 209
  misgivings about "strong-arm"
    actions, 16–17, 145, 146, 152, 153,
    204–5
  testimony of, 14, 145–7, 148, 205,
    206, 266
Berkowitz, L., 252, 253
Bettelheim, Bruno, 287
Booker, Louis, 22
Boyd-Carpenter, John, 44, 45–7
Boydstun, James, 178
Breland, Michael, 230
British internment policy, *see*
    internment policy, British
Brown, Roy Wade, 82–3
Browning, Christopher R., 111–12
Brzeczek, Richard, 60, 83, 84, 85, 86
B'Tselem, 213, 214
Burge, Jon
  background of, 61–2, 65, 76
  investigation of police officer
    murders by, 23, 25, 68, 69, 76, 77
  Wilson's suit against, and
    subsequent investigations and
    trials, 60–87, 158–68, 225–41, 242
bystanders, behavior of, 247–56

Caballero, Florencio, 36
Cambodians, 180–1
Cannon, Darrell, 162, 237
Carrington, Lord Peter, 3, 4, 43, 88,
    135, 195, 196, 245, 246, 259, 263
Catholic Church, 28, 111
CBS, 139, 147, 150
Center for Victims of Torture, 181
Chamous, Azam Hafeth Beni, 218

Chicago Lawyer, 66, 160
Chicago Police Board, 226, 228,
    229–31, 232, 234, 235
Chicago Police Department, 32, 34,
    252
  Office of Professional Standards,
    83–4, 86, 226–8, 232, 237, 239, 242
  Wilson case and related accusations
    against, 21–6, 60–87, 158–68,
    225–41
Chicago Sun-Times, 225, 236
Chicago Tribune, 35, 225, 228
Chile, 175, 182
Citizens Alert, 226
Clark, Mark, 66
Clarke, Joe, 39, 42, 125, 185, 196, 244
Coleman, William, 165–6, 232, 233,
    277
"Communist Interrogation and
    Indoctrination of 'Enemies of
    the States,'" 127, 174–5, 260
Compton, Sir Edmund, 41–4, 244, 245
Compton Report, 41–4, 188, 244
concentration camps, 35, 111–12, 133,
    134, 173, 177, 179, 182
*Confessions d'un professional de la
    torture* (Vittori), 112, 174, 175
Cook County Circuit Court, 231, 232
Cooper, Julio, 107–10
Costello, Declan, 186
Coulter, Andre, 22, 23
Coventry, Dale, 84–5
Crossen, Patricia, 71, 85
Cunningham, Cyril, 43–4

Daily Express (London), 137, 187
Daily Mail (London), 136–7
Daily Mirror (London), 166
Daily Telegraph (London), 137, 187
Daley, Richard, 67, 84, 226, 227, 228,
    229

Daly, Dr. Robert, 126–36, 184, 188, 260, 263

Darley, John, 247–50, 255

Davis, Julia, 81–2

Davis, Larry, 81–2

Deas, Milton, 85

Defender, 24

defining torture, 37–8, 209–10

Dehan, Segen Gavriel, 268–9

Dmadi, Kmal, 222–3

Donat, Alexander, 35

Donnelly, Michael, 42, 194–5

Downs, Levada, 65

Doyle, James, 23

drowning, near, 92, 103–4, 107, 170–1, 177

Duff, Judge Brian Barnett, 60, 65, 66, 80, 87, 158, 159–61, 163, 164–5, 166–7, 225, 226, 231, 232, 280

Dzagulones, Don, 113–21

Edgar, Jim, 236

Eichmann, Adolf, 99, 212

electric shock, 32–3, 90, 92, 104, 107, 112, 117–18, 170, 176–7, 212

    evidence of Chicago police's previous use of, 158–59, 162–5, 230, 234, 237

    Andrew Wilson's claims of, 26, 60, 69–72, 76–7, 79–81, 83, 85–7, 165, 227, 230, 234, 240

Estudias, 172–3

European Commission of Human Rights, Republic of Ireland's complaint, 47, 125–37

    appeal of, *see* European Court of Human Rights, Republic of Ireland's case

    expert witnesses, testimony by, 126–36

    illustrative cases, 129–36

European Convention for the Protection of Human Rights and Fundamental Freedoms, 125, 258

European Court of Human Rights, Republic of Ireland's case, 137, 185–7, 191, 213, 245, 246

Ezra, Gideon, 215

Fahey, Mike, 229

Fahey, William, 21–2, 60, 71, 76, 78, 86, 229, 231, 235, 241

families of torture victims, 182

Faulkner, Brian, 41, 187

Fawcett, J. E. S., 257

Ferro, Mario, 71

Fianna Uladh (Warriors of Ulster), 131

Finklestein, Menachem, 52, 58, 142, 143–45, 151, 153–4, 157, 200–1, 209

Fishman, Alex, 55

Fitzmaurice, Sir Gerald, 187, 258

"five techniques," 6, 39, 40, 45, 123–5, 187–8, 213, 245, 255

    distinguished from classic methods of torture, 137, 187, 213

    effects of, 8, 39–41, 123–5, 127–36, 184–5, 188–98

    European Commission of Human Rights case and, 127–9, 135, 136

    European Court of Human Rights case and, 186, 187, 213, 246

    history and development, 45–6, 127–9, 258

    investigation of, 41–7, 129–30

    lasting effects on victims of, 123–5, 129–36, 184–5, 188–98

    see also specific techniques, e.g. sleep deprivation; standing, forced

Fogel, David, 226–27

food deprivation, 6, 32, 34, 43, 128, 212, 213–14
France, 31–32, 112, 113, 174, 247, 253, 254, 286
Fraternal Order of Police, 236, 279
Front de Liberation Nationale (FLN), Algerian, 112

Gabriel, Danny, 17, 56
Gall, Allen, 167–8
Gallardo, Miguel Rodriguez, 175
Garcia, Hugo, 102–7, 112, 175
Gardiner, Lord, 44–5, 47
Gefen, Ziv, 56, 210
Genefke, Dr. Inge, 179
General Security Service, 13, 55–6, 57, 143, 147, 152, 153, 157, 207, 216
torture methods of, 212–15
Geneva Convention, 44, 116–17, 214
Genovese, Kitty, 247, 249
Germany
criminal code of 1532, 29, 30
Nazi, *see* Nazi Germany
Gettleman, Judge Robert, 235
Gibson, Janice, 88, 93, 95
Givati Brigade, 140–2, 199, 270
Goldenberg, Amnon, 143, 146, 152, 154, 155, 157
Goldston, Michael, 227–8, 237, 239, 242
Golani Brigade, 16, 154
Greece, 93–6, 136, 175–6, 177, 246, 255, 284
Griffiths, Keith, 83–4
Grondona, L. St. Clare, 44
Guardian, 124, 125, 245
Guest, Iain, 175

Ha'aretz, 56, 141–2, 148–9, 160, 200, 213
Haas, Jeffrey, 66, 85, 161, 166–7, 225
Hadashot, 55, 148

Ha Ir, 148
Halevi, Judge Benjamin, 139
Hamael, Jihad, 218–19
Hamous, Samir, 156, 220
Hampton, Fred, 66
Hannaway, Kevin, 8, 39–40, 123–4, 190, 191
Hardin, Dwayne, 22
Harel, Zev, 179
Haritos-Fatouros, Mika, 88, 93–6, 284
Harizat, 'Abd a-Samed, 213
Harrower, Molly, 89
Hawara, West Bank, 17–19, 219–24, 242
court-martial of Yehuda Meir, 59, 139–57, 199–201, 205, 216, 242
investigation of beatings at, 48–59
Hazan, J. B. R., 135–6
Heath, Edward, 4, 41, 47, 125, 188, 246, 259, 263
Helmreich, William, 179
"Helping a Distressed Person: Social, Personality, and Stimulus Determinants," 253
Herzog, Mike, 13, 265
Hinkle, Dr. Lawrence, 127–8, 174–5
history of torture, 27–34
Hobley, Madison, 239
Holmes, Anthony, 162
Holmes, Lee, 238
Holocaust Kingdom, The (Donat), 35
Hooded Men, The (McKenna, CBC documentary), 260
hooding, 43, 47, 129, 169–70, 213, 214
purpose of, 5, 41–2, 103, 244
Hope, Edgar, 23, 24
Hopkins, Ernest, 32–3
Horn, Yuval, 200–1, 267
Howard, Stanley, 237, 279
Howary, Jihad Hamdan, 17–18, 142, 147, 156, 157, 222
Howary, Muhammad Jihad, 18, 19, 219, 266

Human Rights Watch, 213, 214
Hyman, Larry, 71

Innocent IV, Pope, 28
International Committee of the Red
    Cross, 213, 214
internment policy, British, 4, 5, 40,
    242, 244–7
    Republic of Ireland's complaint
    against, *see* European
    Commission of Human Rights,
    Republic of Ireland's complaint
intifada, 11, 12–13, 139–40, 204
    CBS filming of beatings of
    Palestinians, 139, 147, 150
    court-martial of Givati Brigade
    soldiers, 140–2
    court-martial of Yehuda Meir, 59,
    139–57, 199–201, 205, 216, 242
    investigation of beatings, 48–59
    "strong-arm" policy in reaction to,
    13–20, 48, 57, 139, 142, 154–6
Irish Republican Army (IRA), 4, 43,
    135, 189, 193, 197, 245, 246
Israel
    General Security Service, *see*
    General Security Service
    intifada and, *see* intifada
    Meir court-martial, *see* Meir,
    Yehuda, court-martial of
    reaction to revelations of intifada
    "strong-arm" policy, 141–2, 206,
    255
Israel Defense Forces (IDF), 11–20,
    48–59, 57–8, 138–57
    court-martial of Givati Brigade
    soldiers, 140–2
    court-martial of Yehuda Meir, 59,
    139–57, 199–201, 205, 216, 242
    Givati Brigade, 140–2, 199, 270
    Golani Brigade, 16, 154

manifestly illegal orders and, *see*
    manifestly illegal orders
    military police, 49–54, 266
    Nahal Brigade, *see* Nahal Brigade
Israeli High Court of Justice, 56–9,
    212, 214–15
Israeli secret police, *see* General
    Security Service (Shin Bet)
Italy, 31

Jackson, Rev. Jesse, 24
Japan, 31, 133, 177, 181, 182
Jerusalem Post, 13–14
Jones, Melvin, 158–59, 162, 163–4,
    230, 234
Journal of Applied Social Psychology,
    88, 94
Journal of Humanistic Psychology, 88, 95
*Journal of Personality and Social
    Psychology*, 248, 250

Kafr a-Dikh, 149, 152, 154
Kahana, Boaz and Eva, 179
Kedmi, Justice Yaakov, 58, 59
Kelly, Douglas, 89
Kfar Kassem, 138–9, 202, 204, 208,
    211, 267–9
KGB, 31, 45, 127, 128, 255
Kirschner, Dr. Robert, 78–81, 160
Kochva, Omri, 112, 206–10
    carrying out of "strong-arm" policy
    by, 13, 14, 15–16, 17–18, 56, 157,
    206, 211
    investigation of Beita and Hawara
    beatings and, 48–53, 58, 202
    testimony of, 143–44
Korean War, 129, 177, 181, 182
Korn, Dr. Geoffrey, 71–2
Kunkle, William, 67, 72–6, 78, 79–80,
    86–7, 161, 166, 225, 231, 233

Lancet, 45
Landau, Justice Moshe, 212–13, 272
Langbein, John, 29, 30
Latane, Bibb, 247–50, 255
Lawlessness in Law Enforcement, 32–3
Lebanon, 149–50
Le Chambon, France, 253, 254
Leigh, Dr. Denis, 134
LeMoyne, James, 36
Lerner, Melvin, 251
Levin, Justice Dov, 58, 59
Lifton, Robert Jay, 111
Livne, Ze'ev, 16–17, 19–20, 145–56,
    205–6
London, Perry, 252, 290
Los Angeles Police Department,
    33–4, 233

Ma'ariv, 142
Macaulay, J., 252
McCarthy, James, 67, 77, 82, 86, 166
McClean, Paddy Joe, 8, 39, 42, 130,
    131–6, 195–6
McGuigan, Francis, 8, 192
McKenna, Sean, 123–4, 188
McKenna, William, 60, 72–73, 76, 87,
    158, 232
McKerr, Gerard, 39, 42, 189–90
McNally, Patrick, 39, 193–4
Malinki, Shmuel, 138–9, 268–9
Maloney, Judge Thomas, 237–38
Mandressi, Dr. Liber, 169–70
Maniateas, Yannis, 94–5
manifestly illegal orders, 138, 141,
    202, 208, 211
    court-martial of Yehuda Meir and,
        59, 139–57, 199–201, 205, 216, 242
    defined, 139
Manila, 180
Mannion, Judge John, 237, 280
Martin, LeRoy, 226, 227, 228, 232, 241

Martinez, Irena, 170–2
Massu, Jacques, 112, 247
Maulding, Reginald, 43, 44, 244, 245
Meir, Orna, 202, 203
Meir, Yehuda, 11–12, 13, 201–3, 207,
    211
    army career of, 149–50
    court-martial of, 59, 139–57,
        199–201, 205, 216, 242
    defense of, 142, 150–54, 202
    investigation of Beita and Hawara
        beatings and, 52–5, 57–9
    promotion of, 48, 51, 147, 202–3
    "strong-arm" policy and, 13, 16–17,
        152–3
Melman, Yossi, 35–6
Meltzer, Yehuda, 148
Mexico, 182
Miami Herald, 212
Milgram, Stanley, 96–102
Miller, Doris, 24
Miller, Jill, 62–5
Miracle, A Universe, A (Weschler), 36,
    169–70, 172
Miskiw, Gregory, 166, 232
Missios, Chrones, 175–6
Mitzna, Amram, 146, 147, 148–9,
    151–3, 154, 155–6, 201, 205
Mnangagwa, Emmerson, 176
mock executions, 35–6, 104, 171, 179
Montgomery, Michael and Doris, 189
Moody, Erma, 61–2
Moore-King, Bruce, 89–93, 112, 113,
    121–2
Morgan, Solomon, 24–5
Morrissey, Judge John, 237
Mufala, Muhammad Beni, 156–57,
    215–16
Mugabe, Robert, 92, 176–7
Mulvaney, William, 71, 72
Murphy, Maureen, 67, 82–3
My Lai massacre, 88–9

Nafsu case, Israel, 212
Nahal Brigade, 11–13, 48, 149–50,
    207, 242
  Beita and Hawara beatings and, *see*
    Beita, West Bank; Hawara, West
    Bank
  see also names of individuals
National Commission on Law
    Observance and Enforcement
    (Wickersham Commission),
    32–3
Nazi Doctors, The (Lifton), 111
Nazi Germany, 35, 89, 99, 111–12,
    177, 179, 182, 246, 252–5
Nemir, Nemir Saleh, 223
New York City Police Department, 33
New York Times, 36, 179, 236
nightmares, 133, 179, 181, 182, 194,
    196, 197, 221
"Night of the Broken Clubs, The," 56
noise bombardment, 5–6, 42, 43, 213
  hypersensitivity to noise following,
    131, 132, 195
Northern Ireland, 3–10, 35, 39–47,
    123–37, 169, 184–98, 242, 244
Northern Ireland Civil Rights
    Association, 195
North Korea, 129, 177, 255
Noy, Oz, 141
Number 300 bus affair, Israel, 212

obedience to authority, 96–102, 110
Obedience to Authority (Milgram), 98–9
O'Brien, Richard, 21–2, 60, 65, 71, 76,
    86, 241
O'Brien, Judge Thomas, 231
Ofer, Shalom, 268–9
O'Hara, Patrick, 60, 71, 72–3, 76, 87,
    158, 225, 227, 228, 229, 230–1,
    233, 236, 242
Oketch, Richard Juma, 181

Okon, Boaz, 143
Olmert, Yirmi, 55, 57
O'Malley, Dr. Patraig Pearse, 134
Ordinary Men (Browning), 111–12
Our Lawless Police (Hopkins), 32–3

Palestinian uprising, *see* intifada
Papoutsis, Vlasis, 95, 96
Parker, Lord, 44, 45–7
Parker Commission, 44–7, 244
Patterson, Aaron, 237, 279–80
People's Law Office, Chicago, 66–7,
    158–63, 165–7, 226, 231–5, 237
People v. Gregory Banks, The, 238–9
People v. Madison Hobley, The, 239
Peres, Shimon, 224
Peters, Edward, 29, 31
Petrou, Michaelis, 96, 284
Physicians for Human Rights,
    139–40, 269
Police Executive Research Forum,
    240
Porat, Tizra, 217
Porch, Willie, 163, 164–5
Poree, Lawrence, 162
Posner, Judge Richard, 231–2, 235,
    236
Powell, George, 162
psychological torture, 35–7, 38, 104
  lasting effects of, *see* victims, lasting
    effects on
Psychology Today, 88

Question, La (Alleg), 112, 113, 247

Raba, Dr. John, 83, 84, 86
Rabin, Yitzhak, 213, 224
  court-martial of Yehuda Meir and,
    142, 153

Rabin, Yitzhak (*cont'd*)
   denies giving orders, 149, 151
   "strong-arm" policy to suppress the
      intifada of, 13–14, 56, 139, 142,
      154–6, 201, 204, 205
Rabin, Yoram, 48–54, 55, 58, 200, 202,
      209, 210–11
Ragland, Sebastian, 77
Rasmussen, Dr. Ole Vedel, 170, 179
Re'a, Wein, 270
"Reactions among Allied Prisoners of
      War Subjected to Three Years of
      Imprisonment and Torture by
      the Japanese," 173
Red Cross, 52, 54, 202, 213, 214
Rees, Merlyn, 246
Refideyeh Hospital, 266
Reidy, Dan, 230
*Report of an Enquiry into Allegations of
   Ill-Treatment in Northern Ireland,*
      257
Republic of Ireland
   case before European Court of
      Human Rights, *see* European
      Court of Human Rights,
      Republic of Ireland's case
   complaint against Britain, *see*
      European Commission of
      Human Rights, Republic of
      Ireland's complaint
"Rescuers: Motivational Hypotheses
      about Christians Who Saved
      Jews from the Nazis, The," 252
research on torture, problems in
      conducting, 121, 178
Rhodesia, 89–93, 176
Ripley, Herbert, 173, 175, 177, 180
Rizzi, Judge Dom, 238–9
Rodgers, William, 137
Rodriguez, Matt, 231
Roman law, 27–8
Ron, Jim, 214, 273

Roots of Evil (Staub), 89, 110, 254
"Rorschach Records of the Nazi War
      Criminals: An Experimental
      Study after Thirty Years," 89
Rosencof, Mauricio, 172
*Routine Torture: Interrogation Methods
   of the General Security Service,* 214
Rovner, Judge Ilana, 237–8
Royko, Mike, 228–9
Rubin, Jeffrey, 67

Saachi, Dr. Hugo, 172–3
Salem, village of, 150, 199
Sanders, Francine, 227, 228
Saor Uladh (Free Ulster), 131
Sarid, Yossi, 55–6, 148–9, 200, 269
scapegoats, 110–11
Schindler, Oscar, 58
Schoffman, Joshua, 57
Shabback, *see* General Security
      Service
Shadur, Judge Milton, 228
Shami, Hani al-, 140–2, 199, 269–70
Shamir, Yitzhak, 217
Shamseh, Natham Hafeth Beni, 218
Shani, Ilan, 13, 14, 56, 144, 206, 210
Shannon, Liam, 190
Shefi, Shmuel, 15, 144–5
Shihad, Shehadeh Abdallah, 220–1
Shin Bet, *see* General Security Service
Shines, Gayle, 227
Shivers, Patrick, 8, 39, 40, 42, 129–31,
      133–6, 189
Shomron, Dan, 55, 56–7, 153, 155
Silkin, Sam, 185–6
Simmons, Carolyn, 251
Simon, Dan, 56
Sims, Tyrone, 23, 24
sleep deprivation, 6, 29, 32, 34, 36, 43,
      107, 117, 128, 129, 212, 213
Smith, Ian, 92, 93

Smith, Patricia and Alvin, 23–4
societal conditions and human rights
     abuse, 110–12
Somnier, Dr. Finn, 179
Spiegelman, Art, 179
Stainthorp, John, 66, 68, 85, 160, 161,
     166–7, 225
standing, forced, 6, 35, 42, 95, 107,
     128–9, 132
Staub, Dr. Ervin, 89, 110, 253–4, 255–6
Strashnow, Amnon, 54–5, 56–9
suicide, 182
Sunday Times (London), 212, 224, 244,
     245, 272
Supreme Court, U.S., 239

Taylor, Flint, 66, 77, 85, 160, 161,
     166–7, 225–6
Taylor, John, 187–8
Thornton, Adolph, 24
Times (London), 43–4, 137, 246
toilet access, deprivation of, 6, 35, 36,
     42, 94, 107, 129, 213–14
*Torture and Ill-treatment: Israel's
     Interrogation of Palestinians from
     the Occupied Territories,* 214
"Torture and Plea Bargaining," 29
Torture and the Law of Proof
     (Langbein), 29
Torture (Peters), 29
torturers, 88–122
     indoctrination, 90, 95, 104
     obedience to authority, *see*
          obedience to authority
     orders, following, 99–102, 106–7,
          108–9, 111, 141, 143–56, 204–5,
          206, 208–9
     as ordinary people, 88, 89, 95, 96,
          101–2, 110, 121–2
     rationalizations, 42–3, 45–7,
          99–101, 111–12, 142, 153, 244–57

severe training and, 90–91, 94–5
societal conditions and, 110–12
see also names of individuals
trial by jury, development of, 30
Tuzo, Harry, 188, 246–7, 260

Uganda, 181
United Kingdom
     defense before European
          Commission of Human Rights,
          125–6, 136
     defense before European Court of
          Human Rights, 185–7
     denies lasting injury to victims, 43,
          46–7
     history and development of five
          techniques, 45–6, 127–9, 258
     introduction of internment, 3–5, 40
     investigations of abuse of internees,
          41–7
     rationalizations for use of torture,
          42–3, 45–7, 136–7, 187–8, 244–7,
          258, 262–3
     see also five techniques
United Nations definition of torture,
     37–8
United States
     educating foreigners in torture
          techniques, 107, 109
     history of torture in, 32–4
U.S. Army, 88–9, 113–19
U.S. Seventh Circuit Court of
     Appeals, 231–3, 235
U.S. State Department, 140
Ursano, Robert, 178
Uruguay, 36–7, 102–7, 107–10,
     169–70, 172–3

Valenzuela, Andres, 175
victims of torture, 110–11, 169–83, 244

victims of torture (*cont'd*)
coping mechanisms of, 172–6
dehumanization of, 111, 115, 116
devaluing, 100, 251, 252
lasting effects on, 123–5, 129–36,
172, 177–83, 184–5, 188–98, 216
supply inaccurate information, 6–7,
113, 170
see also five techniques; *names of
individuals*
Vietnam Veterans against the War,
116
Vietnam War, 61, 76–7, 177–8
U.S. Army interrogators in, 112,
113–21
Viltzig, Mose, 155–6
Virginia, 33
Vittori, Jean-Pierre, 112, 174, 175

Warpeha, Dr. Raymond, 78, 80, 81,
165
water, 174
dehydration, 116, 130
deprivation, 6, 42, 43, 213
near drowning, *see* drowning, near
Watson, Cassandra, 162
Weschler, Lawrence, 36, 169–70, 172
West Bank and Gaza Strip, *see*
intifada; *specific villages, e.g.*
Beita, West Bank

Wheatley, Richard, 178
White, Donald, 24
White Man, Black War (Moore-King),
92–3
*White Nights: The Story of a Prisoner in
Russia* (Begin), 34
"Who Is Afraid of Colonel Yehuda
Meir," 55
Wickersham Commission, 32–3
Wilson, Andrew
background of, 62–5, 73–4
murder of police officers, 21–2, 60,
71
torture claims and resulting
investigations and trials, 25–6,
60–87, 158–68, 225–41
Wilson, Jackie, 21–5, 65
Wolf, Stewart, 165, 173, 177, 180
Wolff, Dr. Harold, 127–8, 174–5
World War II, POWs in, 133, 177,
178, 181, 182
Wuillaume report, 286

Yucaitis, John, 60, 69, 77, 87, 225, 227,
228, 229, 230–1, 233, 236, 242

Zimbabwe, 92, 93, 176–7
Ziv, Israel, 146
Zucker, Dedi, 269

A NOTE ABOUT THE AUTHOR

John Conroy was born in Chicago, grew up in Skokie, and graduated from the University of Illinois. He has been an editor for *Chicago* magazine, and is at present a staff writer for the *Chicago Reader.* He is the author of a previous book about the troubles in Northern Ireland, *Belfast Diary: War as a Way of Life,* and his articles have appeared in the *New York Times,* the *Boston Globe,* the *Chicago Tribune,* the *Atlanta Constitution,* the *Dallas Morning News,* the *Washington Post, GQ, Mother Jones,* and *Granta,* among other places. He lives with his wife and two children in Oak Park, Illinois.

A NOTE ON THE TYPE

This book was set in Granjon, a type named in compliment to Robert Granjon, a type cutter and printer active in Antwerp, Lyons, Rome, and Paris from 1523 to 1590. Granjon, the boldest and most original designer of his time, was one of the first to practice the trade of typefounder apart from that of printer.

Linotype Granjon was designed by George W. Jones, who based his drawings on a face used by Claude Garamond (ca. 1480–1561) in his beautiful French books. Granjon more closely resembles Garamond's own type than do any of the various modern faces that bear his name.

COMPOSED BY CREATIVE GRAPHICS, ALLENTOWN, PENNSYLVANIA

PRINTED AND BOUND BY R. R. DONNELLEY & SONS, HARRISONBURG, VIRGINIA

DESIGNED BY ROBERT C. OLSSON